# Dalit Men's Autobiographies

# Dalit Men's Autobiographies:
## Convergences and Divergences

*Edited by*

**Dr Bijender Singh**

KALPAZ

First Published, 2021
*Published by*

Kalpaz Publications
C-30, Satyawati Nagar,
Delhi - 110052
Ph.: 011-47034999, 9811692060
www.kalpazpublications.com
E-mail: kalpaz@hotmail.com

*Printed at:* Gyan Press, Delhi.

**Cataloging in Publication Data—DK**
Courtesy: D.K. Agencies (P) Ltd. <docinfo@dkagencies.com>

**Dalit men's autobiographies :** convergences and divergences / edited by Dr Bijender Singh.
pages cm
Contributed articles.
ISBN 9789353246341

1. Indic literature—Dalit authors—History and criticism. 2. Autobiography—Dalit authors. 3. Dalits in literature. I. Singh, Bijender, editor.

LCC PK2903.D35 2021 | DDC 891.409 23

# Contents

# Introduction

> Am I a caste-Hindu? But my mother is an untouchable. Am I an Untouchable? But my father is a caste-Hindu. I have been tossed apart like Jarasandha—half within society and half outside. Who am I?
>
> – (Dangle, 1994: 51)

Dalit Literature is being espoused and loved globally, and that is why the autobiography writing has acquired a significant place in Dalit Literature—"the literature of the oppressed" or "the literature against the tide." Dalit autobiographies are the *avant-garde* texts encapsulating pains, problems, struggle and resistance, which have been missing for thousands of years. A Dalit autobiography is the documentary of the truth and frankness, and it is because of this, it touches the hearts of the readers. A Dalit autobiographer is not merely a writer; but he is also a good social worker who knowingly or unknowingly spreads positive vibes in the society. A Dalit autobiography is the mirror image of a Dalit's life and his community. We can call it a living genre, which poignantly delineates truth and nothing except the truth, and exposes the pain of the thousands of the Dalits, which has been thousands years old.

Only those people, who have experienced the pain, can better understand the sufferings of the Dalits. Many Dalit autobiographies have been written and translated into several languages of India and those of the foreign countries and the main objective behind these autobiographies is to make the maximum number of people access these autobiographies so that the banner of revolt may be raised against the Dalit discrimination. These autobiographies have not written with a purpose of criticising the upper caste people or making the Dalits get angry. The purpose behind them is only to establish equality—in every walk of life, at every place, and at every moment because all are equal as human beings.

With the advent of 21th century, a new current of consciousness and awakening has been initiated by these Dalit autobiographies because several of such Dalit autobiographies are being translated from regional languages into English. As a result, the readers all over the world have an easy access to them In Dalit autobiographies, the Dalit writers have foregrounded the pain, anguish, suffocation, subjugation and exploitation of the entire Dalit community, and this pain has been inflicted by the so-called upper caste people who have preconception or misunderstanding in their minds that the Dalits are born only to serve them and to do all the menial works for them. After being forced to live in an age-old slavery, discrimination, and inhumanity and after their noticing the change in the cultural and social scenario, they decry that the age-old structure of caste discrimination is soon to be pulverised. Thus, the seeds of new consciousness can be easily found in Dalit autobiographies.

Dalit literary works, in particular Dalit autobiographies, have explicitly revealed how the Dalit people have lived in an atrocious, ruthless and cold social system where human sentiments have no place. Dalit autobiographies have given voice to many aspects of Dalit people because such aspects have been deliberately concealed from them since time immemorial. The Dalits have been known by different names since ancient times and as such, they were deprived of their fundamental rights for thousands of years. They want to taçk all their problems together after having been inspired by Dr B. R. Ambedkar commandment "*educate*, *agitate,* and organize".

If Dalit autobiographies are called an important document of Indian Dalit Literature, then it will not be an exaggeration.

The people who are living their life at the fringe level have learnt a lot through Dalit autobiographies and they have become more conscious and aware of their rights. Ever since Dalit autobiographies have been written, Dalit society has admitted that only education can bring radical changes in their lives. Thus, Dalit autobiographies have germinated the seeds of awakening and new consciousness in the society.

Autobiography writing gives much succour to the writers because autobiographies remain very close to them. That's why it can be called an old and the most interesting genre. The oppression and exploitation of the people at the caste or class level is very appalling and condemnable.

Dalit autobiographies do not merely weave the web of the words, instead these are the groundbreaking narratives and the most strong documentaries to bring the radical change towards equality and liberation of the Dalits in the Indian society and especially in the rural areas where the problems of caste discrimination is very severe and sometimes life-threatening.

At the advent of Dalit autobiographies in 1960s, a new phase was introduced in Indian Writing in English and it can be called a revolutionary phase. Gradually Dalit autobiographies acquired central importance by the 1970s and gained momentum in the subsequent decades. Dalit Literature is being written in different genres such as poetry, novels, short stories, plays, and autobiographies and among all these, autobiographies are called the most powerful genre.

At the outset, Dalit autobiographies were written in Marathi language and after getting enthused or influenced; people started writing in other languages of India too. The most remarkable thing about these autobiographies is that nothing piquant, incredible or mind-boggling is found in these autobiographies just like other fictions and non-fictions. The narration is real and unfeigned and no mendaciousness of glitziness can be found in Dalit autobiographies. If we put our sharp eyes on these, the core concept of Dalit autobiographies can be better understood. In Dalit autobiographies, Dalit writers have wryly penned down the most harrowing and tormenting memories of their sufferings and have revealed the real pictures of human beings. While giving creative form to the events of the past memories, the writers' past wounds revive and they have to undergo almost the same kind of pain. These writers get submerged with pain and their pain gives impetus to those tragic moments. Thus, Dalit autobiographies appear capable of expressing the inner pain of a writer and the whole Dalit community.

Dalit autobiographies have the urgency to break out the narrow-mindedness of the so-called upper caste people and give inspiration to other poor people so that they may come out of the abyss of sorrow. These autobiographies have remained successful in unmasking the false Hindu social system. The fact cannot be ignored that the pain of Dalit life is unbearable and experiences are excruciating, leading the Dalits to their mental anguish and finally such bitter experiences become an abiding literary expression in the form of an autobiography. Through these autobiographies, the writers have shaken the whole social system and unravelled the fragile foundation on which Indian social system is placed.

So far as Indian Writing in English is concerned, different writers have enriched it through novels, plays, stories, poetry, biographies, autobiographies, *etc.* to add an extra charm to the existing Indian literature. All the works of Indian writers have voiced the serious concerns about the unpleasant happenings in our society, and their concern is found expressed through the portrayal of their characters.

In many cases, it is also seen that while writing their novels, the men writers do not give importance to the female characters and they have given a primary importance only to the male characters and in doing so, they have made their female characters play their secondary roles both at home and in the society. Similarly, female writers have written their works giving importance to feminism and they have depicted their female characters playing equal roles like men both at home and in the society, or they have also remained busy in writing about the world of women. All such fiction writers have not focused their attention on the trials and tribulations of the 'socially inferior class' known as 'Dalits'. It has been left to the Dalit writers, both men and women, to write literary works of their own so that they can bring to light how the entire Dalit community all over India is taken for granted by the upper caste people. They also focus how the upper caste people do not consider Dalits as human beings at all. Thus, entire Dalit community suffers endlessly without any remedial measures. They are discriminated, humiliated, and treated as sub-human beings unfit to live along with the human beings of other socially superior classes.

The twenty-first century has witnessed a sea-change in the lives of Dalits. More of the Dalits have become educationally and professionally empowered in the society but being Dalits they are not at all considered equal in the society. Many Dalit writers have made their presence felt in the field of Indian Writing in English by producing literary works of some merit equal to those written by the writers of upper middle and middle-class. It has resulted in the existence of a new branch in Indian Writing in English called 'Dalit Literature'. Now Dalit Literature has attained its privileged place and it enjoys a separate but a special entity of its own among all Indian Writing in English. Many Dalit writers find this new branch of Indian Writing in English as a perfect medium for them to bring their existential predicaments to the notice of all reading public. Yet their agony for being the Dalits cannot be abated and the word 'Dalit' attached to them tortures them for beyond endurance. They are leading their life as a socially ostracised group with the feelings that they are more sinned than sinning.

If Indian Dalit men become the writers of literary works of some repute, they also do not give much space to the injustice done with the women of their own home and community. They also do not portray that Dalit female characters cherish equal rights with men in their home and community, and only upper caste people are doing injustice with them. Dalit women also face the same patriarchal humiliation and discrimination for which male Dalit writers raise their voice in their autobiographies against upper caste people. If Dalit women write, they portray the men of their community and the upper caste people who humiliate, isolate, subjugate and above all, exploit them, both at home and outside.

It is a human tendency that people, irrespective of caste, class, gender, and race, want to see the world from their own perspectives and do whatever gives them pleasure or remains beneficial for them. In this process, all the people, knowingly or unknowingly, do injustice with other people about whose pains and problems they know very little. That is the reason that Dalit people also, showing patriarchal chauvinism, do not give much importance to the girls and women of their family or community. In the hierarchy, every superior human being does, more or less, injustice to the inferior ones just like animals do harm to other weak animals in jungle. Human beings also have instincts and actions like animals and how all the good can be expected from a person who is not humane or well-educated. If fair is fair, it must be everywhere. Dalit people should read Malice Amir Sheikh's searing memoir *I Want to Destroy Myself* how her husband Namdeo Dhasal who superheaded the Dalit Panthers movement, talks about equality publically but remains the most brutal at home showing double standards. My other two anthologies *Dalit Women's Autobiographies: A Critical Appraisal* (2016) and *Dalit Women's Autobiographies: Convergences and Divergences* (2021) are the showcases of inundating pain of Dalit women.

Only proper education can change the attitude of people and India is still a progressive country. I personally feel that it may take some more time to change this human tendency because India lives in villages and a large number of villagers are not educated to that level and cannot behave at all the way our constitution expects from them. Apart from it, there are faults in our education system which does not give much education to students how to live life.

Dalit men also should respect their women and *vice-versa*. If they do not do so, they should not expect due respect from the people of other communities. It is a well-known adage that 'Charity begins at home' and ideally speaking, all Dalit people should macerate this discrimination from their own home first so that Dalit women may breathe in free and liberated air and feel proud that at least the men of their community are not like the upper caste people and the whole fault lies only in the upper caste people. Thus, in the treatment of women, Dalit men are not much different from the men and women of upper and upper-middle class. Any revolution or reformation should first start at home and if this becomes successful, all joining together should see that the change in the attitudes of people towards others on the basis of their social status can be achieved to a greater satisfaction in the society.

Among other genres of Dalit Literature, Dalit autobiography has engraved its indelible impression in the heart of the readers belonging to every stratum of the society. It is not fictional in nature but it brings out the real life physical and mental tortures, meted out to the Dalits as the socially discriminated class.

Thus, it has been left to many Dalit men and women writers to bring their personal agonised life in the midst of the other societal classes through their autobiographies. Their portrayal from their birth to death, whatever they could write, is absolutely true. It is generally an accepted truth in the man-made society that men, irrespective of their social class, have a misunderstanding that they are born to rule. But at the same time, it should also be accepted that women should not be taken for a ride for being weaker sex. They are indispensable human beings to their respective men and they are only the preservers of peace and happiness both at home and in the society.

There is not a unanimous consent regarding the first Dalit autobiography but it can be stated that Hazari's *Untouchable: Autobiography of an Indian Outcaste* (1951), N.S. Suryavanchi's *Things I Never Imagined* (1975) and Daya Pawar's *Baluta* (1978) are the earliest autobiographical masterpieces. Rettamalai Srinivasan's autobiography *Jeeviya Sarithira Surukkam* (1938) is the first autobiographical narrative but it is only a fraction. This autobiography was translated into English by Meera Rajgopalan as *A Brief History of My Life*. Here also Dalit men have set the record to write autobiographies and Dalit women appeared much later on the Dalit literary platform. Unfortunately, many Dalit autobiographies written in regional languages have not been translated into English, but it has been attempted to include some well-known autobiographies written in regional languages also. Dalit men's autobiographies have carved a special niche as compared to Dalit women's autobiographies and are more in number also, but the fact also cannot be overlooked that Dalit women's autobiographies have more touching and soul-crushing expressions and conglomerate more pain than Dalit men's autobiographies.

Like my previous anthology *Dalit Men's Anthologies: A Critical Appraisal* (2017), this anthology entitled *Dalit Men's Autobiographies: Convergences and Divergences* is a one step ahead in the attempt to encompass the maximum possible Dalit men's autobiographies written in English and other regional languages also. The present anthology is a compendium of twenty-nine well-analysed research papers by eminent faculty members, research scholars and great researchers.

The first paper entitled "Silver Lining in Hazari's Dark Clouds of Life as an Untouchable: A Study of His *Untouchable: An Autobiography of an Indian Outcaste*" of this anthology has been written by Prof. D. Amalraj. His paper deals with the ways of the life of the Dalits by belittling themselves without minding the situations in which they are placed. Though Hazari was a Dalit, he was against his own Dalit groups indulging in activities which were nauseating to the higher caste Hindus. He felt ill at ease to see his own people becoming responsible for their ill-treatment at the hands of their fellow Hindus but also for being branded as untouchables. A lone Dalit man, who is highly educated and professionally well-placed like Hazari, cannot bring the desired changes in the life style of his entire Dalit community. Only dark clouds were there in the life of the people of his community and if there should be a silver lining, it lies only in the hands of all the Dalits. They should not be at the peck and call of the higher caste Hindus to carry out all the disgraceful works. His autobiography narrates only his unhappiness about the disgraceful ways of the ignorant Dalits. Prof. D. Amalraj has tried to examine all these core issues in his paper.

The second paper of this anthology has been written by Dr Shikha Saxena. Her paper entitled "*Untold Story of a Bhangi Vice-Chancellor*: An Account of Indomitable Courage and Struggle" is an eye-opener for all the readers who are not aware about the atrocities and incessant marginalisation of Bhangis (Shudra Verna) in the post-Independent Indian society. The author's biography served as a testimony to the fact that he has to overcome all types of social humiliations due to the caste-prejudices in the society but despite all the hurdles and odds, he attained the zenith of his teaching career as a successful Vice-Chancellor of Jodhpur University. Threadbare analysis of all the stake-holders has been done in the Dr Saxena's paper to present the grim state of affairs in the princely state of Jodhpur and the abode of higher education i.e. Jodhpur University. The objective analysis of the facts in her paper can motivate the readers to extend the helping hand to all those who are struggling with these types of issues.

It is needless to say that Dalit autobiographies are also the 'autobiographies of the communities' as they assert the authentic Dalit experience. The paper, "Dalit Consciousness in Tumbadi Ramaiah's *Manegara*" by Dr S. R. Chaitra concentrates on bringing out Dalit consciousness in the Dalit autobiographical narrative *Manegara* originally written in Kannada by Tumbadi Ramaiah and translated to English by Krishna Murthy Chandar. The text gives an insight about Dalit life and consciousness. The misery of the untouchables due to the social exclusion and the emerging consciousness and awakening is well brought out and has been explored by Dr Chaitra in this paper.

The English translation of the Telugu autobiography *Antarani Vasantam* by G. Kalyan Rao was published in 2010, ten years after the publication of the original text. This text has been hailed as a seminal text of Dalit resistance in postcolonial context, pertaining to the plight of the utterly marginalised and subaltern section of Indian society—the untouchables. Today, 20 years after the publication, while the text has been prescribed in various undergraduate and postgraduate courses, Dr Deeba Sarmad's paper entitled "The Untouchability of Spring: The Varna Narrative in G. Kalyan Rao's *Antarani Vasantam*" attempts to analyse the significance of the title of the English translation entitled *Untouchable Spring*.

Dr Suruchi Sharma has written the next paper of this anthology. Her paper entitled "Marginalisation and Identity Formation in Sheoraj Singh Bechain's *My Childhood on My Shoulders*" explores the autobiography of Sheoraj Singh Bechain, a man of dust who touched the ladder of success and became a Professor in the University of Delhi defying all odds. He has the privilege of having an array of published books by now. Dr Suruchi has attempted to analyze how Sheoraj became a self-made man from a very fragile background.

Dr Kusum Kanger's paper entitled "Siddalingaiah's *Ooru Keri*: Projection of Self and Society" aims to shed light on the life and social status of the people of Siddalingaiah's caste.

*Ooru Keri* generally refers to any neighbourhood or any residential accommodation and it is similar to Vasant Moon's autobiography *Vasti*. Dalit people's perseverance among all oddities and their struggle to assert their identity is the main emphasis of Dr Kusum's paper.

Dr Ruchika Katiyar's paper entitled "Representation of the Distress and Plight of Dalits in *Upara: An Outsider* by Laxman Mane" highlights the pitiable condition of the Dalits as narrated by the writer in his autobiography. History has witnessed the sufferings and exploitation of Dalits. Dalit Literature can be seen as a literature of protest against the set defined system which is based on injustice. It cannot be denied that we live in a caste-ridden society. The lower caste people are dehumanised, exploited and treated in a contemptuous way by the upper caste people. The writer and his family members as well have confronted all the discrimination and sufferings that he portrays in his autobiography.

Dr V. Suganthi in her paper entitled "Solidarity and Recreating the Community: Vasant Moon's *Growing up Untouchable in India*" explores the solidarity of the Mahars which enabled them to stand against all odds. Their faith in their unparalleled leader Dr Ambedkar and his principles, the way Mahars stood up for their dignity, their attempt at social levelling up of their status in the society by rejecting the religion that rejects them and converting to Buddhism are discussed by Dr Suganthi in her paper.

Dr Meenu Dudeja paper entitled "The Stranded Strings of Dalit Tribals' Existence: A Reading of Laxman Gaikwad's Autobiography *Uchalya: The Branded*" attempts to analyse the painful childhood memories and the hardships of the author related to his caste and the extreme penury. Gaikwad attempts to analyse wounds of caste discrimination prevalent in India that have left indelible scars on the psyche of tribals. His autobiography is a deep cry of a man from the tribal community and he is the person who raised his voice for equal rights to all genders and all citizens of India. Gaikwad's autobiography is a vivid account of the struggle, oppression, exploitation, marginalisation, and agonies of the Dalit community in different spheres of life and Dr Dudeja has explored all these themes in her paper.

The tenth paper of this anthology has been written by Dr C. Ramya. Her paper entitled "Exploitations of Mahars in Shankarrao Kharat's Autobiography *Taral Antral*" examines the life of Mahars in Maharashtra through Shankarrao Kharat's autobiography *Taral Antral* how the writer's father had to split firewood for a schoolteacher who forces him for this work just for reading a letter for him just because the writer's father was illiterate. His father Rama had to remain hungry until the corpse is not brought out of the well. The exploitation of Mahars remains the main focus of Dr Ramya's paper.

Subhasish Barua's paper entitled "Towards the Dream Project: Dissolution of Differences in Kancha Ilaiah's *Why I am Not a Hindu: A Sudra Critique of Hindutva Philosophy, Culture and Political Economy*" aims to focus on the inherent differences between the upper castes and the Dalitbahujans that work to attest the hierarchy as an eternal one. On the other hand, Ilaiah in *Why I Am Not a Hindu* tries to abolish the differences so that the identity of the Dalitbahujans can be established emphatically.

In the paper entitled "Manoranjan Byapari's *Interrogating My Chandal Life*: Disseminating Dalit Survival Saga," Kalyan Pattanayak delineates how a Dalit teenage refugee suffers from displacement due to partition, becomes victim of untouchability and caste system, struggles to earn a handful of meal a day, is engaged in Naxalite movement and then disillusions, suffers from imprisonment being falsely accused of, learns his first letter in prison during his 20s, acquires acclaim as a man of letters, and finally a member of West Bengal Legislative Assembly. Quest for existence through struggle to survive with dignified identity after dislocation, relocation, exploitation is the focal point of Kalyan Pattanayak's paper.

Sukriti Sobti's paper entitled "Transforming Consciousness, Ushering Mobility: The Role of Education in Dalit Men's Autobiography" explores two key texts—Narendra Jadhav's *Outcaste* and Vasant Moon's *Growing up Untouchable in India* as products of modern education system, whose aim is to challenge Brahminical epistemology and deconstruct outmoded knowledge systems. The protagonists of the two texts underline the necessity of education as a means of liberation and empowerment for Dalits. Though the pathway to education is strewn with difficulties for many Dalits, yet striving towards producing an alternate humanizing paradigm of education is the only way out to cast away caste.

N. Padmapriyadharshini's paper "Exposing the Social Inequality and the Pursuit of Identity of Marginalised People in Sharankumar Limbale' *Akkarmashi*: An Analysis" is an attempt to present the social inequality and the pursuit of identity by the marginalised people through a brief study on Sharakumar Limbale's *Akkarashi*. Exposing the realities of autobiographies and the importance of Dalit autobiographies, her paper speaks strongly about the pain and sufferings of people belonging to Dalit community. The social injustice forced Dalit people to lead such a pathetic life. Padmapriyadharshini's paper also speaks how Dalits are doubly marginalised in their own community and how people from the other communities treated them in the society by presenting Sharakumar Limbale as an instance. Thus, by analysing and throwing light on the plights of Sharankumar, her paper encourages the Dalit people to gain knowledge and improve their educational standards to bring a balance in society.

Abdul Wahied Wani has written the next paper of this anthology. In his paper entitled "Mohandas Naimishray's *Apne Apne Pinjare*: A Groundbreaking Document of the Neglected," he has written how Mohandas Naimishray and the people of his caste lived a neglected life among the upper caste people. Such a social system has been narrated in this autobiography that exploits the poor, neglected and oppressed. Abdul Wahied has examined this autobiography from the perspective of a diversified social canvas that gives birth to exploitation.

Guni Vats' paper "Deconstructing the Identity of a 'Dalit' in Bhanwar Meghwanshi's Memoir *I Could not be Hindu: The Story of a Dalit in the RSS*" is an attempt to unveil the caste prejudices of the NGO that claims to build a Hindu Rashtra through Bhanwar Meghwanshi's autobiography. Her paper is a detailed deconstruction of the narrative divided in neat columns that contributed to the saga of the writer's realisation of his caste identity. Guni Vats' paper is an attempt to unveil the caste bias that lurks in the political organisation that preaches higher human values but treats its own members as second-class citizens.

Sanjay Kumar's paper entitled "Unpleasant Childhood Memories Pertaining to Poverty and Untouchability in Aravind Malagatti's *Government Brahmana*" explores Dalit sufferings, caste discrimination and untouchability in Aravind Malagatti's autobiography *Government Brahmana*. It is a counter-hegemonic autobiography, and Aravind Malagatti's revelations about caste and quest for equality are the main emphasis of Sanjay Kumar's paper.

Dr Avinash Kumar has written the eighteenth paper of this anthology. In his paper entitled "Writing Resistance: Journey from Marginality to Centrality in Surajpal Chauhan's *Tiraskrit* and *Santampt*," he has written how Surajpal Chauhan had to struggle in his life and had to live in utter poverty conditions. His journey of life from a labourer to a manager through his two autobiographies has been analysed by Dr Avinash Kumar in his paper.

India has earned a bad name across the globe for the special type of social stratification prevalent in the form of castes resulting in untouchability. Though untouchability has been prohibited under article 17 of Indian constitution, there is no denying the fact that discrimination against Dalits on the basis of caste can still be noticed rampantly. Dalits are, even today, victims of humiliation, oppression and exploitation. In his paper entitled "Traumatic Experiences amid Struggle for Education: A Study of D. R. Jatava's Autobiography *A Silent Soldier*," Dr Vinod K. Chopra has tried to explore how D. R. Jatava's autobiography *A Silent Soldier* is an authentic document of the author's mortification and excruciating struggle for education. Meanwhile, the author has cited the examples, just to validate the truth, from the life of B. R. Ambedkar who, too, suffered humiliation during school days.

Dr Tamanna has written the next paper of this anthology. In her paper entitled "Refugee Dalits and the Fight for Survival: A Study of *Surviving in My World* by Manohar Mouli Biswas", she has attempted to analyse the painful childhood reminisces after the Partition of Bengal and the problems of Dalit refugees and the cold response of the people in Uttar Pradesh and West Bengal. Many such issues have been tried to unearth which remain unnoticed, unseen and unattended by the mainstream and Dr Tamanna has tried to bring equipoise of all such issues in her paper.

The next paper of this anthology has been penned by Dr Budhanath Pratihast. His paper entitled "Voicing the Miseries of Dalit Lives: Rereading Omprakash Valmiki's *Joothan: A Dalit's Life*" showcases the untouchability and caste discrimination in Valmiki's autobiography *Joothan*. Omprakash was born in a very poor Dalit family and he faced many problems in getting his education especially due to the upper caste students and even by his teachers. The miseries and helplessness of Dalits have been examined by Dr Budhanath in his paper.

Dr Ritika Agnihotri's paper entitled "Combating Caste Discrimination through Education: A Study of Y. B. Satyanarayana's *My Father Baliah*" highlights the role of education in questioning the hegemonic dominance of the upper castes and eliminating the prejudices against the Dalits. Through a biographical account of his family, Dr Y. B. Satyanarayana has justified that education has proved to be a powerful tool in the emancipation of Dalits from the shackles of ignorance and subordination.

In the next paper entitled "Daya Pawar's *Baluta*: An Armature of Humiliations of Dalit's Existence in Shinning India," Dr Parul Aggarwal has highlighted the pathetic conditions and living situations of the marginalised Mahar community in which the writer himself spent all his life facing humiliations and discriminations based on the caste system in Indian society. In this autobiographical work, whatever the author has depicted about the pain and agony of every downtrodden who wants to get a place in this caste ridden Indian society, has been clearly presented in Dr Parul Aggarwal's paper.

Harish Mangalam's study of B. Kesharshivam's autobiography *Poorn-Satya* attempts to explore the various kinds of traumatising and nightmarish experiences of untouchability with cruel, appalling, inhuman treatment, atrocities and injustice in the Indian four-fold stratified social structure, during his schooling and service period. The autobiographer weaves untouchability as a malediction which has been chasing him and his Dalit community constantly without a little pause—even a fraction of a second. The autobiographer struggles very hard to help the unprivileged and underdog people—the Dalits of rural areas and being a revenue authority, he gives lands from the surplus lands of village lakes and herbages to enable to uplift them economically and fights for their fundamental social rights of potable water from the village well. The autobiographer follows the ideology of Dr B. R. Ambedkar with full commitment and battles against the irrepressible caste system. He becomes gruesome in his life and faces a macabre dance of injustice made by the upper-castes peoples to Dalits. All this has been narrated and analysed by Harish Mangalam in his paper.

Dr V. Brinda Shree's paper entitled "A Study of the Untouchables in Subaltern Literature with Special Reference to K.A. Gunasekaran's Autobiography *The Scar*: A Clarion Call for Dalit Assertion and Emancipation" seeks to explore Dalit autobiographical narratives written by contemporary Dalit authors. The literature of the oppressed has surpassed the records of history and has also acquired a transition into a socio-political tool that symbolises the wretchedness of the poverty, predicament and injustice that was administered to the Untouchables in India. In this genre, the autobiography of the Dalit writers emerged as a weapon for Dalit to assert their identity, individuality and made them challenge the social order and protest against the oppression for centuries. Amongst the many autobiographies written by Dalit writers, *The Scar* by K.A. Gunasekaran, goes beyond self-expression and signals the exploitation of Tamil Dalit's life. Dr V. Brinda's paper proposes to summarise the quest of the oppressed class to reclaim their identity and ascertain their individual rights and also portrays their fight for freedom and liberty from the oppressors with an optimistic note.

Dr B. Manivannan's paper entitled "Intertextuality of Self and Indigenous Society in Narendra Jadhav's *Outcaste: A Memoir* or *Untouchable*" aims to explore how an individual self is effectively interacting with the other aspects of familial and social selves and deals with Dalit identity which emerges from time and space, which is indigenous in nature. Narendra Jadhav's *Outcaste: A Memoir* or *Untouchables* is studied in the light of Julia Kristeva's linguistic theory "Intertextuality" and is considered an Intertext, that is manifold reflecting on his personal, familial and social life centred round outcastes especially Mahars in Maharashtra.

Dr Suchitra Gupta, her paper "Trauma of Being a Dalit in Govardhan Wankhede's *My Life*: *The Journey of a Sociologist*: From Bleeding Dignity to Healing Humanity," tries not only to probe and examine the struggles of Dr Goverdhan

Wankhede against the complexed difficulties of his life but also it unfurls the resilience that led him to acquire one of the coveted position in the academia. Notwithstanding severest form of discrimination and indignity, the narrative does not satiate self pity. "Together We Can" is the message that finds explicit dissemination through this narrative. Dalits' traumatic experiences and their struggle for survival are the primary concerns in Dr Gupta's paper.

Dr Ashok Verma, in the second last paper of this anthology, seeks to expand the meaning of the term Dalit beyond narrow caste rigidities and advocates for the inclusion of authors like Santram B.A. who pioneered the cause of the downtrodden section of the society in the 20$^{th}$ century by not only preaching but also practicing what he preached in doing away with his caste surname and replacing it with his educational qualification. The author successfully brings to limelight Santram B.A.'s copious creative oeuvre that clearly reflects birth-based caste prejudices and the resultant humiliation and angst; and thus establishes his autobiography as the first Dalit autobiography.

The last paper of this anthology has been written by Dr S. Chelliah. In his paper entitled "Balbir Madhopuri's *Changia Rukh: Against the Night*: Dynamics of Caste Prejudice and Dalit Resistance", Dr S. Chelliah has analysed how the caste and untouchability remain the core issue behind the pains of Dalits. In this paper he has depicted how Balbir Madhopuri and the members of his family and community have borne the sting of casteism.

I hope that this anthology will be very useful for the research scholars, faculty members, Dalit activists, independent researchers and general readers as well just because it has been attempted to include the maximum Dalit men's autobiographies and memoirs. This anthology makes itself unique from other reference books just because many books are available on Dalit Literature but it is very difficult to find a voluminous book like this on Dalit men's autobiographies.

I am immensely indebted to all those persons who helped me in this arduous and time-consuming journey. First and foremost, I would like to express my gratitude to all the contributors who took all the pains in writing the papers on the topics assigned by me. It was not less than a challenge for them but they did this job very meticulously, and consequently, this book has become very unique at this stage. I am also indebted to my several friends who helped me at every step.

I cannot forget the mental support and encouragement of Prof. S. Chelliah, the Dean of Arts, Humanities & Languages, and Professor, Head, and Chairperson of School of English and Foreign Languages, Madurai Kamaraj University, Madurai (Tamil Nadu) whose valuable pieces of advice, from time to time, did not let me feel that I am alone in this academic journey.

I am also thankful to my family members: blessings of elders, support of siblings, love of spouse and back-up of my cute children Saumya and Naitik. This task was not viable without the support of my family members.

Last but not least, I would like to offer my sincere and deepest gratitude to Mr Amit Garg, the Managing Director, Kalpaz Publications, New Delhi who has been doing the commendable work of publication of numerous books on Dalit Literature for the past several years. I owe to him for all the support and understanding in all my academic ventures and publishing this book with all professional care, adequate speed and the optimum quality. I am equally thankful to the whole editorial team, technical hands and the production unit who rendered their services tirelessly and assiduously in producing this anthology so skilfully, adroitly and promptly.

**Dr Bijender Singh**
Editor

# Contributors

**Prof. D. Amalraj** began his teaching career in October 1969 in Kandasamy Kandar College and retired from his service on 31 May 2004. After his retirement, he has worked as the Head and Research Supervisor in Vivekananda College of Arts and Science, a self-financing Women's College at Tiruchengode from June 2004 to 31 December 2011. He again worked as a Part-Time Professor in Bishop Appasamy College, a self-financing college at Coimbatore for one year from 2012 to 2013. He is a writer of literature oriented Study Aid Series on five plays of Shakespeare. He is the author of a reference text titled Research Methodology for Literary Research. His sixth and revised edition 2020 with an ISBN has been published by Omkareswar Press, NOIDA. This reference text is purely meant for the students and scholars pursuing MA, MPhil, and PhD in English Literature. It contains all the prescribed guidelines of three prescribed reference texts such as Assignment and Thesis Writing 4th edition by Anderson and Poole, and MLA 7th and 8th editions. It is a prescribed reference text in Periyar University at Salem and PSG Arts and Science College at Coimbatore. His memoir *My Life My Flight* (2020) and *Literary Terms, Techniques and Devices* (2021) are his latest publications.

**Dr Shikha Saxena** presently works as Professor and Head of the Department of Humanities in Maharaja Agrasen Institute of Technology, Delhi (Affiliated to GGSIPU, Delhi). She is having more than 20 years of teaching experience. She is a poet, a short-story writer and ELT expert. She has 36 papers to her credit in reputed national and international journals and edited anthologies. Her poems have been published in reputed international journals. She has also attended various workshops.

**Dr S. R. Chaitra** works as an Associate Professor in English in Maharaja's College which is a constituent college of University of Mysore, Mysuru, Karnataka. Her areas of interest are Stylistics, Indian Feminism, Marginal Literature, Black Feminism, Dalit Feminism, Diasporic Literature and Post-colonial Literature. She has presented papers at various national/international seminars and conferences. Her research papers have been published in different national and international journals.

**Dr Deeba Sarmad** is an Associate Professor of English, and has taught for over 20 years both at the UG and PG levels. She specialises in Diaspora Studies and under the general rubric of diaspora, she engages with the themes of migration, minorities, displacement, homelessness, exilic perspectives and identity questions. Her present position as Dean, Humanities and Liberal Arts, Cluster University, Srinagar, involves developing academic programmes and performing other administrative functions. She also supervises various aspects of the faculty and student body and participates in university long-term planning and policy setting.

**Dr Suruchi Sharma** (MA, PhD, UGC-NET) is an Associate Professor in RKSD College, Kaithal, Haryana. She has done her PG from KMV Autonomous College, Jalandhar, Punjab. She has been awarded PhD in English on Khaled Hosseini. Her areas of interest are Diaspora Studies, Critical Theories and Cultural Studies. She has presented her papers in many national and international seminars and conferences. Her papers have been published in many national and international journals and seminar/conference proceedings and several edited anthologies.

**Dr Kusum Kanger** (MA, MPhil, PhD) is an Associate Professor in BAR Janta College, Kaul, Kaithal, Haryana. She has earned her MPhil from Kurukshetra University,

Kurukshetra. She has been awarded her doctoral degree on Angela Carter and Bapsi Sidhwa from NIMS University, Jaipur. She has presented and published her papers in many national and international seminars and conferences. She has published her papers in many national and international journals and edited anthologies.

**Dr Ruchika Katiyar** (MA, PhD) is an Assistant Professor in APB Government PG College, Agastyamuni, Uttarakhand. She has completed her PG from Pt. LMS Government PG College (Autonomous), Rishikesh, Uttarakhand. She has been awarded PhD in English on Rabindranath Tagore. Her areas of interest are Indian Writings in English and the Literature of Diaspora. Having an experience of more than 9 years, she is a member of English Language Teachers Association of India and Indian Association for Commonwealth Literature and Language Studies. Her papers have been published in various international journals and seminar/conference proceedings. She has presented her papers in several national and international seminars and conferences.

**Dr V. Suganthi**, Assistant Professor in the PG & Research Department of English in Thiruvalluvar Government Arts College, Rasipuram, Tamil Nadu, has 26 years of experience in collegiate teaching. Her specialisation is African-American Literature. She has guided 4 scholars in their doctoral research. She has authored 3 books, contributed 16 articles in edited anthologies, and has published 50 papers in journals. She has been the editor of special issues of journals, and resource person for symposiums, workshops, and seminars. She has been the member of Doctoral Committee for 15 candidates. She has presented papers in national and international seminars and conferences.

**Dr Meenu Dudeja** is working as an Assistant Professor in Maharaja Agrasen Institute of Technology, New Delhi. She is having more than 17 years of teaching experience. She is having more than 12 papers to her credit in reputed national and international journals. She has attended various workshops. She has authored three books entitled *Communication Skills for Professionals*, *Communication Skill Part 2* and *Lab Manual for Professionals*. Her areas of interest are American Literature, Indian Writing in English, Gender Studies and Communication Skills.

**Dr C. Ramya** (MBA, MA, MPhil, PhD) presently works as an Assistant Professor of English in E.M.G. Yadava Women's College, Madurai, Tamil Nadu, India. She has completed her master's degree in English, master's degree in Business Administration, Master of Philosophy and doctoral degree in English. She has eight years of teaching experience. She has authored/co-authored eight books and has published 120 research papers in peer-reviewed/CARE-listed journals and several edited anthologies. Her areas of interest are Psychoanalysis, Spiritual Studies, Dalit Literature and Comparative Literature.

**Subhasish Barua** is an Assistant Professor, Department of English, Nabagram Hiralal Paul College, Konnagar, District Hooghly, West Bengal and a PhD Research Scholar in Department of English in Vidyasagar University, Medinipur, West Bengal. He has published his papers in journals and edited anthologies. His areas of interest are Dalit Literature, Tribal Literature, Literature of the Subalterns and Gender Studies.

**Kalyan Pattanayak** is a Lecturer in the Department of English, Ghatal Rabindra Satabarsiki Mahavidyalaya, affiliated to Vidyasagar University, Medinipur, West Bengal. He has completed PG from Chhatrapati Shahu Ji Maharaj University, Kanpur. Presently, he is pursuing PhD from the Department of English, Seacom Skills University, Birbhum, West Bengal. He is also an Academic Counsellor of Department of English, Netaji Subhas Open University, West Bengal. His area of research is Indian Writing in English. His areas of interest include Subaltern Studies, Diaspora, Ecocriticism, etc. He has presented many papers in several national and international seminars, webinars, and conferences. He has published research papers in UGC CARE-listed journals and other journals of international repute, and contributed book chapters too. He has authored the book *An Objective Approach to Literature in English* published by a Kolkata-based reputed publisher.

**Sukriti Sobti** teaches English Literature at Sri Aurobindo College, University of Delhi. She has more than seven years of teaching experience at various colleges of University of Delhi and Indraprastha University. She has been fortunate to have taught seminal Dalit texts such as Kalyan Rao's *Untouchable Spring* and Srividya Natarajan and S. Anand's *Bhimayana* to undergraduate students of Delhi University. Her writings have been published in several reputed national journals and newspapers. She has also authored a book for aspiring academicians who are preparing for UGC-NET. She has worked with School of Open Learning as a Visiting Fellow and created e-content for them. Her prime research interest lies in the field of myths and mythopoesis.

**N. Padmapriyadhshini** (MA, MPhil) is pursuing her PhD from the Department of English, Madurai Kamaraj University, Madurai. Her research work focuses on complexities in human relationships and identity crisis. She has presented four papers in international conferences. She has published one article in an international peer-reviewed journal with impact factor. She has participated in two workshops—one on the social evils in literatures and another regarding the usage of online materials for research.

**Abdul Wahied Wani** (MA, CBSE-NET, J& K-SET) is a PhD Scholar in the Department of English at Lovely Professional University, Phagwara, Punjab. He has published his papers in national and international journals and edited anthologies. His areas of interest are Indian Writing in English, British Literature, South Asian Diaspora and Dalit Literature.

**Guni Vats** is a PhD Scholar in the Department of English at the University of Lucknow, Lucknow. She has completed her Master's degree in English Literature from Central University of Rajasthan and she has earned the Bachelor's degree (Honours in English Literature) from the University of Delhi. She is a keen reader, budding researcher and an enthusiastic writer who takes immense pleasure in looking at diverse aspects of life from a psychoanalytical bent. She is keen to research on the Indian women writers and carves a niche for them in the predominantly masculine world. She is currently attempting a thesis tracing the feminist waves in Indian literature and analyzing them through translations. She has many publications in reputed journals and literary anthologies to her credit.

**Sanjay Kumar** (MA, BEd, H-TET, C-TET, UGC-NET, HP-SET) is a PhD Research Scholar at Lovely Professional University, Phagwara, Punjab. He is presently working as an English Lecturer at GMSSSS Bhuna, Fatehabad (Haryana). His areas of interest are Indian Writing in English, Gender Studies, Dalit Literature, American literature and Post-colonial Literature.

**Dr Avinash Kumar** (MA (Gold Medalist), PhD) is PhD holder from Patna University who has a penchant for Afro-American Literature and Indo-English Poetry. He has a wonderful command of Feminist Discourse and Dalit Literature. He has contributed immensely to esteemed journals and edited books from reputed publication houses. He evinces keen interest in publication of insightful research articles on Post-colonial and Feminist Literature in journals of home and abroad and edited anthologies. He has published few books on English Literature.

**Dr Vinod K. Chopra** earned his PhD from Himachal Pradesh University, Shimla in 2002 on the topic "Community, Communalism and Gender: A Study of Short Stories on Partition". He is an honorary faculty member at Career Point

University, Kota, Rajasthan. He has guided thirteen MPhil scholars and at present, he is supervising four PhD scholars. He has published a book *Partition Stories: Mapping Community, Communalism and Gender* in 2009 and he has translated a monograph *Saga of a Revolutionary Hero: Pt. Inderpal, a Freedom Fighter* into English. He has published ten research papers in national and international literary journals and six papers in different anthologies. He has also presented eight research papers on literature and education in national and international seminars. He is a permanent member of Indian Association for the Study of Australia (IASA), The English Language Teachers' Association of India (ELTAI) and English Teachers' Forum (ETF).

**Dr Tamanna** [MSc (Mathematics), MA, MPhil, PhD (English)] is serving as an Assistant Professor in the Department of English at Mahila Mahavidyalaya, Jhojhu Kalan affiliated to Chaudhary Bansi Lal University, Bhiwani. She has attended quite a few seminar and international conferences. She has already published many articles on R.K. Narayan and Mulk Raj Anand in reputed journals. In addition to Narayan and Anand, her area of interest is chiefly related to Indian Writing in English, Post-Colonial Studies and Diasporic Literature.

**Dr Budhanath Pratihast** is an Assistant Professor of English at Bihar Institute of Law, Patna. He has done PhD in English Literature from Patna University. His articles have been published in many national and international journals, and edited anthologies. His areas of interest are Indian Writing in English, Diasporic Literature, and English Language Teaching.

**Dr Ritika Agnihotri** (MA, MPhil, PhD, UGC NET) is currently working as an Assistant Professor in the Department of English, Public College, Samana, Patiala, Punjab. She has been teaching undergraduate and postgraduate classes for more than twelve years. Her research interests focus on Feminist Studies, Cultural Studies, Diasporic Literature and Dalit

Literature. She has attended various national and international conferences and has published research papers in reputed peer-reviewed and UGC approved journals.

**Dr Parul Aggarwal** presently works as an Assistant Professor in the Department of Humanities and Social Sciences in Shri Guru Ram Rai University, Dehradun, Uttarakhand. She has published five papers in peer-reviewed national and international journals. Her areas of interest are Dalit Literature, Indian English Literature and Feminism. She has delivered an expert talk as eminent speaker on *Obstacles in Teaching & Learning English at School Level Before & During Pandemic Situations* in a Seven-Day National Web-Workshop organised by Govt. Lahiri PG College, Chirmiri.

**Harish Mangalam** is a Founder Member and General Secretary of the Gujarati Dalit Sahitya Akademi, Ahmedabad. He was an Additional Collector in the Government of Gujarat. He has published 14 books in different genres and apart from these books; he has 30 edited anthologies to his credit. He has received 12 literary awards from various organisations including Gujarat Sahitya Akademi, Government of Gujarat, Gandhinagar and Gujarati Sahitya Parishad, Ahmedabad. He has successfully organised National and International Seminars/Conference under the banner of The Gujarati Dalit Sahitya Akademi, Ahmedabad. He is the editor of *Hayati Quarterly*, a mouthorgan of the Gujarati Dalit Sahitya Akademi, since 23 years. As a General Secretary of the Gujarati Dalit Sahitya Akademi, he has published 110 titles of Gujarati Dalit Literature in Gujarati, Hindi, English and Sanskrit, etc. He has presented his scholarly papers and delivered speeches on Dalit Literature in different universities and organisations all over India, including at the prestigious Indian Institute of Advanced Studies in Shimla. He is the leading figure among all the Dalit authors because of his commitment to raise Dalit's issues through his Dalit literary creations and field work of 'Annadhamm Yojana'.

**Dr V. Brinda Shree**, who is presently the Head of the Department of English at TIPS College of Arts and Science, Coimbatore, Tamil Nadu, has over 10 years of teaching experience whereby she has facilitated the undergraduate and postgraduate students of Arts, Commerce and Science faculties. She also has been facilitating MBA and Architecture students at The TIPS Global Institute and also the Engineering Students of Anna University. She is a member of English Language Teacher's Interaction Forum (ELTIF), Indian Association of Social Sciences Research (IASSR) and also a certified Cambridge English Examiner for BEC Examinations. Dr Brinda was awarded Doctorate in English from the Bharathiar University, Coimbatore. She has presented several research papers in various national and international journals and has also participated and presented numerous papers in many national and international conferences, seminars and also has attended many workshops and symposia.

**Dr B. Manivannan** (MA, MPhil, BEd, PhD) has been retired as an Associate Professor from the Department of English in VO Chidambaram College, Thoothukudi. He is a Tamil poet, author, translator, soft-skill trainer and environmentalist. He has edited a book titled *Studies in Indian English Poetry: From Aurobindo to Laksmi Kanna*. He has published his articles in many national and international journals and edited anthologies. He is one of the Preliminary Panel Advisers, Award Committee, Sahitya Akademi, Govt. of India. He has been the Chairman, PG English Examination Board, MS University, Tirunelveli, University nominee, PG Board of Studies, Sadakatullah Appa College, Tirunelveli, Member, PG Board of Studies, MS University, Tirunelveli, Member of Editorial Board in Outreach: Multidisciplinary Research Journal. His poems and short stories have been published in Tamil magazines. He has received Loyola Literary Media Award (2014) and Kavi Venthar Award (2015) for being the best poet among more than 300 poets in Tamil Nadu in 2014, conferred by Anantha Jothy Literary Circle and Meera Publishers.

**Dr Suchitra Gupta** is a Professor of English at Govt. VYTPG Autonomous College, Durg (Chhattisgarh). She has 35 years of teaching experience. Her area of specialisation is Indian Writing in English. Her areas of interest are Classical Criticism, Indian Writing in English and Colonial and Postcolonial Literature.

**Dr Ashok Verma** is a Professor in the Department of English, Bhagat Phool Singh Mahila Vishwavidyalaya, Khanpur Kalan (Haryana). His areas of interest include Translation Studies and Marginal Writings. He has published sixteen research papers and has presented papers in more than twenty seminars/conferences including one in Germany and another in Norway.

**Dr S. Chelliah** is the Dean of Arts, Humanities & Languages, and Professor, Head, and Chairperson of School of English and Foreign Languages, and Special Officer for Planning & Development at Madurai Kamaraj University, Madurai (Tamil Nadu). He did his MA in English Literature from Madurai Kamaraj University, Madurai and got his PhD degree in English from the same university. He has produced 25 PhD scholars, more than 209 MPhil scholars and 196 MA projects. He has published 11 books and 317 papers in various national and international journals and edited anthologies. He has served as the Dean for Curriculum Development of Madurai Kamaraj University, Director for Board of Studies Section, Director for Spoken English Institute of Madurai Kamaraj University, Co-ordinator for CBCS Wing, Liaison Officer for SC/ST Cell of Madurai Kamaraj University and Member of Board of Studies of both UG/PG of Pondicherry University, Manonmaniam Sundaranar University, Bharathidhasan University, Trichy, Bharathiar University, Coimbatore and Gandhigram University and an Examiner of various colleges and universities at both

PG and MPhil levels and also Co-ordinator for UGC remedial coaching scheme for SC/ST/OBC and minority categories. He has been awarded the Best Research Publisher Award (Highest Profile) and DLitt for excellent contribution in English Literature and Language by International Economics University (SAARC Countries).

# 1

# Silver Lining in Hazari's Dark Clouds of Life as an Untouchable: A Study of His *Untouchable: An Autobiography of an Indian Outcaste*

*Prof. D. Amalraj*

Every human being is born only as a free man on earth and not as a subordinate or a slave to any other human being who is better in social status. He is God's dignified creation and he leads his life of freedom only to fulfill his heart's desire. The moment his heart's desire takes a concrete shape, he establishes his individual and independent identity. He does it not only by braving all types of natural and man-made obstacles but also by becoming victorious over all such obstructions. William Wordsworth has said in his *Ode on Intimations to Immortality from Recollection of Early Childhood*, "Heaven lies about us in our infancy" (67). He does not mean to say that heaven lies about the infancy of only those born in a higher caste and not to those who are born in a discriminated lower class. Heaven lies about the infancy of all the infants irrespective of their social status. But the self centered higher, higher middle, and middle class human beings convert the heavenly earth into an extremely unpleasant and unlivable one for the socially inferior Dalits who are also dignified human beings as the creators of one and the same God.

The segregation of the Dalits as untouchables from the mainstream of societal life is not the fault of the Creator but that of the people of the forward, backward, and the most backward communities. It is only the inhuman attitudes of these people that have paved the way for the existence of caste divisions in the society. The pity is that the all powerful Creator of human beings remains voiceless like the blindfolded Goddess of Justice in the court of law. The Creator simply sees His one set of people in the Dalits having been sidelined as socially inferior. Hence, both the genders in Dalit group are forced to lead their societal life as insignificant and discriminated beings before others. Jean-Jacques Rousseau, the French Philosopher, has said, "Man who was and is born free, but he is everywhere in chains" (qtd. in Bluhm, 359). This is the real condition of the life of the Dalits in India and Rousseau's saying has become really true in the present set up of the Indian society. The Dalits, though born free, are metaphorically in chains everywhere without any freedom to do anything. They cannot go anywhere in the society, move with others with equality, enter into the places of worship to pray and lead their life as a dignified one.

The Dalits from their birth to the death cannot see any silver lining in the dark clouds of their discriminated and isolated life. Their earthly life has only one season round the year and that is only winter. They cannot be hopeful of seeing spring during their earthly life however advanced they are in education and profession. As far as their life is concerned, Shelly's prophetic line "If winter comes, can spring be far behind?" (*West Wind,* 75) flatters to deceive them. All Dalits, though they are born as Hindus, are not treated on par with their fellow Hindus just because they are untouchables. India has become a Digital and New India but the condition of the entire Dalit community has continued to remain the same as it has been in the past without any traces of advancement in their living conditions. The Brahmins think of themselves higher than all other Indian castes even though some other caste people also belong to the forward communities. Yet all other classes join together and enjoy seeing the plight of the Dalits and in doing so, they are equally sadists as Hitler had been towards the Jews.

All the Dalits being untouchables have experienced and continue to experience public disgrace. As Indian voters, all the Dalits are treated like Gods and Goddesses at the time of the elections but after the elections they become unwanted and good for nothing people meant only for carrying out filthy works such as cleaning the ditches and sweeping the streets. Their life is like the Vinayga who is praised like anything on his birthday but after a week his statues become good for nothing ones, fit only to be thrown into all dirty waters. Only when the Dalits realise their weaknesses inherent in their nature, they can avoid being disgraced by others. Hazari's autobiography *Untouchable: An Autobiography of an Indian Outcaste* highlights how his own Dalit people have been mainly responsible for their endless hardships. He feels distressed at the attitudes of his people. Their failure in realising that God would not have created a man with the thought that one man should consider another man as his inferior and untouchable though both follow Hinduism.

The higher caste domination over the Dalits in Hinduism has been a regular occurrence from time immemorial. If the higher caste Hindus do not change their attitudes towards their fellow Dalits, there can be only dark clouds without silver lining in the life of every Dalit. Gandhiji has already opened up his heart about an Indian treating another Indian as an untouchable in his *Epigram.* According to him:

> The Indian Hindus of higher caste consider their fellow Hindus as untouchables just because the fellow Hindus are the Dalits by birth. Untouchability is a hydra-headed monster but the practice of it in Indian society is very subtle because some of the practices can never be easily detected. Since the eradication of the practice of untouchability is by and large impossible, its practice continues to be an

> [indelible] blot on Hinduism and it is a canker eating into vitals. (n.pag.)

Since the Independence of India in 1947, more than seven decades have gone, and many changes have taken place in the lives of the Indians but there is no end to the practice of untouchability towards the Dalits till this day. Just like the saying 'Only the wearer knows where the shoe pinches, only the Dalits who experience untouchability know how beastly is the practice of untouchability by fellow Indians belonging to the same Hindu religious group.

India is a free nation but the Hindu Dalits continue to be the slaves of other higher caste Indian Hindu groups. They are not free in following their own ways of life. It is the fault of both the higher caste Hindus and the Hindu Dalits. Dr Sivakami Paramasivam in her book *Human Rights—A Study* expresses her concern over the right of the Dalits in Hinduism:

> Though India is totally committed to the principle of secularism, [it is unfortunate that] the caste systems and untouchability still prevail. In rural areas of India, caste feeling is very strong and uncontrollable. Hence, there always exists chaos and confusion in the life of the rural people just because they are from the class of untouchability. Indian government appears to be struggling hard in order to eradicate Casteism and untouchability. However, the act of the government in this regard becomes meaningless as communal clashes continue to spoil the peaceful living of all together. (208)

Hazari being a Dalit has been no exception and his life from his childhood till he has voiced against untouchability and established his independent individuality has always been at the mercy of the higher caste Hindus. He has described the life of untouchability under the guise of a fictitious name. Since he has been placed in a piquant situation to identify his caste, he used to say that he is a Christian without mentioning his caste.

Neither has he mentioned his parents and his relatives as untouchable ones. It is presumed that he has done this kind of act only to avoid his disgrace as a Dalit in public.

Hazari was born in one of the villages in the district of Moradabad in Uttar Pradesh as the son of the untouchable parents. His parents have been unskilled workers and their duty has been to look after the rich Hindus and Muslims, keep the markets, roads and public latrines always neat and clean for the use of the higher caste Hindus. Besides, as and when they have happened to see the animals lying dead in the streets, they have become over-joyous. They have also belittled themselves in doing such acts which the higher castes never do. Hazari has brought out such shameful acts of his people:

> As regards the dead animals, His Dalit people [have] watched them in the same way as the vulture watches; there is no difference between the vulture and the [untouchable] sweeper in this respect. As soon as an animal such as a cow, or a horse, or goat is seen lying dead, his [Dalit people] have brought it to a field to skin it. [They then] take the meat for cooking and eating, and the skin as and when it is dried, it is to be sold. [They have] left the carcass for the vultures to clean, and, when the vultures [have] had finished, they would collect the bones, which they sell for money. (7-8)

As all his Dalit people have been meant only for menial works, their health has been greatly affected. Being unhealthy, they do not mind their children being unhealthy. This is the way of their life and hence, they are always kept at a distance by the higher caste Hindus. The concerned officers in the government have never paid any particular attention to the state of affairs in the families of the untouchables. As a result, many Dalit children for want of medical care, healthy surroundings, and healthy food have met with death even before they have come to know what life has been. Despite such unhealthy living conditions, many Dalit children have miraculously escaped death. As boys, they could not attend schools for their educational advancement. Instead, they have gone to work so that they could be of some help to their parents. With their timely help, their parents can tide over their financial difficulties to a certain extent and feed themselves. Being innocent, these boys have not been aware whether their parents have enjoyed life or suffered a lot, but the boys have remained in darkness not knowing what kind of sufferings their parents have experienced in the society. Children working to help their parents have made Hazari say, "Every young and innocent child of an untouchable family has to be a father before he is a child" (51).

Almost all Hazari's people do not have any landed property of their own. They have to depend on the higher caste rich Hindu farmers and work as their agricultural labourers for livelihood. Being ignorant and innocent, they do not know the ways of the world. They get always cheated by the rich agricultural land owners when they do not get the rightful salary which they deserve for their hard labour. They accept whatever is given as their pay without voicing their dissent. If they point out the less pay for their more hard work in the fields they do, they have to remain at home without any work and starve. In this way, Hazari's parents and his caste people have been exploited. Being dependent on the rich farmers, they do not have money to send their children to school for education. Even if some children go to school for education, they face humiliation at the hands of the upper caste students. The higher caste teachers are no exception in meting out all types of ill-treatment in words outside and inside the school in the presence of other students. Hazari as a student has been no exception to this kind of discrimination.

Hazari feels hurt at the attitudes of his people who have remained indifferent to the affront at the hands of the higher caste Hindus and bitter experiences they have had as and when they have gone and attended both the weddings and the funerals in the houses of the rich and higher caste Hindus. He cannot but silently stand by looking at the attitudes and behaviour of his people. His people have never hesitated to do any kind of menial work because "[they] receive food and grain as recompense for [their] work as well as money" (9). Moreover, they are used to standing in a line and waiting outside with a great reverence before the houses of the higher caste Hindus where marriages are conducted. They have got used to standing outside such houses with their hands placing across their chests as if they were their slaves. They have been eagerly looking forward to getting the left-over food from the dinner tables. It has been due to their birth as untouchables and poverty that have made them belittle themselves. Sometimes, they have been made "to carry messages, either from one village to another or within the town itself" (9). Soon after the marriage, when the bridegroom goes to his house in a procession led by the untouchables, the higher caste Hindus throw money over his head so that he can be saved from the evil spirits. It is done because the people of his Dalit community who have been leading the procession are treated "as the harborers of evil spirits" (10). It has been the belief of the higher caste Hindus that If money is thrown over the bridegroom and if it is collected by the untouchables leading the procession, "It is a way of asking the evil spirits to be kind to their bridegroom and bless his marriage" (10). Hazari has been heavily hurt at his people being treated as evil spirits.

As far as the funerals in the houses of the higher caste Hindus have been concerned, Hazari's people have never looked reluctant to do all sorts of works outside such houses without minding their degradation. Hazari could not but simply stand looking at his people involving themselves in all sorts of unhygienic works as if it had been their karma. He has, thus, described in his autobiography about the attitudes of his people:

> As soon as the dead body is ready to be taken from the house of the higher caste Hindus to the Ghat, the male

> untouchables line up in front of the procession. Money, flowers, and certain fruits are thrown over the body . . . No sooner does the cortege advance toward the Ghat than most of the higher caste people except the close relatives and a few untouchables accompany the body. When the body reaches the Ghat, it is laid on the ground a few yards from the running waters of the Ganges, and, after a short prayer by a sadhu or pundit, it is laid on the plinth built of wood. Then all the outer coverings are taken off the body and given to the untouchables. Sometimes a body will have as many as ten shawls, some of which may be worth up to 500 rupees. These in turn become a few of the occasional sources of the untouchables' worldly riches to be cherished forever. (11)

The untouchables have never thought of anything other than doing service to the higher caste Hindu people in this way but they have failed to realise that their acts have not only belittled them but also pained the heart of those empowered men and women of their community like Hazari. Their lack of education and ignorance of the ways of the world are the causes that bring down their morale in the society.

One should be fortunate to have been born in a Dalit family, which is quite different from other Dalit families. Hazari has been such a fortunate Dalit. His family has not stayed like other Dalit families in one place for ever. It has migrated from one hilly place to another in search of part time jobs better than unskilled works other Dalit families have been doing. Hazari's parents have started serving the British families of the hilly area where they have come into contact with some English men and women with liberal attitudes towards all Indians, irrespective of their religious and caste differences. However, as part time workers, they have been made to update their knowledge in English to a certain extent. Their learning of English has certainly augured well for Hazari. It has resulted in his pursuing his school education in a school run by a mosque. Since he has not been able to continue his schooling after two years as his parents could not pay his fees though he has been good at studies. However, his two year schooling has created in him a lot of interest in reading books like the *Ramayana*, *The Legends of Prithiviraj* and the *Holy Koran*. In spite of his literacy, he has not been able to find any silver lining in his life. He has been only treated as an untouchable by the higher caste Hindus. Moreover, the higher caste Hindu people have appeared startled when they have come to know that Hazari has been literate and he has read books like *Ramayana* and he has had some knowledge of *Koran* too by heart. However, Hazari has been determined to come up in life through education without minding all types of discrimination by the higher caste Hindus.

Hazari has fortunately found himself in the seventh heaven of bliss when he has come into contact with the Congress and Muslim League because they have started schools for the people of untouchability like him. But his happiness has lasted only for a short period the moment he has realised that both the parties have started educational institutions only for getting the votes of the Dalits and not for bringing their advancement in life through education. He has felt shocked to know that the entire country has been only against the entire Dalit community. In spite of this bitter truth, he has been in support of the political parties hoping that there should be some changes to light up the darkness of his Dalit life and bring in equality among all Indians irrespective of the caste differences. But their political attitudes have saddened his heart further. However his faith in God has not let him down when he has seen silver lining appearing in his dark life as a Dalit. He has seen such a silver lining in the guise of Mr Newman from England as his teacher in Aligarh University. Since no higher caste Hindu teacher has been willing to teach him for his being a Dalit, and his fellow students have been mostly Muslims, he has been in great dilemma whether his education is more important than religion or a change himself from a Hindu to a Muslim for his permanent escape from his man-made ordeals as a Dalit Hindu. He has thought of it himself:

> I had to think very hard what I really wanted to do [in my life]. Did my [advancement and social respect in] life lie in the pursuit of education or in a change of religion? I realised that education without religion meant nothing to me; my studies must be related to spiritual life. It seemed I would have to turn to Islam, where the community is a true brotherhood and not merely a formal system. (181)

Just because Hazari believes in the brotherhood that Islam teaches, he is not a total believer in Islam either. He is critical of some of the beliefs Islam entertains. Similarly he does not have complete faith in Hinduism. No human being who is considered to be a non-believer in any religious beliefs is unfit to live along with other believers in their respective religion. God who is considered to be the creator does not differentiate his creations on the basis of their religious faith. All are equal to Him. After his mentor Newman has left India for his native country, he continues to support Hazari for his independent identity through his education. Since then, he has continued to establish his cordial relationship with all the Muslims in India. Yet the feeling that he is still an untouchable one however educated he is and whatever his religion is remains rooted to his heart:

> There was something I could never erase - the fact that I was born an untouchable. At times, this kept me away from the more exclusive society, as I could never discuss either my family or my childhood [with my friends]. I could never tell a friend that when I was young I did this and that. I could not tell anyone why and how I was receiving an allowance from an Englishman. I tried to live as they did, yet I had no background and no social foundation on which to stand. I confided in no one since I dreaded sympathy and condescension, with the result that, in the midst of all these friends, I was lonely and homesick. (188-189)

India is only for all native Indians who follow different religions, belong to different castes and speak different languages. It can never belong to one religion, one caste, and one language. India's strength lies in its declared dictum "unity in diversity." All are equal and no one is inferior or superior to the other. One may be rich or poor but it does not indicate that all those who are rich are superior and all those who are poor are inferior. No religions except Hinduism categorise one group of people as untouchables and the other group is above the reach of all other groups. It is only Hinduism that discriminates people on the basis of their birth and castes. When other religions do not consider the Dalits as untouchables but only as equal human beings, it is only the higher caste Hindus who always keep the Dalits at a distance thinking that the Dalits are the spoiler of the purity of their caste and religion. If the higher caste Hindu people are to be socially boycotted as the most dangerous ones to the unity of India, nobody knows what their fate will be but such a thing is nothing but impractical in the social set up.

## Works Cited

Hazari. *Untouchable: Autobiography of an Indian Outcaste*. Frederick A. Praeger, 1969.

Paramasivam, Dr Sivakami. *Human Rights—A Study*. Sriram Computer Prints and Offset, 1998.

Rousseau, Jean Jacques. "Social Contract and Discourses." *Words of Wisdom: Introduction to Philosophy*, J. M. Dent and Sons, 1920.

Shelley, Percy Bysshe. "Ode to the West Wind." *The Golden Quill: An Anthology of Poetry*, edited by P.K. Seshadri, Macmillan, 2017.

Tikekar, S.R, editor. *Epigrams from Gandhiji*. Publication Division, Ministry of Information and Broadcasting, 2017, pp. 1-342.

Wordsworth, William. "Ode on Intimations of Immortality from Recollections of Early Childhood." *The Oxford Book of English Verse: 1250-1900*, edited by Arthur Quiller-Couch, 1919, p. 536.

# 2

# Untold Story of a Bhangi Vice-Chancellor: An Account of Indomitable Courage and Struggle

*Dr Shikha Saxena*

The autobiography by Prof. Shyamlal *Untold Story of a Bhangi Vice-Chancellor* is a firsthand realistic account of a protagonist who fought against the invincible citadels of society where there was a class divide based on caste system. A Shudra by origin and a Brahmin by profession Prof. Shyamlal had to struggle a lot for his education; grabbing equal opportunity for profession and the worst thing he has to face is the custom of untouchability in the society. To quote from the text:

> Amongst all the castes in the four-fold Hindu society, the Bhangis are the lowest and most backward community. Insensitive to their inferior position, they are not conscious of their slavery. (Shyamlal, 1)

The entire narration of personal experiences exhibits that he has to undergo an incessant ordeal since his childhood. He has given a comprehensive account of the duties that a member of Bhangi Community has to perform. They have to do number of strenuous tasks to meet their both ends. The writer gives a brief account of the duties in the following words:

> The work was of strenuous nature, often involving a great deal of lifting of heavy loads and carrying them to distances

> of more than 2 or 3 miles. The loads consisted of all the refuse of the household. If these duties of the high caste communities were not carried out daily, we could not meet our both the ends. In the Princely states, we, as a Bhangi caste had no other work or profession but to keep the city clean and in fact to do all the work of scavengers, sweeping roads, cleaning public and private latrines and salvaging dead animals. (Shyamlal, 2)

In the Princely state of Jodhpur, the colony of the author was located under the shadow of Mehrangarh Fort. The following excerpt from the text gives us a glimpse of his childhood. They must live in dirty unhygienic Bastis named as Lakharon-Ka-Bass. The writer penned down his recollections of childhood thus:

> I was the true child of untouchable, where there was no drain, no light, no water, and marsh land, where I lived amongst the public latrines and in the stink of their dung scattered about here and there of the world where there the day was like dark night and nights pitch-dark. I had wallowed in its mire, bathed in its marshes, played among its rubbish heaps and my list-less, lazy manners were the result of my surroundings. I was a friend and companion of the flies and mosquitoes, since my childhood. (Shyamlal, 6)

The entire narrative is overcast with the inhuman practice of 'untouchability' prevalent in the society. The so-called high-caste members of society did not allow the 'untouchables' to fetch water from public taps 'as if the water would be polluted' (6). As a child the author becomes inquisitive to know the reason behind 'untouchability'. He deep delves to know the cause behind this inhuman treatment and the answer he gets for his query clearly exhibits the social hypocrisy of upper-caste members of the society. To quote from the text:

> They always abuse us. Because we are Bhangis. Because we touch Dung. They hate Dung. That is why they do not

> touch us, the high caste Hindus....For them we are sweepers, sweeper—Untouchable, Untouchable, Untouchable! That is the word! Untouchables. We are Untouchables. (Shyamlal, 6)

The obsolete inhuman practice of untouchability was not only practiced by uneducated and orthodox members of the society it was also practiced by so-called educated people of the society. To quote his experiences from the text:

> During my middle school days, we had offered Sanskrit as the second language. There was a Brahmin Sanskrit teacher in the middle school. His name was Magha Dutt Shrimali.... He particularly hated the Bhangi students. He used to beat us daily with sticks during the class room. This teacher had left scars on the life of the Bhangi students....The teacher neither touched our note books nor did he ever asked us to recite poems or put questions to us for fear of being polluted. (Shyamlal, 14)

The Bhangis were the worst sufferers in the princely state of Jodhpur. They must announce loudly 'Paiyas Paiyas' (keep distance). They were not allowed to move freely on the streets. "The Bhangis had no right to see their 'Raja' because they belong to a low caste" (12).

The author felt sad for observing all such inhuman practices by his mother. She did not want to invite the wrath of upper caste Hindus, so she also used to cry 'Paiyas Paiyas' to safeguard the upper-caste Hindus from her touch.

One more incident from the autobiography gives us the glimpse of grim state of affairs in the Princely state Jodhpur. The author with his friend was passing through Tripolia Bazar in Jodhpur and he felt thirsty. To quench his thirst, he went to water-hut. The waterman asked about his caste and he shared it as Mali (Gardner). The waterman started pouring water from Ramzhara. In the meantime, some orthodox high caste Hindus recognised him and they were infuriated by the sight that a

Bhangi is drinking water from a Ramzhara. To quote from the text is heart rending.

> They shouted Bhangi, Bhangi. There was uproar in the Bazaar People became conscious. The waterman was red and pale and shouted at the highest pitch of the voice "Bhangi" beat him. I was perplexed. I was dazed....With terror in my mind of beating, I entered my house. (Shyamlal, 19)

The closed-minded inhuman practices were not confined to common people. In higher education center like Jodhpur University the Professors also could not come out from their traditional mindset. The author recollects a particular incident when he was asked to deliver a lecture. He accepted but the moment it was notified by a professor in the class, the upper caste students reacted badly. They quizzed, "What could a Harijan deliver a lecture to high caste Hindu students and others from advanced society?" (27).

Despite all these incessant ordeals of life, the author believed in cosmopolitan philosophy of life. They followed the cult of Kabir school of thought which propounds the philosophy of equality for all members of the society. Their belief is, "Jat Pant Puche na Koi, Har ko Bhaje so har ka hoi" (9).

In all such grim circumstances, education can be the only game-changer. The author gives the credit of his education to his mother. The apprehensions were in society that as they are poor people, so they will not be able to afford it. But the author's mother took it as a challenge, "She vowed to educate her sons, even if circumstances compel her for begging for it. My father felt much relief to see the courage of her wife" (Shyamlal, 8). At the later stage, he also gave the entire credit to his mother. He gave the credit of his success to his mother in the following words:

> Born in a poor family, struggled throughout her life and passed her life more than five decades as widow, my mother was the first Bhangi woman who by her boldness, matured

> brain, intelligent, sincere, honest, loyal and with a wonderful memory made a profound impression on her coming generation. She was a family reformer and was regarded by all men and women as family builder of four generations that followed her. (10)

She inculcated the art of living among all her children. Even in their limited means of living the author and his family were happy. He recollects all such precious moments of his life in the following words:

> The months that followed the death of my father were very critical for all of us. Mother's salary had not been sufficient to feed the whole family. My mother and sisters had to go without shoes, in spite of the scorching heat in Jodhpur. These were days when we could get only one meal and that too a very dry and poor one. We could not afford milk, butter, or meat. Despite all these odds our family life was always happy and there was no discontentment amongst any of his members. We were always glad... (10)

Prof. Shyamlal also appreciated the government policies to give scholarships to all such poor Bhangi students. But he also shared his bitter experiences and callous attitude of clerks in the Jodhpur University campus. Following incident is an example of the biased attitude of clerks at the university campus.

> As regards the submission of the application forms for the scholarship and its disbursement the clerks shrewdly mis-behaved, harassed, humiliated and insulted. For hours together, we had to wait in line for the payment of scholarship and that too was not paid to us in time. On campus, we were the most hated students and branded as a liability on the university. What was worse, was that they labelled us, "Congress ke Damad" (Son-in-laws of Congress Government). We felt humiliated in the campus. There was hardly any involvement in any activities. (21-22)

The entire text has been divided in 15 chapters. Each chapter reveals about a specific phase and time-line in Prof. Shyamlal's life like 1st Chapter has been titled as 'My Childhood Days and Social Background,' then second and third are about student life and family life. There are some specific chapters devoted to his experiences as Vice-Chancellor and revelation of caste-based politics in Jodhpur University campus. Specific mentioned chapters are like 'Seminar on Bhangis' and 'The Bhangis and Bhils'.

The author has given the dates, years and timeline with all the narration in such an accurate way that it seems that he used to write a daily diary and later on he narrated the incidents in his literary work. As a precursor of the moment for abolition of untouchability, he organised various seminar on Bhangis 'exclusively for the Bhangis and by the Bhangis' (107). Magazines, journals and newspaper articles were also written by Prof. Shyamlal. The entire narration in 15 chapters by the author serve as a window for the internal functioning of the university. It was full of politics, caste-based prejudices and overall the author has to work hard to retain the prestige and reputation of the Jodhpur University.

The author with honesty shares his bitter experiences of his life but it was not a demeanour for him. With utmost honesty he accepts and inspires others by his example that hard work and sincerity finally paved the way for him. In the following words he confesses:

> These personalities (Baba Ram Devji Maharaj, M.K. Gandhi, Dr Ambedkar, Jai Narayan Vyas, Mama Achleshwar Prasad Sharma and Saint Kabir) gave me strength and the modern education gave me a weapon. I faced cruel attacks and received merciless blows....Lastly the hard work I undertook and ability which I showed as Vice-Chancellor of J.N.V. University Jodhpur, crowned my work as a successful Vice-Chancellor. What more an untouchable can do? Self made

> and self-elevated as a matter of course, my morning life was dusty and noon bright. (40-41)

In the literary scenario, the present literary work is a literary monument as the author shared his firsthand encounter with the social hegemony that was rampant in contemporary society. His entire odyssey inspired others to break these hegemonic obsolete structures of the society. The inhuman experiences were narrated in an unbiased objective way that left the reader sometime bereaved. The entire ordeal was presented in such a way that it becomes the commendable literary piece of art. Such literary pieces can be the eye-opener for the so called social patrons of the society. From the title to various chapters the author boldly accepted that he is a bhangi. The text with certain facts can be a piece for literary canons and a valid document for sociological research. The book invites comparison with other literary pieces like Bhagwan Das' *Mai Bhangi Hun*, Om Prakash Valmiki's *Joothan*, Anand's *Untouchable* and Gayatri Spivak's *Can the Subaltern Speak*?

## Works Cited

Limbale, Sharankumar. *Towards an Aesthetic of Dalit Literature: History, Controversies and Considerations*. New Delhi: Orient BlackSwan, 2014.

Rajinkar, Ashwin. "The Prisons We Broke: Saga of Dalit Women's Pathetic Condition" http://ashwinranjanikar.blogspot.in/2013/11/dalit-women-autobiography-baby-kamble.html?m=1 Accessed 10 Dec., 2017.

Shyamlal. *Untold Story of a Bhangi Vice-Chancellor*. Jaipur: University Book House, 2001.

# 3

# Dalit Consciousness in Tumbadi Ramaiah's *Manegara*

*Dr S. R. Chaitra*

"Dalit is a category of self-definition of Untouchables in post-Independence India; it signifies a state of radical consciousness and seeks to interrogate and challenge the previous stereotypes that caste Hindu society had employed to describe untouchable as well as near-untouchables castes and communities" (Nagaraj, 21). Dalits, from time immemorial, have lived a precarious existence by being denied the basic human rights. They are rejected and discriminated by the upper caste Hindus in the rigid social structure of the Indian caste-based society.

Dalit Literature is the voice of the people who have lived a voiceless existence. The emergence of Dalit voice in the form of writing is of great significance as the voice reveals a purpose of awakening conscious among the Dalits. Ruman Sutradhar states that at a time when there were no means of communication with Dalits, pen was the only solution as Brahmins controlled the media and therefore Dalits began their own magazines and wrote about their pain, not with ink, but with their blood, they wrote from their own cuts—the cuts being basically mental, with instincts of physical in them. Hence "Dalit Literature is a struggle of new life. It is a soul of humanity. It is a life story which faced the states of death" (Awad, 4). The writings of Dalits document the realistic experience accompanied by anguish, protest and questioning of the unjust treatment in the Hindu caste-ridden society. Unlike the mainstream literature which reveals the universal thoughts and emotions in the highest order which consequently give aesthetic pleasure to the readers, 'Dalit Literature' has no such thoughts and emotions, but a 'purpose'. The 'purpose' is to expose the unjust social order and hegemonic tradition of caste system and resist the culturally rooted exploitation on the basis of 'caste' in India and subsequently assert the identity of the marginalised, dispossessed and disempowered people. Hence Dalit Literature is a literature of protest, rejection, resistance and an attempt to reconstruct their lives. Dalit writing is a literature of marginality which focuses on the social, religious and casteist oppression. These writings reveal the multiple oppressions which the Dalits have suffered.

These sufferings are common to all the Dalits. They have been downgraded and degraded from ages by the upper caste Hindus in the name of religion with concept of 'purity' and 'pollution'. They have lived a life of poverty, oppression and despair in an unhealthy and insanitary condition. Thus, Dalit Literature is a literature of commitment. Arjun Dangle, the Marathi Dalit writer, editor, activist says that Dalit Literature is marked by 'revolt' and 'negativism' since it is closely associated with the 'hopes for freedom' by a group of people who, as untouchables, are victims of social, economic, and cultural inequality. He further says Dalit Literature is nothing but the literary expression of this awareness (Limbale, 1). Hence, 'Dalit Literature is not simply literature ... Dalit Literature is associated with a movement to bring about change... at the very first glance, it will be strongly evident that there is no established critical theory or point of view behind them; instead there is new thinking and a new point of view' (Dangle, vii-viii). Thus, Dalit Literature is a voice of resistance against the marginalisation, oppression and discrimination faced on a daily basis in different arenas of life by a major section of the society.

Dalits have contributed to the emergence of a literature by voicing their plight in the form of various genres to the mainstream Indian literature. Dalit testimonies have served as an excellent area of research to explore the socio-political and economic conditions of their lives. Autobiography is a platform for narrating and commenting their personal experiences. Mini Babu on commenting on autobiographies writes:

> Autobiographies are generally written by eminent personalities towards the end of their lives and who have got much to evidence before the world, while Dalit autobiographies are penned at an early age when the author is neither distinguished nor eminent but noted for its depiction of a poignant past that has affected the history of a community. These autobiographies deal not only with the caste system as oppressive but also depict how economic deprivation and poverty are handmaids with caste discrimination. (Babu, 2)

As Dalits have always been marginalised and exploited, the autobiographies written by them put forth the sorrow 'from the core of the bleeding heart'. These autobiographies reveal the firsthand experience of the oppressed who are socially, culturally, economically, politically and religiously segregated and exploited individuals. Therefore, Dalit autobiographies are also 'autobiographies of the communities'. They are the assertion of authentic Dalit experience. They reject the tradition, aesthetics, and language of the 'mainstream' literature. Dalit Literature rejects the mainstream 'language'. Thus, the minute details of every day struggle are written in a language that is opposed to the upper caste 'language' which is refined and proper. Thus, the language in Dalit Literature is often crude and uncivil.

The present paper concentrates on bringing out Dalit consciousness in the Dalit autobiographical narrative *Manegara* originally written in Kannada by Tumbadi Ramaiah and translated to English by Krishna Murthy Chandar.

The autobiography focuses on the trials and tribulations of narrator who belongs to an extremely backward community called Madiga. Dalits in Karnataka are classified into the 'left hand' Madigas and the 'right hand' Holeyas. The narrator belongs to the category of Manegara. Manegaras are the 'left hand' Dalits coming under the category of Madigas. As Manegaras are the messengers of the news of the death, they are considered to be of bad omen in contradiction to people who bring good news.

*Manegara* as an autobiographical narrative exposes the inequality, cruelty, oppression and injustice besides the experiences of pain, suffering and anguish. The narrative also brings out the agony of victims due to social and cultural brutalities. The narrator brings out his life of humiliation and depravation combined with the existential angst. In the process of the journey of his life, he tastes the bitter realisation of helplessness. The autobiography unravels a series of experiences caught in one frame.

The narrator reminiscences the poverty in this childhood by saying, "sleep outside, biting chill, sleep inside, tormenting Bed-Bugs. *Kure*, the young ones of Bed-Bugs, nested in the only Shirt and Knickers we had" (3). He considers these 'kures' as 'Rakta Beejasuras' who would multiply endlessly and had become one in colour with their shirts and knickers. In an attempt to crush them on their finger nail, their hands would become bloody as if someone had returned from war. Their parents too would help the children in crushing them. The mother would say "all the food that's eaten goes to these lies and kure only" (4). Talking about the 'Ikra' (Indigenous house), the parents reminiscence the way they had built the house with much difficulty. The narrator gives a glimpse of the various jobs undertaken by his father in order to fulfill the needs of his family.

During a government programme named after Sanjay Gandhi to forcibly sterilise men, the narrator's 'appa' (father) too had volunteered and brought food given to him during the operation. The father would do one work in the morning, another in the afternoon, yet another in the evening. He had even taken up the job of cobbling and had been to visit several villages including the Lambani settlements. He would buy Ragi and vegetables to the house. But his business would not be the same every day. Some days he would not get even the first transaction 'boni' and the narrator would be forced to return with his father empty handed and just drink water for the day. The father owned one and a half acres of land besides one acre which he used to cultivate on a share-basis. The government had allotted four acres of land which he ended selling for just eight hundred rupees to clear the loan which he had incurred to celebrate the wedding of the narrator's elder brother. The narrator's father also kept the younger brother as a bonded labour to clear the loan. When the interests were very high, the father had to give away the milking cow and a buffalo. Besides this, the father had also learnt a bit of country medicine where he would treat the cattle for their ailments. He also knew the knack of piercing the nose of the cattle. Pig rearing was another task that the narrator's appa undertook. As the pigs would litter more than ten a year, their numbers would increase rapidly year by year.

Not many ate pork in their locality except four or five houses including the narrator's parents. The pig rearing continued till the narrator joined college in Tumkur. His mother, Sanjeevamma was the mother of many children. She would say to the young girls, "Fourteen were born; only eight have remained now! Six of them died within six months or a year. Only one of them died when he had come of age" (6). When the brothers of the narrator got married and settled elsewhere, his sister Lakshamamma undertook all hard labour starting with lugging mud and stone in order to help the father. The narrator too started working as a casual labour and got involved in stone crushing, bridge construction, carrying and transporting mud, stitching slipper.

The narrator's parents were from Bukkapattana, next to Korategere. His grandfather, Ilu Kempeerappa was reddish just like his name and would wear "white 'panche' till his knees and would tie ceremonial red cloth which was a sign of caste—Madigas" (7). He was the only one who could speak with the same command as the Talawars and was one among the five elders of Panchayati who would deliver justice in and round the seven villages. The grandfather would declare proudly that his grandson, that is, the author was studying in high school. Gollahally was the twin village of Tumbadi which was the place of narrator's other grandfather, Mukundappa. He was also called as 'Maatada' Mukundappa because of his prowess in black magic. The whole village would respect him because of fear as his bag would be full of strange things needed to seal those on whom demons and ghosts had come where three roads met. He had emulets for children and a huge bone which he worshipped with plenty of red vermillion and yellow turmeric.

The narrator gives a glimpse of the nature of the Manegara community. The task of bringing the dead cattle and butchering was undertaken by the Manegaras. The intestines of the cattle were pulled out and dried in the sun. When beaten on a stick, it would produce 'Tamate' like sound. The art that boys of Manegaras community would learn is the art of beating the empty coconut shells which they would at a later stage convert to little tamates and learn beating them. Beating of the Tamate drums was an art hereditarily inherited. This art would not be learnt in a day but was an eternal learning. There were variation in the beats. There were called 'gustis'. There were many gustis such as *Hanumantharaya's* (ordinary) gusti, *Maramma's* (non-vegetarian) gusti and *Kaluve* (canal) gusti.

Doddamma who is one of the seven goddesses was in Bukkattanna where the Talawars were the priests. There is also a temple of Vaaddagere Veerangamma. Though the Manegaras belong to the Veeranagamma and Doddamma '*Okkalu*' (tenants), they are not allowed inside either of these temples.

In every festival the common practice in the village is to beat '*Hare* and *Tamate*'. The instrument of *Hare* was for Holeyas and *Tamate* was the instrument of Madigas. The elders would narrate a story thus:

> The front portion of the Veeranagamma temple was built by one of our ancestors, four-five generations earlier. Even then our Manegaras who were her devotees were not allowed to beat the Tamates there and, along with the Holeyas, were not allowed into the temple. Like all other communities, Manegaras are strict devotees of Veeranagamma. Our houses are full of names such as 'Nagamma and 'Veerakyatharaya'! Still our people could not enter the temple to worship there. We had to stand outside and hand over a coconut which was not husked to someone standing near the entrance. That person would de-husk the coconut as we were not allowed to do so, take it inside the temple, get the puja done and give it back to us. (83)

Though there was not a single Muslim family in Thumbadi village, all communities got together to celebrate Babiah's fair which is a Muslim festival. The narrator says that celebrations continue till this day. Many festivals such as *Ugadi*, *Marnomi*, *Babiah's Jaldi*, *Aarati* to *Anjaneya* and *Maramma* are celebrated. The Manegaras would not take part in the *Marnomihabba* because of the story which the elders narrate in this way:

> One of our ancestors had gone to the Shandy to bring things necessary for this puja. He took his eldest son along to help him. One the way back this son suddenly collapsed and died. Unable to digest this sorrow our ancestor decided not to celebrate Marnomi festival at all and that's how they stopped. This custom continues to this day. (32)

A person of the neighbouring town would invite all the households of the village to participate in Marnomi festival except the household of the Manegaras. Hence the Manegaras would not take part in the festivities but would definitely partake in the meal. On the festivals of *Aarati* to *Anjaneya* which would be held on a Monday and of *Maramma* on Tuesday, the third day would be a sacrifice of Bison which would be non-vegetarian meal for all. Fifteen days before the festival, the Manegaras were given the task to announce with the accompaniment of the beating the tamates. The *Ghate* (earthen pot of liquor) would go from the houses of Manegara. In the process of the narration, the author gives us a glimpse of various castes. Regarding his village, he writes:

> Our village comprised nearly eighty houses; ninety out of hundreds of these households were almost similar in lifestyles or status. Nine belong to *Manegaras (Madigas),* and Nine to *Holeyas,* one each belonging to *Lingayats* and *Hajamas,* the barber community. One belonging to *Tigalas,* seven of *Talavaras,* six of *Vaddas (Bovis),* three *Madiwalas* and two *Jains.* Twenty households of *Kumbaras,* sixteen of *Kunchatiga* families. There were no Brahmins in our village. (29)

As the Brahmins family had eliminated due to disease long ago the whole village depended on *Shanubhoga* for consultation regarding the fixation of wedding, naming ceremony etc. In Bukkapattana the place where his parents hail from, the Talawars would do all the management affairs of the village. The 'Talawars' who would do the 'Gowdikes' (village headman) were from the Nayaka community. The Adi Jambava sages were priest of the Manegaara who would come to collect money. When they realised that the community was finding difficulty to get even one square meal, they stopped coming. Then Dakkakus occupied their place. Though Dakkalu people were believed to be born to Manegaras, they would never step into the Manegara's house, but shout for food, cursing them if there would be any delay in giving them food. The author says that the custom is in practice even now.

The narrator reveals how in the small village of Thumbadi the Manegaras were ill-treated because of their caste. There were just two houses each of Lingayats and Jains, the Jains would 'act like cows bitten by wasps!' (30). If their kids happened to play with the narrator and his community boys, the Jains would drag their children back home, slap them and wash their hands and feet. The attitude of the Holeya community which is also a Dalit community was also strange. They would not draw water from the well given to the Manegaras. When the Holeya women approached their locality they would walk as if they were walking on live coal and would wash their legs with cow dung and cow's urine in order to sanctify themselves. The narrator's brother Veeranagappa who had studied high school much before the narrator, was well built and attractive. Though he was sharp in studies and was well known in school as an intelligent boy, he was hated by the teachers because of the straight behaviour. Due to the evil designs of some communal teachers, he was failed in eighth standard. Having failed twice for no reason, he started sinking and became alone, didn't come for home for a couple of days and after three days his body was floating in the tank in an unrecognizable manner. One day in the blistering sun, when the narrator cycled home on a rented cycle, he saw a group of people in front of the house as a woman of the Bovi community had picked a quarrel with his mother as his mother had touched the pot belonging to that woman near the Bore-well and polluted it.

By living the life of poverty, the narrator grew up in extreme trouble to get educated. The narrator joined high school in Koratagere, till he finished PUC that he writes, "I used to walk to Koratagere from my village, whether my feet wore off or the road itself wore off I cannot say" (85). He made use of one opportunity where a politician for his gains opened a Hostel for the Dalits. But the next year, the Taluk officials made them vacate the building under some pretext. The hostel started functioning from one of those small, Janata houses attached to the canteen comprising just one small kitchen and a room only built by the government for the economically downtrodden families and it was difficult for ten of them to sleep in a single room. When the situation in the hostel started deteriorating, a senior boy who had failed in his PUC told them that they should protest against this injustice and ensure proper functioning of the hostel. The narrator, though initially scared started to raise the issue of the hostel with the principal who happened to be their favourite teacher. The conflict became worse and finally the narrator completed his pre-university education with much trouble.

The narrator joined a college in Tumkur for his BA degree around the time when violent quarrel had started between the Dalit boys and the others. Dalit students became the target of assault everywhere and therefore police protection was given to all the Dalit Hostels. But the assaults on the Dalit boys continued unheeded not caring for the Police too. Those were the days the Dalit Sangharsha Samiti (DSS) was taking shape in the State. When the narrator joined the LLB, course after graduation, he came to know people who had dedicated themselves to this organisation and therefore the narrator too became an active member of the DSS. Around this time, the 'Hamals' came under the umbrella of the DSS hoping that this organisation might help them solve their problems. They were gradually drawn into this movement and became active members and the legs of the DSS. It is on the strength of these legs that DSS started moving around! The DSS then got the maximum support, both human and financial, from these 'Hamals' of the Mandi market. The DSS slowly started making its presence felt in the District. The DSS which started essentially as a movement for the struggle of the Dalits gradually started organising the poor belonging to all communities and castes and engaged in their struggle too. This gave the narrator an opportunity to travel to all the taluqs of the district to personally witness the assaults that were going on the Dalits in numerous ways. When the protests, agitations and struggles launched by the DSS in the District reached its zenith the numbers participating in these also went up substantially. The struggle was peaking as a social movement. "The Dalit movement is the politico-cultural expression of newly self-organised community, signifying strategies of radical negotiation and protest with both the state and upper-caste civil society" (Nagaraj, 21). The Dalit consciousness and Dalit sensibility are linked to Dalit struggle.

The novel gives an insight about Dalit life and consciousness. The misery of the untouchables due to the social exclusion and the emerging consciousness and awakening is well brought out in the novel. The narrative embraces various forms of articulation by depicting the narrator's personal experiences. The text also exposes the rich and cultural aspects of Dalit life. Manu Chakravrati in his foreword to the novel, writes that *Manegara* is an outstanding work that documents the transformation Karnataka has undergone at socio-cultural and political levels. More significantly, *Manegara* gives full expression to the evolution of the Dalit self, both in relation to its struggles for justice and equality and the constant wrestling with experiential truths. Ramaiah's text is an account of the 'struggles with truth' of an evolving self.

## Work Cited

Dangle, Arjun, (ed). *Poisoned Bread: Translations from Marathi Dalit Literature*. Hyderabad: Orient Longman, 1992.

Limbale, Sharankumar. *Towards an Aesthetic of Dalit Literature: History Controversies and Considerations*. Trans. by Alok Mukherjee. New Delhi: Orient Blackswan, 2018.

Nagaraja, D. R. *The Flaming Feet and Other Essays: The Dalit Movement in India*. New Delhi: Orient BlackSwan, 2010.

Ramaiah, Tumbadi. *Manegara*. Bengaluru: Sampada Publications, 2015.

# 4

# The Untouchability of Spring: The Varna Narrative in G. Kalyan Rao's *Antarani Vasantam*

*Dr Deeba Sarmad*

Gayatri C. Spivak, in her seminal essay "Can the Subaltern Speak?" raised an important question regarding the voicing of the concerns of the marginalised sections of society. However, a very crucial understanding of this question in itself demands a redirection of this enquiry to "Are the subalterns heard?", because as it turns out, the subalterns, the marginalised, the oppressed, the downgraded have always been speaking, rather shouting out, about their plight. The problem has not been their not being vocal about their conditions; the problem has always been the lack of attention paid to their voices in the mainstream literary biographies, historiographies and dominant narratives of culture and society.

In the genealogy of Dalit Literature, it is generally accepted that this literature emerged in the late 1950s as a distinct literary corpus. Since its arrival on the literary scene, Dalit Literature has come to be recognised as one of the foremost literatures of resistance in the contemporary times beginning with Marathi Dalit Literature and soon succeeded by Kannada, Telugu, Tamil, Bangla, Hindi and other Indian languages. It encompassed within its corpus, narratives depicting the portrayal of the plight of

Dalits in form of poems, novels, stories, songs, essays, biographies, as well as performative arts. But a close analysis of the text *Antarani Vasantam* by G. Kalyan Rao reveals a different genealogy regarding the evolution and origin of Dalit Literature. Though a work of fiction, refusing any resemblance to actual, factual details, yet the text serves a much deeper purpose. It offers a counter-narrative to the existing discussions and debates regarding history in general and origins of Dalit Literature in particular. Most, important of all, it offers a very personal and subjective account of the issue of Dalits through a frame-tale narrative centred upon the life and experiences of eight generations of one *mala* family (an untouchable caste from Southern India) viz: "Sinasubbadu, Yellana *(Senior)*, ...Yerrenkadu,...Yellana *(Junior)*,...Sivaiah,...Reuben,...Immanuel,... Jessie" (Rao, 2010: 188) and the brave generation of women belonging to the same family viz "Sinasubbi, Latchmi...Lingalu (and Boodevi),...Subhadra,...Sasirekha,...Ruth,...Mary,...Ruby" (Rao, 2010: 188).

The journey depicted by Rao is one based structurally on the framework of the great classical Sanskrit epic the *Mahabharata* with eighteen chapters reflecting the eighteen *parvas* (books) of the ancient epic. In content, too, the novel represents the characteristics of the epic tradition in Indian aesthetics with grand style, grand themes, and equally grand characters/heroes/protagonists, but moulding the epic form within the modern novel genre. The novel stands out distinctly as an alternate-epic to its archaic form and its narrative, also, follows the frame-tale pattern, where the memories and stories from various characters are inter-woven in non-linear and non-chronological sequence to present the nucleus story along with the overall plot. Whether such allusions to the *Mahabharata* are deliberate or purely coincidental, it does stand out as a remarkable feature of Kalyan Rao's *Antarani Vasantam* as he attempts to dismantle the religious caste based *savarna* system that Hindu scriptures have built up over centuries.

Through ages "Spring or *vasant*" has carried a metaphorical connotation of optimistic anticipation and hope of better things to come, and through ages Dalits have been subjected to unacceptable ostracisation, repression and exploitation. Yet, it is with 'hope' of being heard and 'hope' of a dignified future that generations of Dalits have offered sometimes active and sometimes passive resistance to the exploitative and subjugating mechanism persistent in societal systems. The memory text, *Untouchable Spring* is one such act of resistance where the story of seven generations of one Dalit family unfolds, presenting the writer's insights into the question of the predominance of caste and the resolute struggles aimed at bringing about a change in the condition of the Dalits. With a hope of succeeding in challenging and dismantling caste discriminations and prejudices, the novel is a journey into the oldest and cruelest system of unjust power relations that have persisted for centuries.

The book, also, stands out distinctly as an alter-history by virtue of its treatment of the subject matter at hand, offering an alternative version and perspective of the mainstream historiography of the dominant discourse through the lenses of Dalit characters. Rao employs actual historical events like C. P. Brown's Telugu studies in the 1850s, the Great Famine of 1877-78, the famine relief work carried out consequently, as part of the Buckingham Canal (1878), the Lone Star Mission or the Telugu Mission of the American Baptist Missionary Union under John Everett Clough in the late 1860s, and the Sreekakulam peasant uprising of 1976-70. The inclusion of historical details tends to bring authenticity to the fictional narrative which Rao builds through his memory novel. Some of the memories are individual memoirs of personal struggles and survival against caste-system while others are community memoirs of caste atrocities and resistance offered by the mala and madiga sections of society. Taken together,

Much beyond these structural devices employed, Rao raises one important issue centering the oldest debates in Indian history—the origins of caste or *jatis*. To this thematic preoccupation, he also adds insights into issues including the caste conversions, the division of society into classes, the role of art and artistic endeavours in social transformation, the condition of the marginalised in pre and post-independence India, the neo-colonial state mechanism and police brutality, the role of women in revolutionary ideas, and the discussion centring upon the resistance against oppression and exploitation—all through the portrayal of Dalit/untouchable lives and experiences.

> The word 'Dalit' is a word that denotes pride. This term also carries the awareness of oppression and victimisation. The revolutionary sentiment of being continually reminded of the acts of the oppressor class is also embedded in this word. It also has an echo of consciousness. The word 'dalit' makes one aware of a sense of responsibility, and not one of sympathy. It can then be said that along with communicating the meanings of the word 'dalit', the dalit discourse is also geared towards social change and transmission of a 'dalit consciousnesses.' (Ramachandra, 2003: 179)

In *Antarani Vasantam*, Rao has endeavoured to portray the experience of one Dalit family and by extension to the entire identity of Dalits in the pre and post-independence India where despite political emancipation, this section of the society has been relegated to a doubly-marginalised status—one in terms of caste and the other in terms of religion. He raises the issue of caste within Christianity when forced by exploitation and oppression to convert from the hegemonic Brahminical system to Christianity and despite this conversion; the characters in the novel find the idea of hope entirely illusive. It is this hopelessness that culminates in the adoption of violent methods by the later generations, following the Naxalbari uprising, to bring about a substantial change in their social, economic and political conditions. Giving the background of violent revolutions of the late 1970s, the novel ends without showcasing any prominent change in the plight of Dalits, keeping the metaphor of 'spring' forbidden for these marginal sections. At the very outset in the preface to the novel, Rao asserts that "This Spring was forbidden then. Now, too, forbidden. The caste of birth forbidden. The chosen struggle forbidden. It may have been yesterday. Maybe today. Maybe any time. This Spring was forbidden then. Now, too, forbidden" (15) the significance of the preface lies in its declaration that for thousands of years, from one generation to another, the hope of a better future and tomorrow has driven Dalits to resort to all forms of resistance- from subtle ones to the more open revolts- yet there has been no major change in their plight. Prior to Independence from the British, these struggles for a dignified identity and humane treatment were covert, mainly in form of minor localised incidents like the cultivation on the Malla mound, or diverting the waters towards Dalit land patches, the ascendance to higher areas during floods, attending performances alongside the higher castes, and also, through appropriation of art forms to include Dalit voices. All such incidents, however, did not bring about the Spring that these subjugated sections deserve and demand. Then as they found refuge in religious conversions, the ill-treatment even within this caste hierarchy was a natural response, since any change in the status-quo continued to evoke violent and negative response from the Brahminical forces.

The mass conversions of chuhras, pariahs, madigas and malas, often saw fierce counter-resistance from the powerful higher castes. It is no surprise that even the attempt to collect the knowledge of the arts and cultures of these lower castes witnessed a ferocious reponse—the cold blooded murder of Peda Koteshwarudu seems the simplest example of Rao's depiction of the response of the knowledge-power nexus persistent in society. Even within the mission setups, frequent attacks like the one that led to the brutal death of Martin—the Messiah who had saved Sivaiah/Simon, Sarramma and Sasirekha, were a common occurrence. Any challenge to the existing system was seen as a threat to the higher castes and consequently necessitated immediate sometimes brutal responses. As for the later generations, revolutionary ideas of Marxism and communism seemed to be the ultimate way towards hope. But as Rao depicts through the use of police force to quell dissent within independent India, even such attempts seem futile when it comes to the possibility of any change of plight for the lower castes. The prospect of education bringing about tangible outcomes too seem bleak in case of the caste deprivation as evident with Ramanujan and Yenkayi's treatment at the hands of the police-state during water disputes. The forbiddance of a bright and equal future dominated any narrative related to the Avarnas as caste dominates all facets of life and society. As Rao mentions:

> In this country, the air that one breathes has caste. The water one drinks has caste. The field canal that flows and the land that yields harvest have caste. The school, the temple and the village square have caste. The food one eats, the house one lives in and the clothes one wears have caste. The word one speaks has caste. Literature and culture have caste. The state has caste, its laws have caste. Justice and the courts have caste. The corpse and the cemetery have caste. God has caste. Devil has caste. (Rao, 2010: 227)

The domination from higher castes in education, in financial matters, in legal battles, in common discourse hampered any attempt at gaining equal footing for the avarnas as was witnessed in Immanuel's martyrdom in custody. The loss of this boy from the last generation, brings to the fore the impossibility of any hopeful settlement of the issue of caste—the longing for Spring to change their general quandary. Of the women that are left to wait for their sons to embark on a violent path, Rao, however, gives them the power of the pen. As Ruth writes her final letter to her grandson Jessie, her urgency of sharing her thoughts portrays Rao's belief that writing and communicating one's thoughts remains the last resort of humans to bring any peace to their tumultuous lives especially if they are burdened with as much hardships as the Dalits. The narrative of eight generations of one such Dalit family looking out hopefully, reaches millions of readers from across the world by the medium of the written script in Telugu, in every translation done of the novel. In the epilogue titled "Final Word", Rao maintains that "*Untouchable Spring* is not a life that will be completed in these few pages" (265). The narratives of oppression are endless and in a hope to end this oppression and bring eternal Spring, it is necessary for all characters to rise up in Resistance as he suggests that Mary Suvarta needs to speak up against savarna system that cost her a husband and a son. It is hoped that Kalyan Rao sees in such uprisings that demand exposing and challenging forbiddance of spring for the lower castes.

## Works Cited

Kavitha, K. "Dalit Literature in India". *Indian Journal of Research, Paripex.* Vol. 3. Issue 4. April 2014.

Ramchandra. *Hindi Dalit Vimarsh ki Vaicharikta* (The Conceptualisation of Hindi Dalit Discourse). In Devendra Chaubey (Ed.), *Sahitya ka Naya Soundaryashastra* (The New Aesthetic of Literature). Delhi: Kitabghar Prakashan, 2003.

Rao, G. Kalyan. *Antarani Vasantam.* (*Untouchable Spring*). Trans. by Alladi Uma and K. Shridhar. New Delhi: Orient BlackSwan, 2010.

Shukla, A. R. *Hindi Sahitya ka Itihas* (A History of Hindi Literature). Allahabad: Lokbharati Prakashan, 2013.

Singh, Vikas and Vikas Jain. "The Development of Theoretical Principles of Dalit Literature" *Fortell: A Journal of Teaching English Language and Literature.* Issue 34, January 2017, pp. 79-84.

Thorat, V. & Badtya, S. *Bharatiya Dalit Sahitya ka Vidrohi Svar* (The Rebellious Voice in Indian Dalit Literature). Delhi and Jaipur: Rawat Publications, 2008.

Valmiki, O. P. *Dalit Sahitya ka Soundaryashastra* (The Aesthetics of Dalit Literature). Delhi: Radhakrishna Prakashan, 2008.

Valmiki, O. P. *Dalit Sahitya: Anubhav, Sangharsh evam Yathart* (Dalit Literature: Experience, Struggle and Reality). Delhi: Radhakrishna Prakashan, 2003.

# 5

# Marginalisation and Identity Formation in Sheoraj Singh Bechain's *My Childhood on My Shoulders*

*Dr Suruchi Sharma*

Dalits are those poor or ostracized people who live their life at the mercy of others just because they are not accepted by the mainstream society due to their low caste status. Indian social system was formed to cater the requirements of all the people because currency did not play so much vital role at that time, and most of the work was done by the exchange of things. That's why Indian society was divided into different castes.

Ancient Indian Hindu society was divided into four *varnas* and these *varnas* were important in their unique manner. Out of these *varnas*, these were the Shudras who were the lowest of the low and they did all kinds of menial jobs. They had to do all kinds of those works which were detested by the other three *varnas*.

As time rolled by, changes came in the Hindu society also and among these, there was a caste of those people who skinned and disposed of animal carcasses. These people would deal in tanning and leather craft and were known as 'Chamars'. They are known by different names in different states of India who are mainly associated with the working of any form of leather.

They make shoes for the people. This caste is generally found in North India.

There was the reference of various leather goods in the *Rigveda*, the ancient Hindu scripture. Tanners and leather workers would help the society in warfares in ancient times by making leather shields and armours. Thus, this caste has been very helpful since ancient times. In the present time, it is generally seen that hardly few people in Indian villages make leather *jutis* as a main profession. But this profession was much prevalent in Northern India just a hundred years back.

In this context, a name, Dr Sheoraj Singh Bechain, strikes in the mind when there is a discussion of this caste because his family belonged to 'Chamar' caste which he frankly writes in his autobiography just because he does not want to hide his caste. He was born in village Nadrauli of Budaun district in Uttar Pradesh. It would be a misleading term if his caste is not mentioned here. Sheoraj presently works as the Head and Professor in the Department of Hindi in the University of Delhi. His autobiography *Mera Bachpan Mere Kandhon Par* was published in 2009 by Vani Prakashan, New Delhi and it was published in English in 2018 as *My Childhood on My Shoulders* by Oxford University Press, New Delhi.

Sheoraj Singh Bechain describes how his childhood was spent in utter penury after the death of his father. Present paper deals with some horrific incidents of his life especially in his childhood and the formation phase of his career. The very first chapter of the autobiography "An Untimely Death" narrates how the mountain of sorrows falls on their family when his father dies leaving behind his small children and a young wife. Dr Kusum Kanger writes that, "It was the phase of his life which made him tough to face every kind of adversity of life" (Kanger, 234). The opening lines of this autobiography clearly depict Sheoraj's family profession:

> It has been almost thirty years since my paternal uncles, Beedhe Phupha and Gangawasi, earned their livelihood through petty business in scavenging, skinning carcasses of cattle, and trading in the remains of dead beasts. (Bechain, 1)

When Sheoraj Singh Bechain was merely five or six years old, his father passed away. There was no source of income in the family and they had to live from hand to mouth. Some people of his caste would also show the superiority complex though they were also not rich.

Sheoraj describes how his father Radhe took him to the wedding at his Chhoti Bua's village by putting him on his shoulders. His uncle Pyarelal was also with him. Sheoraj's mother was much worried about him as the village was at a distance. His father rested at several places on the way and gave him water to drink at the wells. Sheoraj describes that his Bua's in-laws were also very poor and none of the children would go to school.

Sheoraj Singh narrates in his autobiography how the people of that village would believe in superstitions and blind-beliefs. His father Radhe did not drink but some people somehow persuaded him to drink. His health deteriorated. He started vomiting and became dehydrated. There was no provision of medicine in the village and they did not have sufficient money for the treatment. They preferred to call tree *Ojhas* or the wise men who tried exorcism. His father was physically tortured by them because they told the family that Radhe is suffering from some evil spirits, "Three exorcists, in unison, had invoked the spirits upon themselves. Swaying wildly and with strange gesticulations, they swept their arms through the air to plant the soundest of slaps on my father's cheeks" (Bechain, 5).

His condition was getting worse but the wise men were slapping and whipping him saying that they are trying to send the evil spirits away. His father Radhe was saying that no evil spirits have entered his body. He was telling them to call the doctor for his treatment but nobody paid any attention to him and the wise men kept beating and whipping him for three days.

Sheoraj Singh was feeling very listless to see his father in this condition. His mother, great uncle and uncle were also called from the village when his condition got worse. Sheoraj's mother had given birth to a boy around one or two weeks back and the second child was in her lap. In Sheoraj's family, there was dearth of family income just because his Tau and his Gangi uncle were blind and his Bidhe uncle was lame. When the wise men realised that Radhe's health was critical, they took their money and ran away.

When Sheoraj's mother reached at night, his father was taking his last breathe. All the people of the house started wailing after his death. His life was filled with sorrow. Now it was his responsibility to run the family. The cremation scene is also quite moving in this autobiography. A bull-cart of an upper caste person was arranged and Sheoraj, his mother Mukhi and Rambhrose were sitting at the burning material used for cremation. Sheoraj's father was also sitting at the back of the bull-cart and he was trying to console Sheoraj's mother while she was wailing:

> 'Mukhi Beta, you need to steal your heart. My son has left behind three miniatures of himself. It is your responsibility to safeguard their interests. There is lifetime ahead of you to shed your tears. Think of your children instead.' (Sheoraj, 10)

Sheoraj could not forget this horrific incident in his life. His grandfathers Bhagirath, Gangi and Tau Baburam, were blind. His grandmother, Vidharam was lame. Thus, all these people were handicapped in his family. The family needed at least one young man who would earn bread for this family. Moreover, her mother was only twenty-five years old. After a few days of his father's death, there was nothing to eat in the family. Bechain writes, "In these troubled times, we had nobody to lean upon and despite the scarcity of resources, the people of our *basti* forced us to hold a ritual feast for them on the thirteenth day after the death of my father" (Bechain, 11). It was a big challenge for these people to make arrangements of food. No grain was left in the house after this ritual. Sheoraj, his Tau and grandfather would sit in front of the house so that they may get any kind of labour work.

There is an incident of death of Sheoraj's younger brother, Neksingh who was sick and he could not get any medical treatment like his father and died an untimely death. Sheoraj remembers how he died, "In the end, Neksingh passed away, painfully, bit by bit, in front of our eyes" (13). Sheoraj's mother was married with another poor man, Ramlal in Naura-Baura village. No advice was taken from Sheoraj's grandparents and his maternal grandfather gave this logic for the second marriage:

> 'My daughter is in her early twenties. What has she seen of life? We are not Brahmins or Banias that we can afford to keep our widowed daughters unmarried, nor are we Chaudhuris whose daughters can feed off the fat of their lands. We are Chamars. This is our custom. On whose support can we keep our daughters home? Is there any prospect of sustenance to be provided from your end?' (Sheoraj, 19)

Sheoraj's step-father was also very poor and he started quarelling with Mukhi after some time saying that he cannot feed her children. He wanted that she may leave the children at her grand maternal uncle's home but Sheoraj's mother did not want it. Thus, money becomes the main cause of quarrel in the family.

Sheoraj's Jeeja Gangawasi's death was also another blow of fate for them. The people of the neighbourhood came forward for the cremation and a man named Bande helped them a lot in the cremation. Sheoraj writes about it, "How affable these people were! The women had tears in their eyes when we left. These *jhuggis* were inhibited by Dalits who were rich in the emotion of love" (Sheoraj, 81). This family was so helpless that they did not have enough money for the creation. Bechain's mother was filled with remorse and she uttered the following words:

> You are dead, son! And we could do nothing about it! You must forgive us. You must convey our helplessness to God in Heaven. We are praying for you with our heart and soul that in your next birth you are born in a more fortunate home. (Sheoraj, 82)

Sheoraj's mother was married again with Bhikari and this man adopted some crooked methods to get rid of Mukhi's children. He took advance money from a contractor and started sending Sheoraj and his sister Maya to work at the brick-kiln. Sheoraj and Maya were now merely children and their bodies were not grown enough to handle this work. Thus, the children's future was bleak. Sheoraj narrates about it, "Amma could clearly see that the very man she had chosen to secure our futures was hell bent on destroying them but she had no alternative arrangement for us if he refused to feed us" (45).

Sheoraj had to do any work he got from anybody. He started polishing boots at the railway stations, hotels and cinema houses in Chandausi. Sheoraj and his mother would do menial jobs in order to run the family. He had to carry a heavy load on his head.

Sheoraj faces many problems in getting education. His step-father did not want to pay his school fee and he would quarrel when Sheoraj would study in the light of the kerosene oil. Sheoraj narrates many other incidents of miserable life in his autobiography. S.M. Michael writes, "The aspirations of contemporary Dalits are completely different from those of Dalits in traditional India. This change is due to the difference in the vision perceived by the Untouchables of the past and of today. Visions set the agenda for both thought" (Michael, 14).

Sheoraj Singh Bechain writes about the problem of child marriage in this autobiography. It was not considered a social evil in the society because most of the people were not aware of it. Sheoraj Singh comments about it, "In my village, child marriage is the norm among the people of our community. It is practiced even to this day" (68). His sister was married to Gangawasi who was ten or fifteen years older than his sister. When Sheoraj would go to her in-laws' home, he would get good hospitality. He was given sweets also to eat which he usually did not get without any hard work. He cherishes this memory and writes about it, "Sheoraj had never eaten sweets without any hard work in his life and this was the first time that he had eaten these sweets without any work. He narrates about it, "For me, sweets or good meals were hard to come by and perhaps, it was for the first time since my father's death that I was getting to eat without having to work for it" (71).

He describes one incident when his leg got badly injured while cultivating the fields of his Massaab with the bullocks. He was crazy for poetry at that time and he would write poetry while ploughing the fields. Some thoughts struck his mind and he stopped the harrow for some time so that he might pen down his poem. He lost balance and his leg was narrowly escaped from being amputated. He painfully narrates this incident:

> One day the moment I put my hand in the pocket to bring out a pen, my attention got diverted from the bullocks and the discs of the harrow struck a solid lump of soil and toppled over. I lost my balance and my left foot went under the disc of the harrow. Two-and-a-half inches of the flesh over my toes got scraped off and flipped over. The bones of my foot lay exposed. (209)

His wrapped towel tightly on his leg and somehow reached Massaab's house. Sheoraj's relatives do not utter any words of sympathy for him and rather speak very disheartening words, "Looks like you have deliberately got your foot injured so that you can sit back and eat some fleshly made food by me for about fifteen days or more. Well, you'd better give up daydreaming because I am not giving you a sip of water without your working for it" (210).

Thus, Sheoraj had to face many problems in his life but he did not succumb to the adverse situations. His autobiography is an account of the pains and problems of his life. He suffered much caste discrimination in his village and outside also but he never surrendered. Anupama Rao writes, "Caste discrimination required a rewritten history of the Dalit and redress through modern political measures, such as the franchise and a constitutionally mandated regime of affirmative action" (23). Sheoraj remained a marginalised figure even among the marginalised and he asserted his identity by dint of his hard work and strong will power. Dr Sadhana Agrawal aptly writes about it, "Life can take a turn at any time in anybody's life and hard work and determination can make anything possible" (Agrawal, 30).

## Works Cited

Agrawal, Sadhana. "Childhood Memories as Narrated by Sheoraj Singh Bechain in His Autobiography My Childhood on My Shoulders." *Different Dimensions of Dalit Discourse*. Ed. Bijender Singh, New Delhi, Altantic Publishers and Distributors, 2019, 28-36.

Bechain, Sheoraj Singh. *My Childhood on My Shoulders*. Trans. Deeba Zafir and Tapan Basu. New Delhi: Oxford University Press, 2017.

Kanger, Kusum. "Dalit Marginalisation and Caste Atrocities in Sheoraj Singh Bechain's My Childhood on My Shoulders." Eds. S. Chelliah and Bijender Singh. *Dalit Literature: Journey from Repression to Resistance*. New Delhi: Kalpaz Publications, 2019, 233-41.

Michael, S.M., ed. *Dalits in Modern India: Vision and Values* (1999). 2nd ed. New Delhi and London: Sage, 2007.

Rao, Anupama. *The Caste Question: Dalits and the Politics of Modern India*. London: University of California Press, 2009.

# 6

# Siddalingaiah's *Ooru Keri*: Projection of Self and Society

*Dr Kusum Kanger*

An autobiography is a record of somebody's experiences and it makes the past memories of the writer much fresh, novel and permanent. The form and scope of Dalit autobiographies has undergone a sea change in the last three decades and many new Dalit autobiographies have been written in different languages and some of these have been published in English but there are still many autobiographies which have not been published in English even after many years of publication. There are few autobiographies which attracted the attention of some people who took pains to translate these autobiographies. *Ooru Keri* is also one of those autobiographies. This autobiography was originally published in 2006 in Kannada by a Karnataka based writer Siddalingaiah. He can be called one of the foremost Dalit writers. This autobiography was translated by two persons at different times. Dr Ramesh A. Landage writes that, "Siddalingaiah's *Ooru Keri* portrays his life-long struggles with poverty, hunger, and humiliations in the village Magadi of Karnataka" (Siddalingaiah, 10).

Many Dalit autobiographies have been written in regional languages but these autobiographies have limited scope because only the readers of that language can read these autobiographies and the readers of other languages are deprived of the opportunity to read. It is English, a global language, that has a wide readership across the globe and the people of all languages can read this autobiography. Martin McQuillan writes about autobiography that, "Autobiography seems to depend on actual and potentially verifiable events in a less ambivalent way than fiction does. It seems to belong to a simpler mode of referentiality" (McQuillan, 172).

This autobiography depicts the hunger, poverty, caste discrimination and marginalisation of Dalit people in a village Magadi in Karnataka state. 'Ooru' can be called a village or town where the people of the upper caste live with all the basic amenities. 'Keri' means a geographically separated place where only low caste people live with limited resources. In this way, *Ooru Keri* depicts the life of the low caste people who are living in the same village. This autobiography presents the picture of subhuman treatment with Dalits. This book reminds the readers about Vasant Moon's autobiography *Vasti* which is all about caste and class discrimination.

The low caste people had to go to a far off place to fetch water just because they were not allowed to touch the wells belonging to the upper caste. The people of his caste were very poor and they were depended on the leftover food offered by the upper caste people. This incidence reminds us Omprakash Valmiki's autobiography *Joothan: A Dalit's Life* in which the people of Omprakash's caste were given only leftover food in marriages. Their mothers worked as sweepers and they were humiliated for their low caste. They would bring leftover food from the upper caste people. Siddalingaiah's childhood pictures have been depicted in *Ooru Keri*. S. Bhartiraja writes in this context, "Siddalingaiah's childhood was submerged into poverty. His family belongs to farm labourers and gets low-income, and sometimes nothing" (Bhartiraja, 76).

Siddalingaiah's family lived at Megalahatti. One day there was the news of the arrival of a minister, "The minister is coming today" (Siddalingaiah, 9). All Dalit children were curious to see the minister. Many people were standing on the road waiting for the arrival of the minister but he did not come and the crowd got angry at this incident. The hired chairs were also sent back.

Siddalingaiah was admitted in the village school by extra efforts of his mother. His class teacher, Nagappachar was very strict. One day there was an educational tour of an inspector. All the students were kept in the school for a long time. Siddalingaiah did the mimicry of the school inspector and he became famous in the school. One day their teacher tells the students to sing a song. A boy says, "Sir, he can show inspector lips" (Siddalingaiah, 12). His teacher asked Siddalingaiah to do the mimicry of the inspector. He said, "What is it... come on, show it to me" (Siddalingaiah, 12). It was a good occasion for the enjoyment of the students.

This autobiography has some similarity with Bama's *Sanagati* (*Events*) because several incidents of Dalit community have been depicted in this autobiography. Siddalingaiah writes about a slum area Srirampura where quarrels, fighting, affair, exploitation, and chaos were very common. It was the hub of several events. People would drink and quarrel among themselves. Most of the people belonged to the lower stratum of the society. Shrinivas K. remarks about it, "*Ooru Keri* narrates the story, with a light tone and humour, of an active student in Bangalore slum who has migrated from a village due to poverty" (Shrinivas, 124).

Siddalingaiah writes about it, "Some sang song in whatever manner they could. Their love for their wives and children brimmed over. Some would try to have sex with their wives in public" (Siddalingaiah, 24).

This autobiography depicts how Dalits have not been escaped from the cruel clutches of blind faith. Few of them are possessed by gods and goddesses but not a single person of the upper caste is possessed by them. He narrates many episodes of ghosts but he writes that he is an atheist, "By that time I had already lost faith in God" (72). Though he believed in God in his childhood but later he became atheist. Aravind Malagatti was also a theist in his childhood but he also became a staunch atheist.

*Ooru Keri* describes that Dalits live much separate from the upper caste people. If we read Omprakash Valmiki's *Joothan: A Dalit Life*, the same kind of depiction can be found in the opening lines of this autobiography. Ainoru are the upper caste people in *Ooru Keri*. There were caste barriers in their village and Siddalingaiah writes that, 'Ours was the last house in the colony' (Siddalingaiah, 1). The roof of the house was in a very bad condition. It was just like a temporary settlement. Some people of his caste had to keep moving from one place to another. The people of his caste were very poor and they had to face humiliation by the upper caste people. Dr Ramesh A. Landage writes about it, "Siddalingaiah's *Ooru Keri: An Autobiography* is almost reminiscent of distorting the hunger and humiliations of Dalits in Karnataka" (Landage, 5). The writer and the people of his caste would feel inferiority complex. The people of his caste would feel depressed to see their pitiable conditions. The writer describes that the people of his caste had to face very bad situation during draught:

> That was a time of drought everywhere. People had to struggle even for a morsel of food. Some threw ceremonial fests to appease the rain gods. During fests, the Holeyas were made to sit in a corner. We were noticed only after people of the upper castes had been served. I felt contented with whatever little food came my way, and wouldn't think too much about the discrimination. (Siddalingaiah, 7)

Siddalingaiah held his self esteem high. He was born in a poor low caste family but he was a bit different from others. A Brahmin teacher Andalamma would give him food and other basic things. In spite of his poor background, he did not reveal his poverty to anybody. Free study material was provided by the government but Siddalingaiah did not receive it. His teacher showed a soft corner and helped him as much as he could.

When his family settled at the slum called Srirampura in Bangalore, Siddalingaiah started concentrating on his studies. He also tried to improve his communication skills. When he was merely a student in his school, he was assigned the task of reading out the letter in the village. Whenever any letter would come in the village, he was called with full respect and he was given delicious food to eat. He made the people happy not only by reading the letters but also explaining the meaning of the statement.

> People felt very happy because I not only read the letters but explained their meanings also. Some would make me write letters to their relatives. I would then get, besides a generous amount of eats, some money as well. For the handful who got love letters, I was equal to god. (Siddalingaiah, 33-34)

Siddalingaiah was told to write people's letters for which he was given money and he would use this money to buy his books. Siddalingaiah's father was a woodcutter and there was no good source of income. That's why his mother also had to work at Shivanahalli tank. Siddalingaiah had to see very tough time in his life. Dr Sumitra Singh writes in her paper, "In his autobiography *Ooru Keri*, Siddalingaiah describes how he used to stay in the graveyard" (Singh, 217-18).

Siddalingaiah joined a Dalit hostel in Srirampura where his mother would work as a sweeper. Thousands of students lived in this hostel from different parts of Karnataka and would speak different languages. The hostel was divided into four languages. It was a rumour among the students that ghosts live in the hostel. One night when he was on his bed, the ghosts were singing a song and they snatched his chopper. He woke up and started dancing with them without being frightened. The ghosts also became his friends. This is merely a narration which does not have any logic. It is generally seen in the hostels that some naughty students try to terrorize other students by such activities.

Siddalingaiah was inspired by Ambedkar and his movement. He thought that only education can change the course of his life. Siddalingaiah remembers how his father was beaten by two men. He writes that the agents of the moneylender beat him, "My father had become a huge debtor...One day two toughs beat him on the street" (Siddhlingaih, 37). His clothes were torn and he was crying with pain on the road. Siddalingaiah narrates that Dalits were treated mercilessly at several occasions. The writer's father was also unable to pay his debt on time. He did not get any work sometimes and he also became a huge debtor. He would remain in tension and that's why he would drink. Through this event, Siddalingaiah wants to draw the attention of the readers towards money lenders' cruelty. Most of the poor people would live there and they had to borrow money from these moneylenders. These moneylenders would give them money at a high rate of interest.

The writer gives an example of a woman who borrowed money from a moneylender on weekly interest. She could not return the money even after four weeks. The moneylender took his son away from her and the woman had to sell her cauldron in order to pay the amount. Only after paying the amount, she could get back her son.

Siddalingaiah writes how an upper caste teacher in Government Arts College, Bangalore told him to bring water but as soon as he came to know about his caste, he refused the author boy to fetch water, "Why he still chose me to fetch water became a subject of discussion in class. He had mistaken me for a Lingayat. I was liberated from the task of fetching water after he came to know my caste" (Siddalingaiah, 76). Siddalingaiah focused on his studies and gained knowledge. He earned his MA in Kannada language and secured a position of research Assistant at Kannada Research Centre. He started delivering lectures and lost his faith in God. He said, "If God does exist, will it stop me speaking" (Siddalingaiah, 81). S. Bhartiraja writes that he lost faith in God just because God did not help him in his adversities, "All through his growing up, hungry, suffering, and humiliation at odd jobs while studying are his chief memories; they made him lose faith in God, and also mark the beginning of his Dalit introspection" (Bhartiraja, 76).

Siddalingaiah's autobiography, like several other Dalit men's autobiographies spills the pains and anguishes of the Dalit people of his caste. The poverty and caste of these people remain the main cause of their sufferings. They do not have faith in God; instead they are God fearing people. They lost their faith in God and had to live a neglected life as Ram Kumar writes:

> Regarding *Ooru Keri,* it is true that *Dalits* have not escaped from the clutches of the blind faith. They are not God-loving but a God-fearing people. The sufferings and humiliations are an integral part of the *Dalit* struggle. As a result of this, Siddalingaiah is forced to live a neglected life and carry out the traditional roles without proper welfare. (Kumar, 223)

## Work Cited

Bhartiraja, S. "Siddalingaiah's Self Sprung Achievement in *Ooru Keri—An Autobiography*: A Study, in Development of Scheduled Castes in India." Ed. Rao P. D. New Delhi: Serials Publication, 2012.

Kumar, Ram. "Dalit Autobiographies Telling the Pains." *IMPACT: International Journal of Research in Humanities, Arts and Literature (IMPACT: IJRHAL)*. 6.2 (Feb 2018) pp. 219-226.

Landage, Ramesh A. "Cultural Assertion in Siddalingaiah's *Ooru Keri. Aayushi International Interdisciplinary Research Journal (AIIRJ).* Special Issue. Jan 2018. pp. 10-15.

McQuillan, Martin. *Deconstruction: A Reader.* Routledge: New York, 2001.

Shrinivas, K. "Dalit Movement and Kannada Dalit Autobiographies Translated into English." *The Criterion: An International Journal in English.* 7.3 (June 2016). pp. 123-27.

Siddalingaiah. *Ooru Keri: An Autobiography.* Trans. S.R. Ramakrishna, New Delhi: Sahitya Akademi, 2003.

Singh, Sumitra. "Hollowness and Shadow in Siddalingaiah's *Ooru Keri.*" *Dalit Men's Autobiographies: A Critical Appraisal.* Ed. Bijender Singh. New Delhi: Kalpaz Publications, 2017. pp. 223-228.

# 7

# Representation of the Distress and Plight of Dalits in *Upara: An Outsider* by Laxman Mane

*Dr Ruchika Katiyar*

## Introduction

Dalit people have been considered as inferior since the beginning of the era. They have been treated badly always and thought of as less than human beings. It is due to the caste system in India which has prevailed since the ancient days. There is no evidence of their existence in history as well because they were always denied the basic rights of living and education by the upper caste people. That is why, they always pen their history in a more expressive way highlighting their culture. Autobiography can be perceived here as the personal expression of their grievances through literature. It is the consequence of their desire to set up their social history with the help of the story of their life. These autobiographies get published in various Indian languages and translated into English. Omprakash Valmiki's autobiography *Joothan*; Laxman Gaikwad's *Uchalaya*, Arjun Dangle's *Poisoned Bread*, D.P. Das's *The Untouchable Story*, Kumud Pawade's *Antaspot*, Balwant Singh's *An Untouchable in the IAS* and many more are the several autobiographies translated into other European languages besides English.

An autobiography is not only a written literary record but it can be also be considered as a plea by the sufferer. Autobiographies are generally thought of as an expression of truth. They are an effort to give human life a linear narrative. They are composed not to be taken in a judgmental role reaching to a conclusion but to be written in the language of adventure glorifying the achievements of a person. A literary work is an adventure of language on the contrary. This is the second issue in relation to an autobiography. An autobiography can surpass as well as avoid these two limitations to become a literary composition and a conscious effort is necessary for that purpose.

There is a difference of opinion among the critics regarding Dalit Literature. Some think that it is an ineradicable mark at the global level while others witness it with contempt as a plan to transform the predicament of the Dalit for their own advantage. Ambedkar and Rettaimalai Srinivasan are the predecessors of the Dalit autobiography. Their autobiographies are in the form of accurate notes. It seems like both the autobiographies have been penned in 1939. The foreigners are aware of the stigma known as untouchability in India. But they are unaware how frightening and ghastly it is. Ambedkar himself perceived that a Dalit in a village isn't allowed to socialise with the upper caste. It is not like that all the autobiographies written by Dalits in India are similar to those written by Ambedkar or Rettaimalai Srinivasan but some elements are akin to their writings. The most brutal aspects of untouchability can be seen in Dalit autobiographies. According to Arjun Dandle, the Dalit people begun writing much before the Ambedkar movement started. Dr M.N. Wankhade notes: "The pens of the Dalit writers are ready as levers, to lift the people's democracy out of the mud of the anarchy" (Dangle, 319).

## A Reflection of Sorrow in *Upara: An Outsider*

Laxman Mane is a Marathi writer and a social activist from Maharashtra who has portrayed the suppression and exploitation of the Dalit people. He belongs to a tribal community. His autobiography *Upara* is an excellent endeavour to project all the grievances and gloom of a person because of his/her caste. An individual is lost in the fathoms of obscurity of oppression and marginalisation through alienation. He has made a successful endeavour to depict the problems and issues of the marginalised people. He became famous when he published his autobiography in 1980. It is a turning point in Marathi Dalit Literature. He got Sahitya Akademi Award in 1981 and Padma Shri in 2009 for his autobiography penned in Marathi language and translated into other languages later.

Although the writer has to confront a lot of difficulties and distress in his life yet still he does not feel stressed. The upper caste people made his course difficult, insulted and degraded him. But still he never feels lost. The injustice done to him inspires him to fight for his cause. He acquires success in every phase of his life. He gets education and knowledge despite of every obstacle imposed on him by the upper caste people. After receiving proper education, he gets to know that an individual cannot be judged on the basis of birth and caste, but on the basis of his moral and spiritual values instead. The writer gives encouragement to the other suppressed people as well. He suggests other people that they should not tolerate any kind of injustice done towards them.

Mane has depicted the problems and issues faced by the nomadic tribals. *Upara* has been translated by Shri A.K. Kamat in English in a very nice and expressive manner. The author has successfully attempted to portray the socio-cultural circumstances of the lower class and his Kaikadi tribe.

There are several such kinds of communities who are living an unrefined life in the entire world including India. These people are forced to lead their lives like beasts. They are kept away from literacy and civilised life since ages. Most of the ancient texts are in Sanskrit. It is written in the *Manusmriti*:

> Only Brahmin intellectuals should read religious texts authoritatively and indoctrinate it to their Shishyas (students).....No Brahmin should teach Sudras any religious principles to keep him (Brahmin) safe from going to hell.... Neither Sudra can be a spoke person of the king... In case, if he tried to be a religious pedagogue a king must pour hot oil into his ears and mouth. (Nareke, 600)

If someone achieves success in such predicament, one gets surprised at one's success. Laxman is bewildered when he reflects on the predicament of his community people. The lacuna of the basic facilities for the people of his community distresses him greatly. Several questions come across his mind:

> Is the life of nomadic tribals really going to change? Will they change from within? Will our society allow them to change? Will they settle in a particular place and will they accept the new way of life? Will they lead a life as partners of a new culture? In the areas of power, wealth, prestige, philosophic thinking, arts, will this stream of nomadic tribals merge into the body of a larger human culture after effacing the stigma of Upara from their foreheads? Will their humanness be respected? Will their basic necessities such as food, clothes and shelter be looked after? Will the society accept them as humans? (Mane, 12-13)

Mane knows that many schemes by the government for the goodness of his community people, but the fact is that all these schemes are not executed in a well-defined way. Only education is able to widen their horizons and illumine their lives. The nomadic tribals are generally the wandering communities and as a result of which their children don't have an opportunity to receive education. The very less number of people of his community who stay at one place think of it to be useless and unworthy. Laxman has begun an enlightening movement for the tribals. Laxman's father got him registered in the school without taking into consideration the opinion of his mother and the community. He was of the view that only education can help them to live a better life in comparison to the present dirty life. The schooling of Laxman was disturbed as his father generally didn't stay at one place continuously and went from one place to another living a nomadic life. As they went to a new village, the head master of the school didn't want to admit him to school. His father requested him a lot for the same. The teachers possessing the upper class mindset said: "You funny guy! Do nomadic beggars go to school? ... If they study, who will weave our basket? Nothing doing! You want to study, Huh!" (Mane, 360). It appeared to him as if the lower caste people take birth in order to endure the abusive behaviour of the upper class. The teachers themselves had the fear in their minds that if the lower caste people will study and will adapt to a better way of life then who will perform the trivial odd tasks of theirs. The writer witnessed the humiliation of his father whose eyes were filled with tears. He at that time decided to be a teacher as his father wanted him to be so. It is very complicated for the nomads to live a serene life as they have to confront a lot of hardships in their life.

The author writes about the episode of going to school, very bitter and painful. When his father decided him to go to school, Laxman pondered that his father must have consumed alcohol. The imagination of the writer of going to school liberated him from many menial tasks like trampling over dung hills and the thrashes of his father etc. He wants a tiny space for himself to raise his life above the dirty ways. The presence of Laxman in the school was indeed, a surprise for the upper caste children. So they exclaimed, "A Kaikadi child... in school?" (Mane, 20).

The writer thought teacher to be nice as he gave him the permission to sit near the door. The students of the upper caste neglected him and his slight physical touch as well. Laxman was unable to understand the language of the teacher as it was different from his mother tongue. He slumbered when he noticed that the teacher was not looking at him. He went to Indya and Khagya and didn't return home as a consequence of which his mother became anxious. She blamed her husband for that:

> Why don't you kill him? Poor Lakshya? Or burn him, and be happy. To think that he will study and be officer! "... Father reacts—Yah! Let him be street mongrel and run across the streets! Why should I send him to school? You Bitch of a wife! You want him to be a beggar? I'll certainly send him to school and make him a teacher or an officer. Who are you to poke your filthy nose into any affair, woman?" (Mane 21-22)

It was due to his father that Laxman got education and knowledge. He really feels very bad when he reflects over the matters of the tribals leading an oppressed and alienated life at the borders of the hamlets and struggling hard for their existence and survival. He utilised the "Ford Foundation Fellowship" by going through the tents and huts of the nomads.

Narayan and Bapusaheb played a very important part in organising the wedding of the writer. The marriage took place within two and a half hours. The entire expenses of the function were twenty-one rupees only. Everything happened in a nice manner. The author wrote a letter to his parents after the marriage. They all abused and cursed Laxman and Shashi. The mother said, "Why did you not die when you were born?... You have blackened our face in the community.... We brought you up....wearing out our bones... And you pissed into our mouth!" (Mane, 177-178).

When the father of the writer inquired about the caste of Shashi, Laxman told him that she was a Maratha. The utterances of Appa represent the mentality of an individual entirely blindfolded by casteism:

> What's the proof that she is Maratha? What's the proof that she is not Mahar... And as for you, was your own caste

> dead?...Does she know your caste is?..... That girl must be a lower caste. That's why she came with you. Otherwise do you think the girls of higher caste get married to the boys of the lower caste? (Mane, 148)

According to the writer, the inter-caste marriages should be there. Therefore, he talks about the Mahar community. When the family members of Laxman left from there, Shashi's utterances are very significant, "I thought that we Marathas alone were insanely proud of our ninety six generations of Maratha lineage, but what I witnessed just now appears to be even worse" (Mane, 185).

The nomadic tribals have been in such a situation because of their superstitions and dogmatic traditions. The writer has written about an incident in his book *Band Darwaja* (*Closed Door*) in which there was a sexual relation between a Pardhi woman and her son. It is very problematic to satisfy illiterate and superstitious individuals. But Laxman firmly determined to work for such type of people till the very end of his life. The author endeavours to make them aware continuously with the help of agitations and meetings. The writer and his mother performed the job of cleaning the ground covered by the porch at the time of wedding ceremony in a rich family. They didn't prepare meals on that day and waited for the guests to attend the wedding feast so that they can have the leftovers. When they did odd and menial jobs at the house of the owner, they behaved as if they were themselves the owner of that particular house. When the guests dined, they were given the food left by them on the plates made up of jackfruit tree leaves. They gathered the left-overs on the plates collecting it in a cloth before the dogs begin to lick the plates.

## Conclusion

Laxman depicts through various events and incidents the hellish life faced by the oppressed and marginalised people. In his autobiography, he has very clearly described the problems faced by the nomadic tribals. They are treated in a cruel way by the upper caste people who want to suppress the lower ones due to the caste system. His family and he himself has confronted all the hardships being a nomadic tribal. He was able to get out of such sort of life only because of the education. It was because of his father who sent him to school. He endured the insult and humiliation imposed on him when he went to register Laxman in school in the new village. Various other such circumstances and situations were there and the author reveals it vividly in *Upara*. The autobiography is a clear cut portrayal of the distress and miseries confronted by the Dalit people who are neglected always due to the type of job that they perform.

## Works Cited

Dangle, Arjun (ed.). *Poisoned Bread: Translations from Modern Dalit Literature*. Hyderabad: Orient Longman, 1992.

Mane, Laxman. *Upara: An Outsider*. New Delhi: Sahitya Akademi, 1997.

Nareke, Hari (ed.). *Mahatma Phule Gourav Granth (A Festschrift for Mahatma Phule) Dr Babasaheb Ambedkar, Mahatma Phule, aani Rajarshi Shau Charita,* Mumbai: Sadhane Prakashan Samiti, 2006.

# 8

# Solidarity and Recreating the Community: Vasant Moon's *Growing up Untouchable in India*

*Dr V. Suganthi*

## Introducing Dalit Literature

Literature is as old as the existence of man. Literature of every sort records and reflects human life and its relationships. Literature has been used as a weapon and a vehicle. Dalit Literature came into existence as a tool to voice out the feelings of Dalits and as a weapon to fight for their rights. Dalit Literature is a part of fourth world literature that centres on the subjugation of the people at the fringe of the society—the broken class under the caste system. The role of Dalits in the society is significant, yet much ignored, neglected, and demeaned. Dalit oppression has been a global phenomenon, though termed differently in different parts of the world. In India, the term 'Dalit' refers to the community of people who are marginalised, looked down, treated inhumanely, denied their rights as human beings and kept at the social periphery. So, Dalit Literature takes up the task of being the voice of these voiceless. Dalit Literature is the outcome of the social, economic, political, and psychological oppression that has been the agony of Dalits for ages.

The origin of Dalit Literature can be traced back to Buddhist literature in India. This is recognised as a separate genre of literature only recently; but its voice is strongly felt. The voice for the cause of Dalits can be seen in the antique and classical literatures of India. There are novels, poems, short stories, autobiographies and memoirs that form the genre Dalit Literature. In recent years, in Dalit Literature, there are prominent writers like Babu Rao Bagul, Bama, Urmila Pawar, Arun Krishnaji Kamble, Shantabai Kamble, Katti Padma Rao, and Sivakami.

Dalit Literature is a part of Dalit movement. It marks an important development in the political scenario and culture of India. The influence of Ambedkar played a major role in shaping the Dalit movement. In Maharashtra it sped up and strengthened the Dalit movement there. Dalit Literature questions the caste system. It redefines the "social status" that is based on caste and community which are determined at one's birth. Dalit Literature is a verbal protest against the established social norms and practices that oppress the Dalits and help the people of the "higher community" to ride on their shoulders. This protest and the attempt to "reform" the social standards form the crust of Dalit Literature. Dalit writings serve as a clarion call for redefining the status and the lives of Dalits.

## Dalit Autobiographies

Dalit writers and activists felt the need to sketch their lives in writing so that the world would come to know of their quandary. Typically, Dalit autobiographies are not just autobiographies of individual persons; they are the autobiographies and voices of the community to which these writers belong. There are autobiographies written by Dalit men and Dalit women. Writers like Urmila Pawar, Kishore Shanbabai Kamble, Baby Kamble, Bama and Vasant Moon drafted their lives into autobiographies, bringing out through them the predicaments of their community and the ways they find to overcome those predicaments. They are very powerful as they are the voices of the suffered, subjugated, exploited class, voiced by themselves; they are the expression of first-hand experience. The autobiographies of Dalit women are even more significant than those of Dalit men as they are the voices of the doubly and many a times triply oppressed. These Dalit autobiographies strengthened the Dalit movement. Some autobiographies talk about the working out of the suppressing hands in their lives while some other autobiographies talk about the ways they fought against these oppressions. These autobiographies narrate the ways they surmount the oppression imposed upon them and thus, inspire the men of their community to live a dignified life fighting against the subjugation and demand respect from the men of other communities. Bama ruminates in her novel *Karukku*:

> How did the upper castes become so elevated? How is it that we have been denigrated? They possess money; we do not. If we were wealthy too, wouldn't we learn more, and make more progress than they do? But when it comes to it, even if we are as good as they are, or even better, because of this one issue of caste alone, we are forced to suffer pain and humiliation. (27)

These ruminations find expression in Dalit autobiographies.

## Introducing Vasant Moon

Vasant Moon is a retired civil servant and Dalit activist. He is the editor of 17 volumes of the writings and speeches of the architect of the Indian constitution Dr Ambedkar in English. He is a Marathi writer who acclaims Dr Ambedkar and his principles. He is a contemporary writer, voicing out the cause of Dalits. He was shaped and moulded by the education he received despite the humble life of his family and also by the leadership of Ambedkar and his followers and co-workers.

## Introduction to *Growing up Untouchable in India*

Though Dalit Literature and the resultant Dalit movement mark an important development in the political scenario and the culture of India, not much of Dalit Literature is brought to the world outside India through the global language. They were all written in regional languages and so are unknown to the occidental world. Vasant Moon's autobiography *Growing up Untouchable in India*, the first Dalit autobiography to be published in English, is a moving and eloquent testament to a uniquely Indian life as well as to the universal human spirit. It is a record of the events in his personal life which are intertwined with the spread of Ambedkarite principles and Ambedkar's influence on his community. It is the story of Vasant Moon's life in his Vasti and his neighbourhood. It is the story of any Dalit who finds his life miserable in the hands of the 'upper caste'. It is the story of the ghetto. It is the story of the inescapable hierarchy imposed by caste, based on ancient principles of hereditary pollution. It is the story of the influence of the unparalleled heroic Dr B. R. Ambedkar, a significant hero who is described as a 'wave' for India's awakened and newly ambitious Dalits.

*Growing up Untouchable in India* was originally written in Marathi, the mother tongue of Vasant Moon and translated into English by the well-known sociologist Gail Omvedt with an introduction by his research associate and friend Eleanor Zelliot. Written in an easy-to-understand style, the life of Vasant Moon unfurls itself in the eyes of the readers. The events are not chronicled chronologically, but as and when an idea expressed needs mention of an event, it is presented. So, the autobiography does not begin conventionally with the birth of Vasant Moon. As Eleanor Zelliot has mentioned in the Introduction:

> Vasant Moon's story is about a neighbourhood, a community of people who are Mahars, 'Untouchables,' at the bottom of India's caste system. But it is about that group at a time and place when change had taken place and more change was in the air, when the community feeling was stronger than any sense of inferiority when a child could delight in the wonders of an urban slum. Nevertheless the

tale of Moon's growing up must be seen as a statement by a man whose caste was polluting, despised, 'untouchable' by higher castes. (ii)

In this book Vasant Moon uses the term Dalit to refer to those "who want to free themselves from the concept of pollution and from the patronage of Gandhian ideology" (iii). *Growing up Untouchable in India* "... is a story of growing up in a *vasti*, an urban neighbourhood, adds a new dimension to our understanding of India's Dalits, her Untouchables" (iii). Vasant Moon's autobiography is a part of the nation-building process in the social and political history of India. It is more about the leadership of Dr B. R. Ambedkar and his principles which made the Dalits realise their self-worth and rise for their rights than about their sufferings in the hands of the "upper caste" and about Vasant Moon's personal life. To be specific, the personal life of Vasant Moon is intertwined with Ambedkarite principles.

## Vasant Top of Form Moon's Early Days

Though Vasant Moon hailed from a family that had a respectable background, his childhood was dipped in poverty. As his father did not treat his mother well, his maternal grandfather Sadashiv brought them with him, separating them from their father. His grandfather was grown up in the company of Europeans and it was because of him that Vasant Moon got the English alphabet taught. He had progressive thinking which was much ahead of his time. He was visited by many Mahar leaders like Laxmanrao Ogale, Ghadale, and Dashrath Patil who had great reverence and gratitude for him.

Vasant Moon was the only one from the Mahar community to study in the Normal School. Other Mahar children went to the city primary school. In the Normal School, everyone else was a Brahmin and almost all the teachers were influenced by Gandhi's teachings. The teachers in his school "... had compassion for Mahar boys. They never treated me [Vasant

Moon] scornfully" (14). There was no caste feeling in that school, neither with the teachers nor with the students. He fondly remembered one incident that happened during his school days:

> The teachers took care that the poison of casteism never spread among the boys of the class. One day I fell very sick. For three or four days the fever raged. Nobody, not even my mother, was at home during the day. All the twenty or twenty-five boys in my class came to the Maharpura to visit me. They began to examine me. After that they finished off the cold water in our pot. [...] These Brahman boys used to come to school in cars. Even in this there was no feeling that some were great, some small, some rich, and some poor. My bonds of friendship with them remain unbroken. (15)

After his grandfather's time, Vasant Moon's mother had to take care of the family and the income was never sufficient to feed the family's needs. After his fourth grade his mother sought the help of the Patil family for his education. They got him admitted into the Parwardhan High School which was of the highest standard in all of the Central Provinces and where admission was on merit. They paid the fee too in addition to providing him with the books and the stationery items needed. His poverty led him once to steal a drawing brush from his classmate Tambe.

In school, he was never despised for poverty or for belonging to the Mahar community. As his clothes were worn-out, he avoided washing for fear that they might tear off. When the teacher and his classmates came to know of the reason, they '... fell silent. All of these teachers had some kind of social consciousness. He told me to sit down and then told the students purposefully, "Many of you are well-to-do. If someone gives him a shirt and pants outfit it will be a work of merit"' (36). Many of his classmates helped him with clothes, food and stationery. Some took him to their homes and gave him new outfits. People of his caste also gave him clothes. After graduation, Vasant Moon got a job as the Deputy Accountant General in the Department of Post and Telegraph. But he resigned in 1955 to pursue post-graduation.

Despite the poverty that was lurking the family, he had good education that helped him to realise the plight of his community and take meaningful measures to get them out of that mean existence. His acquaintance with politically significant people served as an impetus and inspiration for him to indulge in progressive activities for the sake of his community. He was attracted by the charismatic Babasahib Ambedkar and his principles as all the Dalits too were. The major part of his life was dedicated to the uplift of his community, following the path of Ambedkar.

## Dignity

The people of Mahar community did not want to get any concession in the name of their caste. They had high self-esteem which aided them to lead a dignified life. Though Vasant Moon's fee was excused at his school, there was no government scholarship for the "untouchables" at that time. One day, there was a notice asking for the list of Harijans. When the teacher asked for the Harijan boys to stand up, though Vasant Moon was not the one to respond to questions in class, this time, he

> ... promptly rose and said, "Sir, we are not 'Harijans,' and we don't want the scholarship of the Harijan Sevak Sangh. None of us like to be called Harijans."

Pralhad Rangari also stood up. "We are followers of Babasaheb Ambedkar. None of us want 'Harijan' scholarships. Shende, do you want it?" (37)

No Mahar student in the class defied Rangari. They were faithful and proud followers of Ambedkar and upheld their dignity.

## Vasant Moon's Life with His Father

All that Vasant Moon could remember of his early days with his father was only of his father's drunkenness. Though his father earned a fine salary as a driver for the Parsis, he spent the money on drinking. His father:

> Waman was a widower and had four daughters and one son by his first wife. The oldest daughter was older than my [Vasant Moon's] mother, but still Sadashiv gave his consent [for their marriage]. He must have been concerned whether mother would get married at all after the effects of her accident.
>
> There was one more reason for agreeing to the proposal of Waman. Waman's father, Vithoba Raoji Moon, was a well-known social leader of Nagpur. He had built a bathing place at Ambala tank for the Mahar community; he would collect fees for their ceremonies and so was known as Moonpande (Moonpriest). He would beat drums known as *pongade* for the processions for Shiva's fair. So, he was also called Vithoba Pongade. Along with spreading education among Untouchables, and encouraging them to keep away from carrion, he also organised Mahar conferences. Because Sadashiv was convinced by all of this that his daughter would have a good life in the Moon family he overlooked Waman's being a widower and had his daughter Puranabai married to him. (18-19)

Vasant Moon's father, like every other Mahar father, gave the children's cut of what he drank. One day he gave Vasant Moon liquor till he became tipsy. Unable to bear this, his mother sent a message to her father saying that she could not live and the children were in danger. Her father took them with him.

## Moon's Society—Vasti

Vasti thronged with life—the lively Dalit community. Though there were hunger and deprivation in Vasti, there were also a sense of community, an easy acceptance of petty crimes and violence, the saving grace of sports and organised activities led by caring adults, the off and on aid from relatives and neighbours, the inexplicable cruelty and unexpected generosity, and escape through education. In Vasti, there were Nagpur's heat and the vivid joy brought by the monsoon. There was lively green nature. Indeed, every tree, every fruit, every nook and cranny of the world in and around Vasti played an important part in Moon's story.

Vasti was a square made by four roads. There were separate colonies or settlements for each community—Mahars, Weavers, Brahmans and other caste Hindus. The people of Vasti worshipped whichever God they liked. There were temples of Hindu Gods, Muslim durgahs, people who wanted to become Muslims, and even people who were a kind of atheists. There was Matamai temple which was the sanctuary for the people when there was an attack of an epidemic. There was an empty field called Tar which served as a playground for them. It was the place to sleep for the children. There were his friends whose fathers narrated stories from the Mahabharata, the Ramayana, and other epics. There was a fodder market held on Mondays and Thursdays on the Tar. The Tar later became the Gita ground as an old man who recited the Gita wandered there. He delivered sermons which were listened to by thousands of people. The children of Maharpura were notorious and they indulged in pranks.

The habitants of the settlement were heterogeneous. There were the Bandits—the thieves for whom the settlement was famous. There were wrestlers. Though there were robbers, no one in the community was afraid of being robbed. The girls were secure under their guard. The neighbours took care of the little kids who were left by their mothers who were away on their jobs. "Neighbourliness means giving a bit of our family's food every day to the neighbours and taking some from them.

The love of neighbourliness residing in earthen houses would absorb all the summer heat" (28).

There were elaborate and grand celebrations of festivals in Vasti. There was conduct of games. There were magic shows. There were heat and rain; joy and sorrow. There were fights and quarrels. There were displays of courage and valour. There were compassion and understanding. There were sharing and caring. There was great interdependence in the community in Vasti. The people of Vasti were influenced by Dr Babasaheb Ambedkar who was their absolute leader beyond question and they took pride in identifying themselves as Ambedkarites.

## Solidarity in Vasti

The Dalits or Mahars living in Vasti stood united in fighting against any power that worked against them. The Mahars were the scavengers of the neighbourhood. Around 1930, Dasharath Patil called for a reform and the Mahars in and around Vasti stopped carrying away the dead animals. They faced all the forms of suppression due to this protest. The Hindus boycotted them; shops were closed for them; mills were closed to them; they were beaten. But all these did not lessen their spirit. They started their own market. They also stood united against the looting of their goods by the Hindus. Dasharath's life was at stake and a Mahar Bablya had to bring him food when he went in hiding. The police had to provide protection for Dasharath to come out of the forest. He arranged for the protection of Mahars and repairing of the roads as compensation for the loss they suffered.

Vasant Moon narrates another incident which stands as a testimony for the unity of Mahars in times of need. A gang of Muslims, who were fascinated by Mahar girls, tried to kidnap a girl of the Mahar community in a market.

> Hardas aroused his companions against this. They urged in every community not to send girls to the Mandai alone. Gangs of Mahar youth began to roam through the market,

> and if any girl was grabbed knives flashed. The *goondas* were at first caught by surprise by this counterattack. Later they brought in more boys. Fighting began in the market. Finally the police intervened. Hardas proclaimed, "If the police don't give protection to our women, then we will have to maintain law and order. You should not interfere." From that time on Mahar girls could wander fearlessly in the Mandai. (49-50)

There were differences among the people of Vasti as there were Congressmen and Ambedkarites, there were people who wanted to follow Islam and those who preferred Christianity. There were those who felt that there was nothing in being called Harijans and those who despised the term. But despite all these differences, there was unity and mutual care and help in the neighbourhood.

## Involvement in Ambedkar's Principles

There could not be any despised community that had ever had a leader as meaningful, influential, and charismatic as Babasaheb Ambedkar whose name keeps India's Dalits awakened and ambitious even today. The emancipation of Dalits in India could be first felt in Maharashtra. Even in Vasant Moon's school days, Ambedkar's visit to their neighbourhood was his and every Dalit's dream. *Janata*, the newspaper run by Ambedkar was read in Vasant Moon's community. Everytime Ambedkar came to their neighbourhood, it would be like a festival and celebration. There would be procession and everyone, including the women, would go to the meeting and procession. Ambedkar washed away the attempts of social structuralists to monopolise political power. He made it possible for Dalits to contribute to the politics of India. He made knowledge and power equal for all citizens of India.

## Boycott of Hinduism

In 1935, there was a call by Dr Ambedkar for a conversion

from Hinduism to Buddhism. This caused "a great mental upheaval" (40) in Nagpur. They came to know about it through *Janata* and everyone discussed it. They read in it, "The Hindus' gods were not brought for us; don't do their *puja*. Their festivals are not ours; don't observe them" (43). But, it is excruciatingly painful to abandon the age-old customs and to go against it. There were old people in Vasti who would not go against the norms of the tradition, especially when it came to matters of religion and God. There was a leader Wamanrao Godbole who convened a meeting of the youth of Vasti, explaining them the ways of Ambedkar and asking them to spread it among the people.

> "From now on, don't celebrate Hindu festivals."
>
> "But what shall we do to begin? People will not give up the practice of *puja*."
>
> "To begin with, stop the festivals in your own homes."
>
> "Ambedkar Jayanti, Chokhamela Jayanti. Don't celebrate Janmashtami-Krishna's birthday or Ram's birthday." (43)

So, they had to begin it from their own homes. That was the time of Janmashtami and people were ready to install idols of Kanooba in their houses. The youth were working vigorously to spread the words of Ambedkar and deprecate the celebration of any Hindu festival. When they were on this mission, they were joined by even the pickpocket of the community Dasarya.

> The same evening there was a meeting of the Dal. The youth on the wrestling ground were called. "Wrestling Master, where are you going?" asked Dasarya Pickpocket of Pralhad Khobragade.
>
> "There is a meeting. We have decided not to install the image of Kanoba. But Gulab Tirpude Ustad says he's going to put up a Kanoba idol in his house. This meeting is called to decide what to do."

"Why can't I come? Oh, brother, let my profession be what it is, but don't I regard Babasaheb as a god? Then why can't I come with you?" (43)

Such was the influence of Ambedkar on the people of Vasti that they regarded him as god and saviour who had come to save them from their state of social derangement. The youth broke the idols of Kanoba. There was no celebration of Krishnajayanthi during that year in Vasti. Vasant Moon was in the sixth grade at that time. He also insisted that his mother did not have any photo or idol of any god in their house and she threw away the little statue of Sai Baba that she had got from someone. Vasant Moon had grown involved in and influenced by Ambedkarite principles. From his childhood, he had been exposed to activities based on these principles and when he grew up, his faith in these principles also got imbibed in him. He became a rationalist humanitarian.

## Mahars in Politics

Mahars wanted to have equal footing with others in the society. Their involvement in politics was very active and vibrant. Babu Hardas was the secretary to the union and in addition, he was the first one to bring all the *bidi* workers from Nagpur to Gondiya and Chandrapur under an organisation. He was the candidate of the Independent Labour Party for Kamathi constituency for the elections in 1937. Till then the Congress was considered to be the only national party in India. The candidature of Babu Hardas outraged the Congress. They involved in a lobby with the Independent Labour Party which was a futile effort. They even sent agents to kill Babu Hardas. But all these could not deter Babu Hardas' determination; instead, it grew stronger. He won the election.

In the 1946 elections, for the workers' seat, Sakharam Meshram was the candidate of the Scheduled Caste Federation and Rambhau was the candidate of Congress and for the

Untouchables's seat, Sitaram Hadke was the candidate of the Federation and Hemchandra Khandekar was the candidate of the Congress. But the Congress was not courageous enough to campaign in the Dalit habitation. They had a heated election atmosphere with meetings, strikes, discussions among the activists, thunderous processions of the troops joined by thousands of men and women, physical assaults on the Mahars, resistance to these attacks, disguises, and cases in the court. The names of the Ambedkarite voters were entered in the wrong neighbourhood as a result of which the men had to walk long distances to vote and the women were left at home, ready with weapons. When the men had to go hiding, the women brought them food and support. There were shootings in which an Ambedkarit activist was fired. In all these "... the lawyers of the Mahar community and the activists stood behind their heroes" (99). There were attacks by the Hindu goondas. Even after the election, there were issues of quarrels resulting in riots and the imposing of curfew. It was almost like a war atmosphere, but, the Mahars stood up against all these trepidations with a united heart and soul and emerged victorious, though they lost the elections which showed that "Ambedkar's demands for recognition of Scheduled Caste needs went unheeded" (105).

## Anti-Gandhian Sentiment

The Mahars had an "antagonistic feeling" towards Gandhi, if one could name it so. The Chokhamela hostel management had been arranging for the annual gathering of the hostel every year. In 1941, they decided to invite Mahatma Gandhi. But the Mahars were against this idea. So, the organisers had to get Gandhi down two stations earlier so as to make the Mahars think that he had not arrived. Gandhi's car arrived from the back of the hostel. When the reception committee was trying to shout welcome notes, there was a thunderous roar of the demonstration outside, "Mahatma Gandhi go back!" (63). Despite the antagonistic feeling of the Mahars, Gandhi entered the stage. When an

Ambedkarite Dalit raised a question, the uproar against Gandhi was so loud that the question faded in it. Gandhi was not allowed to speak a word. There was pelting of stones and Gandhi had to be rushed through the back door.

The difference between Gandhi and Ambedkar rose from the difference in their approach and attitude to untouchability. Gandhi thought that untouchability could be destroyed without disturbing the caste system whereas Ambedkar was determined that caste system had to be done away with in order for untouchability to be eradicated. Ambedkar was able to convince the Dalits and win them over to his side as the Dalits were ill-treated in the name of caste. Even in matter of the independence of India, Ambedkar was not sure of the status of Dalits in the political, economic, and social arenas.

## Samata Sainik Dal

The Mahars had a branch of Samata Sainik Dal in their neighbourhood. It was established by Asaram Paithankar, Sadanand Dongare, and others around the year 1938. There was flag-hoisting every day except on Sundays. The flag was their pride. They sang songs in the honour of the flag.

> After the historic 1942 first Scheduled Castes Federation conference, he [Wamanrao Godbole] brought silk cloth for a blue flag and made a flat with his own hands. In the centre of the flag was a sun of white cloth, which symbolised Babasaheb Ambedkar. In the middle of the sun, touching the edges, was a round "SCF" standing for the Scheduled Caste Federation, embroidered in English letters. On the left side of the flat, next to the rope, were eleven stars in the top corner sewn out of white cloth, and the letters "SSD" in the bottom corner. This flag was the united symbol of the Scheduled Caste Federation and the Samata Sainik Dal. The eleven stars symbolised the eleven provinces of India at the time. While raising the flag, care was taken that its edge should not touch the ground or any dirt. (65)

Everyone of the community came to the Dal. There was strict discipline. There was a parade of the soldiers every day. The Samata Sainik Dal of Nagpur was the subject of discussion of Nagpur. Women were not excluded from the membership of the working committee of this branch of the Dal. There were theatre performances arranged by Dal focusing on social awareness and Ambedkarite principles.

## Ambedkar's Influence

There was a conference of the Ambedkarites to take place in 1942. On the arrival of Ambedkar, Wamanrao suggested that they offered him the Guard of Honour which was agreed to by the leaders. He planned elaborately and minutely, arranging the stage, the chair on the stage for him, the photographer, and everything thoroughly and in detail. But when he reached the railway station with his battalion, R.R. Patil with his group had received Ambedkar already in procession. But, Wamanrao was not the one to give up and give in. He, with his people, blocked the main road in his fury, the fury caused by the sense of being betrayed of the opportunity of welcoming the great leader. Everything turned into normalcy only when Ambedkar called Wamanrao to him.

Mahars were not considered Hindus. There were Hindu-Mahar bloodied riots. As the Hindus were dominating the government departments, whenever there was a riot between the two communities, the Mahars were arrested. The Mahars were in strong support of the satyagraha campaign against the Pune Pact which was sponsored by the Federation. "The disciples of Ambedkar had created a tremendous self-confidence in the Dalit community. For that matter, other communities also were awed by the Dalits" (96). It is this sense of unity that prevailed among the Dalits which pushed them forward in their struggle against untouchability.

During the Quit India movement in 1942, while the Hindus wanted independence as a means of gaining power, Ambedkar wanted to be clear about the Dalits' share in this independence. There was the concept of "Congress and Gandhi mean the country" (105) and Ambedkar was portrayed as a traitor who was against the independence of India. But Dalits had unstinted and unshakable faith in Ambedkar. They celebrated Ambekar's birthday for ten days as Ambedkar Jayanti. On these occasions they staged plays on Ambedkarite principles and other social issues.

Around 1946, the only newspaper of the Dalits was *Janata* and the weekly *Dawn* run by N. K. Tirpude, an Ambedkarite activist. Raosaheb Thavare who earlier left SCF and joined Congress, returned then into the SCF. This caused friction between Ambedkarite activists and Thavare's group and this was reflected in the newspapers they ran. The Thavare group who were anti-Ambedkarites were called Harijans—which they considered a demeaning term. The Ambedkarites cut off all social relationship with the anti-Ambedkarites. There existed a strong solidarity among the Ambedkarites. The influence of Ambedkar was so great on Mahars:

> One day a blind man and his lame sighted wife came to beg alms. The two sang together a hymn about Babasaheb Ambedkar in fine, thin voices. Once the words "Bhimrao Ambedkar" came out of their mouths, women and children came out from all the nearby houses and began to listen. While they listened, they filled the couple's begging bags with grain. From then on this pair did the rounds of our neighbourhood for many days. (111)

## Efforts to bring Awareness

Strong and strenuous efforts were there by the youth of the Dalits to arouse the people of their community of their present depressed demeaned state. There were slogans, leaflets, pamphlets, songs and poems written bringing to light the detestable social condition of Dalits. There was a comedy

*Conversion* which effectively demonstrated the ill-treatment that Dalits met with in the society, in the hands of Brahmins. Even when they were put to test, the "Ambedkari dramatists acted according to their word" (112). Poets wandered from place to place singing songs on the principles of Ambedkar. The singers "... were young men who would experience an upsurge of rage about atrocities and the battle for our rights. They were not striving to publish books of poetry. They went from neighbourhood to neighbourhood, village to village to raise consciousness through their songs" (117).

## Buddhism and Dalits

Buddhism gained its influence on Dalits and Dalit activists. They erected statues of Lord Budha in their temple and did puja. The Dalits of Nagpur visited Sanchi when the remains of the two important disciples of Buddha were sent to India by the British government and were to be installed at Sanchi. After their return, they felt a new spirit throbbing in their community. In addition to celebrating Ambedkar Jayanthi for ten days, they decided to celebrate Buddha Jayanti. A cement statue of Buddha was kept in the temple grounds. There were lectures delivered on Buddhism by noted professors. During a visit of Ambedkar to his neighbourhood, there were several questions on Buddhism and its concepts to which Ambedkar gave detailed and convincing explanations and there ensued a lengthy and meaningful conversation.

## The Great Conversion

Though there were talks about the great conversion to Buddhism by Dalits in 1950, it was only around 1954 that Ambedkar "publicly proclaimed that the conversion ceremony would take place in Mumbai" (153). But Wamanrao Godbole and all the people with him felt that it should be held in Nagpur. As Wamanrao had deep knowledge of Buddhism and has read many books on it, he wrote to Ambedkar that there was no place for

Mumbai in the life of Buddha or Buddhism and in fact, there was a mention of "a tooth of the Buddha's being in Nagpur" (153). He also suggested that the conversion should be on the 14th of October 1956, as the date of the bodily death of Buddha could be narrowed down to October 13 taking into account the "description of a shower of flowers on his body" which blossom in September and October. Ambedkar consented. Wamanrao put in all his efforts in preparation for the great conversion. He set up an office room. The place of the office room "... selected by Wamanrao was a plot of fourteen acres near the Vaccine Institute at Shradhanand Peth, which has since been known as the Diksha Bhumi, a place of conversion" (154).

There was complete and absolute unity, discipline, and dedication on the part of the people involved in the task.

> During the planning I [Vasant Moon] made a trip every Sunday from Saunsar, where I was employed at the time, stayed in the conversion office. Wamanrao was drawing up the entire plan and implementing it himself. There was a group of youth from Bardi under his direction. The work of correspondence was given to a gentleman named Manik Domaji Panchbhai. Everyone tended to his assigned task with discipline. Because of dedication, Panchbhai did not even see the arrangements set up at Diksha Bhoomi until the very last day. The mixture of duty and loyalty was natural to Panchbhai. (154)

But, things were not going smooth. One day, Wamanrao was called by Ambedkar to Delhi. There seemed to be some change as Hardas Avale and Akant Mate had some suggestions and accusations on Wamanrao. They wanted to change the place where the conversion had to take place saying that the place was surrounded by Sangh people and was given free of charge. The accusation they held against Wamanrao and which made Ambedkar furious was, "Wamanrao held a *puja* of the place for the conversion ceremony. This *puja* was done at the hands of the Brahman Shri Bhavani Shankar Niyogi" (155). This accusation was dismissed as Wamanrao explained:

> We did *puja* for the Diksha Bhumi but it was at the hands of one of our Buddhists. Shri Laxmanrao Kavade, who has just taken the vow of a *shramaner*, did a programme of *bhumipuja*. Shri Niyogi came walking by. Out of curiosity he stopped to see and joined in the ceremony. There was no kind of *puja* at his hands. (155-156)

When Ambedkar asked him about the place, Wamanrao replied that he had made entire preparations selecting spacious and convenient place in Nagpur, sprawling over fourteen acres and had made complete arrangements for the protection of Ambedkar. Ambedkar could not decide at once. But he decided upon Nagpur after he met with an accident and was saved from death by his wife.

Though the Federation's activists were displeased with Wamanrao, the preparations went on war footing. Establishing committees for various works, allocation of works, cleaning of the land, and works of all kind were done by the members of the committees and volunteers. The Deputy Mayor of Nagpur helped day and night in levelling the ground. Complete care was taken regarding the protection and safety of Ambedkar. Though there were some volunteers standing in close protection, the entire "Maharpura kept a close watch on it" (156). Vasant Moon took great care of the protection of Ambedkar and his seat on the stage. He selected volunteers for his protection and borrowed a special teak chair from a neighbour. The two day programme went on as planned and the conversion ceremony got over. This mass conversion to Buddhism marked epoch-changing, era-making social, political, religious, and cultural phenomena in Indian system. This mass conversion symbolised the rejection of the rejecting. It indicated the renunciation of the humiliated past. It brought to light, it made the entire world know about the barbaric caste system that was prevailing in the

Hindu community in India. This conversion enabled the Dalits to get themselves rid of the feeling of being downtrodden, the caste taboo, and marginalisation.

Ambedkar did not want Dalits to be Hindus because, R. R. Bohle says in his preface to *Buddha and His Dhamma*:

> Since the institution of untouchability is popularly an integral part of Hinduism and since caste is a major tenet of the Hindus, concerted measures should be taken to breakdown such barriers. Buddhism is an ideal for this purpose but it should reach all the corners of the country. Untouchability, unfortunately is not merely an social or an economic problem but also a religious problem. (12)

Further he quotes Ambedkar's speech on the day of conversion:

> Hindu religion offers no opportunity for the untouchables to improve their lot, for, it is based on inequality. On the other hand Buddhism is based on equality and justice. . . I would like to see all India become Buddhist. (13)

## Death of Ambedkar

The news of the death of Ambedkar came as a sudden blow after fifty-three days of the conversion. Tears drowned everyone's eyes. All the trains to Mumbai were crowded. The cremation was at Dadar. Vasant Moon says:

> People described to us the gathering before the funeral pyre of Babasaheb. The mass of people was so huge that the boundary between people and the sea had nearly vanished. When the words "Baba has gone" fell from Acharya Atre's mouth, the whole mass erupted. For some minutes only crying could be heard everywhere. (165)

Such was the influence and reach of Ambedkar. Many poets wrote emotional and revolutionary poems on the death of their impeccable leader. Here is one of such expressive poems by Shridhar Hoval, written after Ambedkar's death:

> This field was tilled by Bhim, here grass and weeds will not grow; Even if the seeds of dissension are harvested, here they will not sprout; Better for the organisation to be widowed than live a feeble married life. We will not leave the lion's gymnasium to study the way of sheep! (118-119)

Some verses that Nagarale composed after the death of Babasaheb testify the power of Ambedkar's very name:

> Whatever we had to be told was said by Ambedkar.
>
> His teachings are finished, his speaking finished, his commands finished.
>
> But don't let your mind be deceived that we are adrift and destroyed-Ambedkar has lifted us up, liberated us.
>
> Don't lose your strength in sorrow, keep the wisdom that is life. There is no benefit in futile sobbing, remember who you are; Don't give scope to treachery, backbiting, infighting. These are such insignificant things, but be wary of them. (119)

Ambedkar was criticised vehemently for his act of conversion, even by his own people. But he was strong in his point. He had answers for all the questions thrown at him. When he was asked by the "Hindus" why he was depriving the Dalits of their income by carrying away the dead animals and why he declined the offer of reservation for Dalits at the State Assemblies and the Parliament, he just asked them why did not the "Hindus" take them instead and benefit. He was sure, "What a man truly needs is self-respect and not economical benefits" (Trans. Own, *Indhuvaaga Saagamaatten* (*I will not Die as a Hindu*) 5).

## Conclusion

The spread of literacy among the Mahars, their craving for a dignified position and status in the society, and the leadership of Ambedkar gave them the ferocity, the daring and panache and above all, the unity with which the Mahars fought against the oppression, politically, academically, socially, and psychologically. Every time they got hit, they stayed strong and stood taller. They pushed boundaries of belief to play fearless but careful and planned part. Injuries and uncertainties were there for them to stumble upon; but those were not necessarily their speedbreakers. They helped them to improve their strategy and fight better against the discrimination. They found the conversion to Buddhism as social levelling up - shedding the identity of Dalit for being a Buddhist and being treated in equal status with the Hindus. Vasant Moon's autobiography *Growing Up Untouchable in India* is an expression of their anger with the society that treats Dalits callously and heartlessly and their indomitable hope to rise up. It is a voice of rebellion, and an account of their painful but heroic attempt to dismantle the caste system that kept them as the lowest stratum of the society. It is the testimony for the power of unison.

## Works Cited

Ambedkar, B. R. *Annihilation of Caste Dr Babasaheb Ambedkar Writings and Speeches* Vol. I Ambedkar Foundation, 2014.

Ambedkar, Dr B. R. *Buddha and His Dhamma*. http://www.ambedkar.webs.com

Ambedkar, Dr *Indhuvaaga Saagamaatten*. Periyaar Dhraavida Kazhagam, www.periyardk.org

Bama. *Karukku*. Trans. Lakshmi Holmistrom. OUP, 2011.

Deo, Veena. "Dalit Literature in Marathi". *Handbook of Twentieth-Century Literatures of India*. Eds. Natarajan, Nalini and Emmanuel Sampath Nelson. Greenwood Publishing Group, 1996. p. 363. ISBN 0-313-28778-3.

http://14.139.211.59/bitstream/123456789/3545/1/Vol.%207%20March%202020_01.pdf

http://www.bookverdict.com/details.xqy?uri=Product-8757212414155.xml

https://drambedkarbooks.com/

https://www.bookdepository.com/Growing-up-Untouchable-India-Vasant-Moon/9780742508811

https://www.bookganga.com/eBooks/Books/Details/4627458641999410862

https://www.goodreads.com/author/show/11894.Vasant_Moon

https://www.goodreads.com/book/show/168.Growing_Up_Untouchable_in_India

Moon, Vasant. *Growing Up Untouchable in India*. Trans. Gail Omvedt. Rowman & Littlefield Publishers, Inc., 2000.

# 9

# The Stranded Strings of Dalit Tribals' Existence: A Reading of Laxman Gaikwad's Autobiography *Uchalya*: *The Branded*

*Dr Meenu Dudeja*

I do not ask
For the sun and moon from your sky
Your farm, your land,
Your high houses or mansions
I do not ask for gods or rituals,
Castes or sects
Or even for your mother, sisters, daughters.
I ask for
My rights as a man. (Limbale, "White Paper" Lines 1-7)

Not only in India but also in the whole world, caste is understood through various prisms. Caste plays an important role in every perspective in public and private life. Caste and Dalit are not separate issues, nor are they external issues, which are unrelated to anyone in caste ecology. They are not peripheral, they have to do with the legitimacy of livelihood—the humanity of common collective existence. They affect the atrocities to a great extent. There can be no Dalit humanitarian tradition without being insulted, attacked and honest with the

Dalit. Therefore, participating in the Dalit struggle is a difficult exercise to speak and listen to the truth. The caste has been divided in India on their *karma* (duty).

They are treated as untouchables. They were forced to live a life of morbid absurdities due to a lack of cripples' family structures. Their condition is worse than animals socially, economically, politically, and culturally. Dalit, Untouchables, and Adivasis, more than make us aware of the caste that is considered untouchables, they are separated from the rest of the castes. In the other words, and they do not have any existence as human beings. Dr S. Chelliah writes about this autobiography, Laxman Gaikwad's autobiography *Uchalya: The Branded* does not deal only with the problems of only male Dalits; it portrays the unheard sufferings and pains of Dalit women of his tribe" (Chelliah 262).

Laxman Gaikwad's *Uchalya: The Branded* is a deep scream of a man from the tribal community who raised his voice for equal rights to all genders and all citizens of India. Gaikwad's autobiography is a vivid account of the struggle, oppression, exploitation, marginalisation, and agonies of the Dalit community in different spheres of life. After 72 years of independence still, they are de-notified tribals. They are the second citizens in India. Laxman Gaikwad expressed his heartfelt pain, suffering, and agony in his autobiography—*The Branded*. In this way he narrates his real pain. This nomadic "denotified tribe" is exposed to cruel treatment by law enforcement. To remain alive, it clings to the thieving profession. In 1998, Gaikwad received the Sahitya Akademi Award for his autobiographical book, which was written in Marathi. This interpretation is crafted by P.A. Kolharkar. The opening lines from the text reveal the pain of the author and his tribal community:

> No native place. No birthdate. No house or farm. No caste, either. That is how I was born in an Uchalya community, at Dhanegaon in Taluka Latur. (Gaikwad, 1)

Laxman Gaikwad illustrates the traumatic condition of their living style. Access to sanitation was a big struggle for them as they had no bathroom and no toilet. Night becomes a horrible dream for them. To quote from the text:

> Nobody would offer work to my father, Martand, as we were known to belong to a branded tribe of criminals. They would not employ my mother, Dhondabai, even as a farmhand. (Gaikwad, 2)

Laxman Gaikwad has given a threadbare account of their community and it proved a window to the entire literary world. No one was allowed to go anywhere without getting permission from the upper class. To quote from the text:

> If anyone from our household or tribe wished to leave the place, he had to obtain a permit from the police, Patil, for the purpose. We were reduced to the level of animals just as permits are needed for cattle to be moved to on places or to be sold in the market, we had to have passes to move about. We had to show them to the police Patil and him where we were going to, and even then, we could stay there for more than three days.. (Gaikwad 3)

Laxman Gaikwad's *Uchalya: The Branded* is a good description of the tribal community. It is Gaikwad's sincere attempt to represent the unheard voice of his community. Panchayat becomes the owner of their life also. Patil, a village headman, in charge of law and order, was supposed to kill anyone.

One day they held a Panchayat and argued that ever since Lingappa Gaikwad of the community had started reporting the names of his colleagues to the police, it had become impossible to go on thieving missions. Nor did the tribesmen get jobs as they were known to be thieves, now he became old and weak and had no strength to bear the beatings and torture by the police, and that some steps had to be taken to stop him for good. Hence it was resolved that he must be killed. One day they broke into his hut through the thatched roof, gagged his grandfather, and hacked him to death with an axe. The Panchayat saw to it that the death was not reported to the police.

His community can't go to the police against the Panchayat. His grandfather was cremated without anybody getting to know of it. Now that grandfather was dead, the people from our community resumed their usual business of thieving and picking pockets without the fear of being reported since then the entire household depended on grandmother.

In the social hierarchy, this community is at the bottom. They are introduced as a thief Santmuchchar Community. Socially his community became so branded and mistrusted, that nobody was ready to offer any work to the people of their tribe.

In Maharashtra, his community is not identified by anyone's name. There are several names by which people of his community are referred to. Some of these names are Pathrut, Takari, Bhamta, Uchale, Girnewadar, Kamati, Ghantichor and Wadar. Thus in different districts and parts, they are known by different names. In Maharashtra, he has to refer to his clan with different names on different occasions. His community is known all over India as a Santmuchchar community. They speak Telugu. Sant means 'market' and Muchchar means thief.

Being disadvantaged and being deprived of fundamental rights, they have educated only on theft strategies. The education of the young trainees for both boys and women would begin with their beating. They had been made to bear bodily tortures in order that they might now not expose the names of others. If any person fails after the training duration, there has been excessive punishment for her or him. Laxman recalls how Manikada was arrested by the police in the market one day. He was tortured and forced to reveal all names. To quote from the text:

> When he returned, he was punished by the people of his community: they abused him, you bastard, f ... k your mother, you are afraid like Ven (merchant) and Baman (Brahmin). When caught red-handed, you revealed the names of the entire gang. You have shamed the name of Jamaat of thieves. (Gaikwad, 6)

He would give physical torture and mental harassment even to the women. They would squeeze the breasts of women and tortured them. The police had naked Manikada and were beating him.. Dada's front and back were blood-red. They took chilli powder and put it in Manik's anus and eyes and continued beating him on the burning sand. Only when he burst with dirt and pee, then they let him go.

Laxman Gaikwad describes how Dalit women are double marginalised. They have to suffer because of their caste and also due to their gender. They belong to the most oppressed group in the world. Both externally and internally, the women of these communities are victims of the cultures, structures, and institutions of oppression. They are physically and mentally tortured and are sexually assaulted. There are many examples of domestic attacks in Uchalya households. The perception that a woman's actual place is her husband's toes and her role is just to serve her husband and his family members. To quote from the text, "Laxman on occasion beats his spouse, Chabbu..... I threw her out of the house" (Gaikwad, 139).

Laxman Gaikwad describes that the people of his community did not know the value of education. For them, education means only to learn how to be a good thief. No school, No books. Their only identity was a thief.

> When Laxman Gaikwad was sent to school, his community opposed this step. They believed that if their children started going to school then their race would be ruined. Despite all the obstacles he regularly attends his school. Education

brings positive changes to Laxman's life. He got rid of his dirty and clumsy habits. (Gaikwad, 33)

When Laxman Gaikwad got a job as a labourer in a spinning mill, he started fighting for the rights of the workers. He protested the exploitation and cruel behaviour of the manager and the chairman of the mill. They were made to work more than normal hours and yet they were not given satisfactory pay and medical allowances. Nobody dared to protest this exploitation. After initial hesitation, Gaikwad formed a union and became a powerful leader. He solved many problems faced by the mill workers. But he was eventually fired. He had a question in his mind that why these officers are not called thieves.

He used peaceful means for the rights of Dalit. Through the Pathruta Samaj organisation, he raised issues of corruption of the so-called eminent people of his community and society. Laxman brings these issues to the attention of the public through the *Daily Deity* newspaper. This fight against the system not only brought a change in the mentality of landowners and policemen but also excluded branded people who began to gain self-respect. He advocated an equal place for heights in society. Her vision of socio-political change raised her voice against an unjust social fabric.

Laxman Gaikwad said if they all have been brothers and citizens of the same country, then why his brothers have not been given jobs. Why they couldn't eat together, why they didn't have land? Why didn't they have their own house? Why they had been beaten with false allegations of theft. In fact, when they had committed no theft, then why did they beat my mother and pulled at her sari? Even now he was frequently surprised why they had been discriminated. He just thinks about why his race used to be branded and treated as a thief community.

Laxman Gaikwad's Uchalya community emerges as a poignant portrayal of trials and tribulations. The narrative throws light on the marginalised existence of Dalit, who are suffering due to the age-old social, cultural, and economic exclusion and discrimination.

This exclusion and discrimination of people at the lowest level in social, cultural, and economic hierarchies make them vulnerable to myriad forms of inequality and injustice. Gaikwad raised his voice against the age-old Brahminical tradition and the hegemonic forces deployed by the state agency. Laxman questions the prevailing dumb social structure. To quote from the text:

> Why is it that the whole community is branded as thieves? Why are we denied opportunities to live a decent life? ... Are we proud of this diverse heritage as we age for these conditions Addicted to? (Gaikwad, 63)

Thus, in this autobiography *Uchalya: The Branded* tribals' sufferings have been narrated. They are exploited not only by the upper caste people but also by the government due to wrong policies and corruption in the departments. Laxman Gaikwad's literary creation gets acclamation from all literary spheres. His personal journey serves as a strong motivation for liberating Dalits from exploitation and deprivation of self-definition. This is the brutal honesty of Gaikwad. This life story is in a way an exercise in self-cleaning. The author addresses terms along with his traumatic past, as well as the trauma of being born into a "brand society." They are supposed to be the SECOND CITIZENS of India—De-notified tribals. Dr Bijender Singh observes in his paper that "Laxman Gaikwad's autobiography is a masterpiece of Dalit Literature" (45).

## Works Cited

Chelliah, S. "Projection of Poverty and Exploitation of Dalit Women in Laxman Gaikwad's Autobiography *Uchalya—The Branded:* An Analysis." *Dalit Men's Autobiographies: A Critical Appraisal.* Ed. Bijender Singh. New Delhi: Kalpaz Publications, 2017. 261-67.

Gaikwad, Laxman. *Uchalya: The Branded* (1998). Trans. P.A. Kolharkar. Delhi: Sahitya Akademi, 2009.

Kumar, Sanjay. "The Curse of Poverty and Casteism: Childhood Memories in Laxman Gaikwad's *The Branded: Uchalya.*" *Different Dimensions of Dalit Literature*. Ed. Bijender Singh. Atlantic Publishers and Distributors, 2019. 127-134.

Limbale, Sharankumar. "White Paper." In Marathi Dalit Poetry Blog.

http://marathidalitpoetry.blogspot.com/2014/07/white-paper-sharankumar-limbale.html. Accessed 15 May, 2021.

Singh, Bijender. "Dalit Resurrection in Laxman Gaikwad's *The Branded.*" *Indian Scholar: An International Multidisciplinary Research e-Journal*. Vol. 1. No. 1, Sept 2014. 49-54.

# 10

# Exploitations of Mahars in Shankarrao Kharat's Autobiography *Taral Antral*

*Dr C. Ramya*

The main contribution in Dalit Literature, at the earliest phase, has been from Maharashtra. The main reason behind it is that the main figure of Dalit Literature Dr B. R. Ambedkar belonged to Maharashtra and he motivated unlimited people to get education and convinced them that only education can transform their life. Many people, after getting influenced by him, got good education and some of these people became writers. This fact cannot be denied that many Dalit people are greatly influenced by him today also. Many well-known Dalit writers from Maharashtra wrote their autobiographies in Marathi by his inspiration.

Shankar Ramchandra Kharat (1921-2001) was also an acclaimed Dalit writer from Maharashtra. He was born in a Mahar caste in Atpati in Sangali district of Maharashtra. His father's name was Shri Ramchandra Tatya Kharat and his mother's name was Smt Savitri Ramchandra Kharat. He had three brothers and three sisters in his family. After his school education, he went to Pune for higher education. He went to Mumbai to do LLB. He met Dr Ambedkar there and became his personal secretary. He also worked at a few other posts under Dr B. R. Ambedkar. He was highly influenced by Ambedkar and that's why he converted to Buddhism. He worked with

Dr B. R. Ambedkar and Ambedkar told him that India have sufficient doctors, lawyers, engineers and other educated people in Dalit community but there is dearth of writers in Dalit community. Ambedkar gave him this opportunity.

B. R. Ambedkar told him that when a non-Dalit writer Shri Venkatesh Madgulkar can raise Dalit issues in his works, at least, Dalit writers must not remain behind in that direction. Shankarrao Kharat made up his mind that he will definitely serve Dalit society not only by writing books on Dalit issues; he fought for their rights in the court also. Dalits of India face the problem of caste discrimination at every step because the mentality of the people cannot be changed even after making constitutional laws. Initially, they were not allowed to get education and it is mentioned in many Dalit autobiographies. Dr S.D. Sargar writes in this context:

> Dalits formed the lower strata in Indian social structure. Hence, they were denied each and every opportunity by the upper caste Hindus. All the efforts of Dalits for getting education were strongly and unanimously opposed by the upper castes for social and political reasons. The upper castes were afraid that if the lower castes were allowed to get education, they would ask for their share in power. (Sargar, 1-2)

Shankarrao Kharat took started writing his books covering different aspects of Dalit people. He served as the Vice-Chancellor of Marathwada University in Aurangabad which is known as Dr Babasaheb Ambedkar Marathwada University. He also became a member of the council of Maharashtra State.

His autobiography *Taral Antaral* was published in 1981 in Marathi. Dr Deler Singh writes in his paper that, "His autobiography *Taraal Antaraal* is considered to be a great work in Marathi literature" (Singh, 196). Apart from Kharat's autobiography, he has written many short story collections such as *Bara Balutedar* (1959), *Tadipar* (1961), *Sangava* (1962), *Titvicha Phera* (1963), *Sutaka* (1964), *Daundi* (1965), *Adgavche Pani* (1970) and *Gav-Shiv* (1970). *Hatbhatti* (1970), *Gavacha Tinpol Guruji* ((1971), *Jhopadpatti* (1973), *Masaledar Guesthouse* (1974), *Footpath Nambar 1* (1980) and *Majhe Nav* (1987) are the novels written by him. Apart from these, he has written several non-fictional books.

His autobiography *Taral Antral* narrates the personal moments and memories of his life and the entire Dalit community. It can be called that his autobiography is a story of an untouchable. It describes how the changes took place in his village and how the caste discrimination was prevalent in the society at that time. Being an established writer, he knew well how he can give better shape to his autobiography. The different characters of his autobiography are revolutionary figures who want a change in society.

Kharat's autobiography narrates different incidents of his childhood. There was a time when he was a school-going child and could not read. There is an incident of a letter. It was late night time and unexpectedly Genubuva Taral came to the door of his house. He brings out a letter from his half-sister and gives it to Shankar's father Rama Mahar. It was a strange thing to him because he knew that being a Mahar, he would deliver letters to people but up to now he had not received any letter from anybody. Rama and Genubuva speculate about the sender of the letter. There were only a few words in the letter. They decide that tomorrow he will go to someone who can read this letter for him. The village clerk and schoolteacher could do this task for him. They decide that he will go to the schoolteacher as the village clerk is out of station.

When Shankar goes with his father to the schoolteacher's house, the teacher's wife had made a *rangoli*. When Shankar puts his step on the *rangoli* by mistake, the Brahman woman bursts out on him and calls him a blind. When Rama tells her that he is merely a child, the teacher's wife says that he is old enough to eat; so he cannot be called a child.

The exploitation of Dalits was so common at that time. The Mahars were given the kind of work which nobody else would like to do. They were considered slaves and did all the work for the upper caste people. These people would not go to school and that's why they remained poor and uneducated. Most of the upper caste people would exploit them and the same happens here also. When Rama goes to the schoolteacher's house, the teacher's wife wants to take undue advantage of this situation. She tells her husband that a Mahar has come at the right time and tells her husband to order him to cut the wood for them for at least a week.

Rama requests the schoolteacher to read the letter for him first. He does not deny the work but the schoolteacher shows cunningness and he says that he is going to take a bath as the water is getting cold. He tells him to split the firewood for him and only after that he will read that letter for him.

Human beings should help each other at the time of need and at least a teacher should show moral values but it does not happen in this case. The village schoolmaster also leaves no stone unturned to exploit Rama. He reads the letter to him only when he gets ensured that the firewood has been split for at least four days. He tells him to come another day so that the wood may be sufficient for at least eight days.

When he reads the letter to Rama, he tells that his half-sister Dhondibai in Mumbai passed away ten days back last Tuesday. Rama was shocked after getting the news of Dhondibai's demise. Tears rolled down from his eyes. When Rama goes home, his wife asks about the delay. Rama tells her the whole incident how the village schoolmaster forced him to split the firewood for him first in lieu of reading a letter for him. Thus, this incident of Shankarrao Kharat narrates how the Mahars were treated like animals at that time.

To understand the nuances of this narrative, the readers easily come to know that even the educated people did not miss the chance of exploitation of Dalits in the past. It is not the first instance of any Dalit autobiography, in Omprakash Valmiki's autobiography *Joothan: A Dalit's Life*, Omprakash's headmaster abuses him and orders him to clean the whole school. His Chemistry teacher did not allow him to enter the practical classes at many occasions deliberately due to which Omprakash failed in that subject. Valmiki writes in his autobiography, "When the results were announced, I was among the failures. I had good marks in all other subjects except Chemistry. I had failed the lab tests" (Valmiki, 65). He aptly writes that, "Caste follows one right up to one's death" (Valmiki, 78).

Mohandas Naimisharay's school teachers did not want to teach in their school just because only the children of the low caste people would come in this school. It is narrated in his autobiography *Apne Apne Pinjare*. Balbir Madhopuri also narrates in his autobiography *Changiya Rukh* how his Sodhi Master would send him, his friend Roshi and other Dalit students to do his personal works in the nearby villages. D. R. Jatava's autobiography *A Silent Soldier* also has a narration when Jatava is declared unsuccessful in his PhD-Viva just because he belonged to a Dalit family and was not teaching in a college. There are many more instances in Dalit autobiographies where teachers also showed discriminatory attitude with Dalit students.

Such events are found in our Hindu epics such as the *Mahabharata* and the *Ramayana* also. Eklavya is not given education by Dronacharya just because he belonged to a Bheel caste. Draupadi refused to marry Karna in the *Svayamvara* just because he belonged to a low caste. In the *Ramayana*, there are instances of two persons Nishadraj Kewat and Shabri who were given due respect only by Lord Rama while many other people did not show any intimate relation with them due to their low caste.

In this autobiography, Shankarrao Kharat describes how the village Mahars were given the responsibility of looking after the dead bodies. The village duties of the Mahars were very difficult. Kharat writes that he "knew clearly the dangers of village duty" (Dangle, *A Corpse in the Well* 1). He further writes that "It was a perpetual noose around the neck of a Mahar! My father was crushed flat by this duty" (Dangle, 1). The incident of the corpse is very heart-wrenching as his father could not eat his meals on time. When Shankarrao asked his father to eat the meal, he said that, "The chief constable and the constable are yet to arrive! They will carry out the inquest; only then can the Mahar rest" (Dangle, 2). His father Rama knew that the head constable had arrived and he was having his meal. The village head has also eaten to his fill. Shankarrao became very angry when his father refused to eat food. He said, "Anna! The constable will come after his meal. The village chief has also filled his belly. Then why can't you too eat your bread? Why must you remain hungry?" (Dangle, 2). His father was very helpless and he told his son that he cannot do it even if he wishes to do so. He is helpless just because he is a Mahar. He just uttered these words to his son, "Who cares if a Mahar lives or dies?" (2).

It is clear from the situation that the Mahars of Maharashtra were trying to come out of the cruel clutches of casteism but it was not possible for them. The string of their life was at the hands of the upper caste people. When the head constable came, he ordered Shankarrao's father to bring out the corpse out of the well. It was a very difficult task for him. He had to face humiliation when he felt reluctant to do it. When Shankarrao raised his voice against this discrimination with his father, his father silenced him saying, "Shut up son. You are not old enough to understand. Don't say a word. I'll have to bear whatever happens" (4). Ultimately, he had to go down in the well. He noticed that a snake was in the well. The village people misguided him saying that it is a reptile and it would not bite him.

Fortunately, the snake did not bite him and he remained successful in bringing the corpse out of the well.

There were also chances of snake bite also. Nobody spoke in favour of him. This incident reminds the pain of a Bakha in Mulk Raj Anand's *Untouchable* (1935) when Pundit Kali Nath tries to physically exploit Bakha's sister Sohini just because she belonged to a lower caste. Rohinton Mistry's *A Fine Balance* also deals with the problems of Dukhi Mochi and his whole family. Thakur Dharmasi leaves no stone unturned to show the cruelty in killing the members of Mochi's family just because he wanted to show his terror in the society.

Shankarrao Kharat became an advocate after completing his education and he devoted his life for the welfare of the Mahars. He supported the Mahars for getting their rights in the caste-ridden society. He writes about the aim of his life in his autobiography, "Only after I myself had become an advocate did I learn that for the sake of this hereditary right—this worthless right—the Mahars had played the game of litigation right up to the High Court" (Dangle, 6).

Thus, it can be stated that this autobiography is a wonderful depiction of the miserable life of Mahars at that time. The upper caste people would exploit them just because they were uneducated and were not aware of their rights. It was the *varna* system that was responsible for it because the Shudras were not allowed to take part in the activities of the mainstream. The same happens in this case also. The upper caste people exploit these Mahars who were called untouchables publically. In this autobiography, Rama cuts the firewood for a Brahman. The touch of a Mahar can pollute them but, in spite of it, the schoolteacher's wife insists on her husband to order Rama to cut firewood for them. It shows the hollowness and hypocrisy of the caste system also. Dr S. Ramanathan writes in this context:

> The four castes are subdivided into multitudinous sub-castes and there is a final stratum of this ethnic division known as

the untouchables, the lowest of all, so impure and despicable that they stood outside the caste and social structure of the Indian people altogether. This final stratum is known as 'Dalits' in modern linguistic terminology. (Ramanathan, 327)

## Works Cited


Singh, Deler. "Dalits and Social Structure: A Study of Shankarrao Kharat's *A Corpse in the Well.*" *Dalit Men's Autobiographies: A Critical Appraisal.* Ed. Bijender Singh. New Delhi: Kalpaz Publication, 2017. 193-199.

Dangle, Arjun. ed. *A Corpse in the Well: Translations from Modern Marathi Dalit Autobiographies.* Hyderabad: Disha Books, 1992.

Valmiki, Omprakash. *Joothan: A Dalit's Life.* Trans. Arun Prabha Mukherjee. Kolkata: Samya, 2003.

Ramanathan, S. "Situating Dalit Literature in Indian Writing in English". *Language in India.* Vol. 14, 12 December 2014. 327-338.

Sargar, S.D. "Dalit Autobiography and Education: An Analytical Study." *The Criterion: An International Journal in English.* 2.4. (2011):1-8

# 11

# Towards the Dream Project: Dissolution of Differences in Kancha Ilaiah's *Why I am Not a Hindu: A Sudra Critique of Hindutva Philosophy, Culture and Political Economy*

*Subhasish Barua*

Being marginalised, Dalitbahujans have to face torture and caste-based hierarchy. To portray that picture, Ilaiah in *Why I am Not a Hindu* refers to certain differences that make the position of Dalitbahujans in the society acute and ignoble. But the author takes up this responsibility to change the traditional orientation of the society by initiating structural resettlement. In due process, Ilaiah intends to highlight those differences to make them defunct.

In the "Introduction", Ilaiah writes about his village that had seen all the episodes of the freedom movement of India to get rid of colonial oppression. It must have left an impression on the consciousness of the author, and thus, he narrates that his 'childhood experiences' constitute 'a narrative of the cultural contradictions' (Ilaiah, x). Dalitbahujans always look into the gap to judge how far they are discriminated. Dalitbahujans have a critical bent of mind to look for the inherent differences to which they fall prey.

Certain practices in the village act as a reminder of the low status of the Dalitbahujans. They have to attend different types of rituals so that they cannot mingle with other members of the 'Hindu' religious fraternity. This exclusion and difference form a general resolution, "I was not born a Hindu for the simple reason that my parents did not know that they were Hindus" (Ilaiah, 1). They are forced to form a sub-group where they have to follow a different religious order. The grand system has left a malicious influence on the internal system of caste. Even Gods and Goddesses come to the Dalitbahujans in a particular ethnic or narrative terminology that is familiar to him, and thus, Brahma, Vishnu, and Eswara were external to his consciousness. He tries to devise the order of the cosmos or universe according to the conception of the activities of local deities. Separate culture is being fostered by separate religions. The culture of the Dalitbahujans is tagged derogatorily as 'ugly' as it follows a different order and practice:

> 'Upper' caste children are taught to live differently from Dalitbahujan children, just as they are taught to despise and dismiss them. Hindu inhumanism becomes part of their early formation; hating others—the Dalitbahujans—is a part of their consciousness. (Ilaiah, 9)

Ilaiah speaks for humanity propagating an inclusive philosophy where another culture is valued and respected. Dalitbahujans are not supposed to touch and read Hindu religious texts. As a Dalitbahujan, he faces different treatment in school, in terms of food and habit, and Ilaiah opines that these differences are "created as part of our upbringing" (Ilaiah, 12). So Dalitbahujans are made to internalise the differences and to make it a part of their life since their childhood. The cultural difference is so acute that even the names of the characters of the *Ramayana* and the *Mahabharata* appear 'alien' to them. On the other hand, there is no mention of local deities like Panchamma, Potaraju, Beerappa, and Kaatamaraju in the textbook. They are filled with references to the upper caste deities which the lower castes do not have access to visit or worship. But that does not mean that they, the local deities, do not have importance and significance. Underneath, or sometimes against, the mainstream text-narrative, the storytelling of Dalitbahujans relies solely on the activities of local deities with which they are closely associated. So their narrative flows with a different and distinct purpose. This marginal story-telling counters and questions the credibility of the grand or mainstream narrative.

Since there is no mention of local deities in the canonical texts apart from the upper caste Gods and Goddesses, the Dalitbahujans are shaped to follow a particular cultural construct, different and far away from their ethnicity. One paradox is at work here. Dalitbahujans become familiar with the heroic feats of those deities in Hindu texts who do not preach for them. They are made part of the larger canonical culture but are also treated as an outsider to that culture. Ilaiah faces this clash of cultures where the call of the greater culture is at odds with the urge to highlight one's own culture. These underrepresented deities also form the centre of the narrative of the downtrodden.

Though independence is there, the taste of freedom, Swaraj, was inaccessible to the Dalitbahujans because the marginalised were not free. Thus, Ilaiah narrates that Swaraj is "a word which even today I fail to understand, the school teacher was against us, the textbook language was against us" (Ilaiah, 14-15). The pathos becomes more intense as he sees two simultaneous and different approaches in home and the world, and any reconciliation or union of these two would invite more hostility, "Our homes have one culture and the schools have another culture....The gap between the two was enormous" (Ilaiah, 15).

So the author is always in a doubt as to which culture he is to follow. Along with that, the question of permanent adherence to the standard culture remains because he has to deal with the outside world where Hindu culture prevails and it will devour up the marginal culture, and if he flourishes with the native culture, he does not find any corresponding culture in the external world, and thus, either he stands neglected and left alone with his marginal culture or his culture gets overshadowed with the grandeur of the mainstream culture. Words in the canonical texts appear unfamiliar to him as they do not appeal to his sensibility and identity formation. This observation makes him comment on how far the orientation of the Hindu canonical texts is different from the purpose of the lives of the Dalitbahujans because to him a courageous man is one who performs certain activities to sustain livelihood like 'sheep-breeding', 'agriculture', 'rope making', diagnosing the disease of the animals as opposed to the image of one as represented in the canonical texts. In a sense, this is a recontextualisation of epic heroes and mythical heroism to suit marginal needs because the call of life is more important than any pompous imagination. Thus, we have two versions of life stories—imaginative or fictional and real or felt. It is obvious that Dalitbahujans are attached to real-life stories where involvement of the self is evident because the story is not narrated with a passive approach; rather active participation of the self is there in its unfolding. This constant binary raises certain fundamental questions in the mind of the author:

> Who becomes a good hero? One who produces varieties of crops, one who faces lions and tigers or one who kills the relatives and friends, simply because what 'upper' castes think is *dharma* and what others think is *adharma*? Where do we begin and where do we end? We must begin by creating our history and we must end by changing this very social fabric. (Ilaiah, 18)

The difference that Ilaiah sees since his childhood produces anguish and anger—anguish because he happens to be the victim of this politics; and anger to initiate a total socio-cultural overhaul to make everything anew. This feeling comes out of a sense of deep loss and constant deprivation. That he gets neglected from accessing the resources causes a sense of humiliation and justified irritation in the self.

Ilaiah values highly and considerably the Dalitbahujan body as it is an integral part of social production. He is a product of society and a contributor to society. The life of Dalitbahujans is of supreme importance to marginalised sections, and thus, their philosophy also talks about performing productive work that would be conducive to the formation of a social self unlike preaching 'divine philosophy'. So the philosophy of Dalitbahujans is grounded on solid materialistic needs contributing at the same time to the intricate relationship between self and society. The upper caste social order runs through a 'deceitful mechanism' that diverts the attention to something immaterial and unrelated. Ilaiah's message to the Dalitbahujans is to make them active to replenish the loss.

The politics of differences shows a heated tension between the privileged macro-cultural establishment and the Dalitbahujan micro-cultural development. How detrimental this vertical social structure is can be understood from the difference:

> The lower the caste of the person, the higher will be the level of obedience, and the higher the caste of the person, the stronger will be the motivation to speak and to command. (Ilaiah, 37)

This social structure helps the upper castes to manipulate social sectors and organisations to maintain hegemony and to exclude the Dalitbahujans from any engagement. Sometimes the difference works at the collective level where the Dalitbahujans endorse the view of communitarianism. So the meaning of existence is coordinated and integrated, not separated. This spirit of living together acts against the politics of separation because Ilaiah believes in the generous policy of the extension of the self to the level of others where 'I' and 'we' are interlinked and can no longer be disjointed. This notion of home to diverse areas is to promote the idea of a uniform India that denies any monolithic policy of compartmentalisation. The more they will be unified, the more they will be nearing the possibility of exercising the power.

Not only in the social arena, but in academic forums also Ilaiah notices discrepancies. He keeps on accusing the upper castes of promoting irrationality to make the masses dearth of intellectuality. On the other hand, Dalitbahujan intellectuals believe in the production of merit which is fostered only by work (Ilaiah, 63). It is the intellectual investigation that must be cultivated to probe into the matters related to caste to make people aware of its demerits. A member of the Dalitbahujan community always believes in a democratic spirit to talk and let others talk. Hence, they improve the pattern of the transaction of feelings and knowledge which is churned by 'life experiences' and 'real-life tasks' which are conducive to living a productive life.

The more the Dalitbahujans make progress, the more the clash between 'Hindu irrationality' and 'Dalitbahujan rationality' becomes obvious and inevitable. To Ilaiah, this clash is geared up by one definite purpose, and this is to evolve 'a new hope of a rational future for this country' (Ilaiah, 65). Unlike that of upper castes, his ideological background has been painted with colourful and diverse activities closely associated with the self. It helps him refashion himself as a leading thinker from the Dalitbahujan community.

The text has built a strong nexus between Ambedkar and Ilaiah in channelising the felt experiences to recreate the self because they take positive essence from the experiences to challenge the upper caste order and to reshape their life and that of the community according to their own will. *The Weapon of the Other* also draws a steady connection between Ambedkar and Ilaiah as both of them fight for Dalitbahujan nationalism 'from a position of disadvantage' (Ilaiah, *The Weapon of the Other* 16). They extract positive support from this disadvantageous position.

Earlier they have only experienced, now they are theorising the experiences and finding out the resources therein which might be helpful for the renovation of the identity. Gradually, they are making advances to the realm of knowledge and thought process which was earlier denied to them. They were just made a part of the experiences, but now they start decoding those experiences to evaluate how deceitfully those events of the experiences have been deployed to push them further to the maximal level of margin.

Ilaiah is happy to invoke a clash between the upper caste 'closed minds' and the Dalitbahujan 'open minds' as it further explores his identity. So the upper caste culture always believes in imposing the authoritarian code of conduct without taking cognizance of the expression of the Dalitbahujans. Their idea of culture is narrow and stagnant, not inclusive. On the contrary, Dalitbahujan culture believes in the convergence of multiple cultures putting emphasis on, and valuing, the words of others. This humanitarian cultural rhetoric of the margin does not preach any stringent oneness, rather holds dearly the belief in that wholistic oneness which is home to many as Ilaiah says, "...the Dalitbahujans have a much more humane and egalitarian tradition and culture than the Hindu tradition and culture" (Ilaiah, *Why I am Not a Hindu*, 101).

The emergence of cross-cultural domains is to accept and nurture the concept of plurality which further heightens the diversity of the nation. Ilaiah says in *The Weapon of the Other* that the purpose of critiquing the hegemonic culture is to orient the consciousness of the people towards building 'Dalitbahujan nationalism' which attempts to create a 'casteless, classless, egalitarian' Indian society, and it is regarded as far better and more benefic than 'religious nationalism' and 'secular socialist nationalism' (Ilaiah, *The Weapon of the Other*, 1).

The aim of the author is to recreate a human being who is both 'collective' and 'secular' with no inhibitions and prejudices. Dalitbahujans believe in the production for social welfare, not for personal benefit. A Dalitbahujan member is driven to utilise the self to create a strong linkage to a social function. Since there is nothing 'private' or 'personal' to Dalitbahujans, each act is meant for the society and for the individual's exploration in the society. Dalitisation is a step towards democratisation of social order which is the only means available to Dalitbahujans. The process of Dalitisation will be very minute and straightforward. It is not to say that the Dalitbahujans will capture everything or take over every possible aspect of society. Rather, Dalitisation does invoke a sense of radical divergence from the upper caste authoritarian hangover with a positive Dalit intent to theorise, implement, and activate the ideas and values long cherished by the Dalitbahujans:

> In order to dalitise society and de-Hinduize it thoroughly, every word and every sentence that has been written by brahminical thinkers, writers, politicians, historians, poets and art critics—virtually everything in every field must be re-examined thoroughly. (Ilaiah, 131)

It must be the expected outcome of the struggle of a visionary artist. The difference, which gives a special privilege to the upper castes, enriches the Dalitbahujans with a unique meta-cultural domain full of interrogative remarks.

Ilaiah ultimately rests his hope on the importance of Dalitbahujan intellectuals who would theorise and lay down the future project of the Dalitbahujan communities. When Ilaiah talks about the responsibility and production of the Dalitbahujan intellectuals, he touches upon the content thought about much earlier by Ambedkar when he comments on the role of an intellectual in *The Untouchables.* Ambedkar speaks for the evolution of an idea to break the stereotype with revolutionary changes and courage. But unfortunately, he does not find any

Brahmin scholar who is ready to undertake the task of reconstituting the model of Hinduism by critiquing it. Herein lies the thematic and crucial difference between a scholar and an intellectual as Ambedkar says that a scholar is 'class conscious' and an intellectual is not bound by any class consideration (Ambedkar, 240).

So, a scholar does not rise above the limitation of his class. Consequently, his opinion is conditioned and determined by his class consciousness, and this class consciousness does not let him accept the suggestions and criticism of others. That scholar becomes closeted, restrictive, and conservative not valuing the spirit of democracy in honouring others. On the contrary, an intellectual is a free being who believes in the transaction of views and reviews. His orientation is towards the abolition of boundaries. Since there is no class consciousness in an intellectual, his rationality does not make him a selfish being.

Ilaiah himself is an intellectual who works to transform society into an elevated state. As he is free from 'internal limitation', he can question the power and position of the upper caste supremacy. That is why Ilaiah is so prompt in advocating for the emergence of Dalitbahujan intellectuals who will be speaking for a wider audience with a humane implication. When an intellectual goes beyond the borderline, it is to emphasise the intrinsic worth of his merit, not his caste background. The relevance of a scholar is very time-specific, but the importance of an intellectual is timeless and permanent.

Born with the differences, Ilaiah presents himself as a man with the difference as he is different in his approach to social functions, caste structure, and concept of democracy. His project of establishing a wider and more conscious community is a response to historical compartmentalisation imposed on Dalitbahujans. Ilaiah takes up the thread of the discourse of 'anti-caste nationalism' from Phule and Ambedkar and wants to disseminate that philosophy among the Dalitbahujans.

All of them want to preach a liberal thought which is not governed by caste, class, and creed.

Ilaiah reconstructs his experiences in the autobiographical text and observes minutely the upper caste attitude to those experiences and his attitude to those steps taken by the upper castes. Instead of mingling with 'the glorious, one-dimensional Hindu past' (Ilaiah, *The Weapon of the Other,* 66), Ilaiah mainly seeks a different and anti-Brahminical school of thought and belief. He is not ready to accept the upper caste concept of civilisation which tends to de-notify the civility of the downtrodden, rather he propounds that concept of civilisation which is constituted mainly by the ignored and neglected. In a sense, it is a welcoming concept of civilisation including all and sundry. When Ilaiah points out the differences to show how influential the system of caste colonialism is in identifying a particular caste, it is quite understandable that his attempt is like that of Ambedkar's organisation of anti-caste movement which is directly meant for a better version of nationalism. This tendency to strengthen and consolidate the marginal forces is to create a space of their own where no one is concerned about the presence and prevalence of the boundaries, and no one will be suspicious of another's identity.

Even Ilaiah adopts a name that is suggestive of communitarian and democratic taste. He prefers to call himself Kancha Ilaiah Shepherd owing to his ancestral profession of sheep flocking and breeding. Apart from that, he envisions drawing a larger picture on a broader canvas by changing his name. In an interview with the *Hindustan Times*, Ilaiah says that just like a Shepherd God who treats the entire flock of sheep with equal judgement, he also cherishes that democratic aspiration by treating all equally (Ilaiah).

Like the Shepherd God, Ilaiah wants to highlight the fundamental values of equality. Under the aegis of this egalitarian philosophy, all the exploited sections must aim to establish a united force to cross the barriers of superiority-inferiority conflict. Broadly speaking, this 'Sudra critique' shows what Ilaiah dreams to achieve in the future, and this effort must be percolated even to the lowest possible member of the society.

## Works Cited

Ambedkar, B. R. "The Untouchables: Who Were They and Why They Became Untouchables?" *Dr Babasaheb Ambedkar: Writings and Speeches*. Comp. Vasant Moon. Vol. 7. Bombay: Dr Babasaheb Ambedkar Source Material Publication Committee, 1990. Web. 10 Aug. 2020.

Ilaiah, Kancha. "Good Shepherd: Dalit thinker Kancha Ilaiah on Name, Caste." Interview by Sudipto Mondal. *Hindustan Times* 27 May 2016. Web. 15 Dec. 2020.

—. *The Weapon of the Other: Dalitbahujan Writings and the Remaking of Indian Nationalist Thought*. Delhi: Pearson, 2010. Web. 6 Dec. 2020.

—. *Why I am Not a Hindu: A Sudra Critique of Hindutva Philosophy, Culture and Political Economy*. Calcutta: Samya, 1996.

# 12

# Manoranjan Byapari: *Interrogating My Chandal Life*: Disseminating Dalit Survival Saga

*Kalyan Pattanayak*

Etymologically the term 'Dalit' is of Sanskrit origin and is derived from the root word *dal*, which means to break, split, be broken or destroyed, trampled down, dispersed, squashed. The word 'Dalit' can be utilised for all of sexual orientations, as a noun and adjective. Arvind P. Nirmal, who pioneers Dalit theology in India, clarifies, "the Dalits are (1) the broken, the torn, the rent, the burst, the split; (2) the opened, the expanded; (3) the bisected; (4) the driven asunder, the dispelled, the scattered; (5) the downtrodden, the crushed, the destroyed; and (6) the manifested, the displayed" (Nirmal 139).

Extensively, the word 'Dalit' is a political term which represents the moderately new identity of class of individuals who were prior known as 'untouchables'. Untouchability, a norm of social alienation, is a profoundly instilled ramification of the social framework of the caste system and is an inappropriate and barbed social custom. When the Indian Constitution was implemented in 1950, this evil social practice was put to an end, legally. Despite its lawful cancelation, untouchability keeps on being rehearsed and polished in various structures and degrees, practically, in all parts of India, even today. Accordingly, the term 'Dalit' unmistakably recommends that caste as a social framework is as yet pervasive in India. Dalits are combating hard against discrimination to recover their pride, dignity and confidence. The ascent of Dalit movements and Dalit writings is an instance of how Dalits have turned into another ethnic group.

According to conventional Indian social power structure, caste system discriminates the whole Hindu populace into two classifications: upper standings and lower ranks. This social division is perpetual and is sponsored by various Hindu strict sacred scriptures, by and large, known as Dharmashastras. More than two hundred Dharmashastras are there, written in Sanskrit, which is one of the traditional dialects much acclaimed by Hindus. The Dharmashastras are essentially law books created by Brahmins to prioritise themselves and impose caste barriers on Dalits. Within the jurisdiction of Dharmashastras, Brahmanvad and Manuvad promote implicit rules composed particularly to manipulate strict approvals of sanctity to the lower castes, particularly Dalits. These approvals, by and large, aided the caste system to re-establish its authenticity even after it was legitimately challenged. Therefore, the casteism, with its multiple varieties and intricacies, continues in all areas of India with various levels of rigorousness.

Dalits comprise around sixteen percent of India's populace, numbering more than 220 million and spread all over India. Apart from India, Dalits are traced in different parts of the globe, diversely known as ati-Shudras, chandalas, panchamas, antyajas, achhuts, asprushyas, Harijans, and the Scheduled Castes in various periods in Indian history. They endure the stigma of untouchability even after the caste system has been proclaimed an offense under Article 17 of the Indian Constitution. They are socially infirm, financially poor, and politically weak. Although a little segment of Dalits has flourished under government support on account of reservation policies in schooling, employment, and legislative affairs and have climbed financially and expertly, socially they remained unaccepted.

It is supposed that the term 'Dalit' came to be operated in broad daylight in the public domain towards the end of the nineteenth century. It was Mahatma Jotibarao Govindrao Phule (1827-90), Indian anti-caste social activist and writer from Maharashtra, who have used the term 'Dalit' to depict the state of the outcastes and untouchables as abused and oppressed individuals who were exploited by the upper castes. Phule particularly accused two groups of elite class—the businessmen and the Brahmins of such caste discrimination. He required the Shudras and Ati-Shudras to meet up and battle against what he called 'caste slavery'. Phule's conscious application of the term 'Dalit', effectively being used in Marathi, started a collective force against the danger of Brahminism all through the nineteenth century.

Afterward, Bhimrao Ramji Ambedkar (1891-1956), the draughtsman of the Indian Constitution and the strongest leader of the Dalit movement, used this term 'Dalit' especially in his Marathi speech and often in his Marathi writings, along with different other synonymous terms; for example, 'bahishkrut' and 'asprushyavarga,' *etc.* Ambedkar considered Phule as one of his masters. Having been vigorously inspired by the progressive ideas of Phule, Kabir and Buddha, he furthered his struggle against caste system unto zenith's height. Ambedkar profoundly contemplated the Vedas, Vedanta, and the Dharmashastras and dismissed the claims made by Brahmins that the caste system was sanctioned and affirmed by the divine God. He offered new translations of these Hindu scriptures and extracted newer interpretations. For instance, in his acclaimed book *The Untouchables: Who Were They and Why They Became Untouchables? (1948)*, he expresses that once the untouchables were included in the Kshatriya community. Since they did unskilled and manual work, they were looked down upon by the Brahmins, and were consigned to the periphery and turned into the untouchables. Contemplating the financial states of untouchables in old occasions, Ambedkar coined the phrase 'the Broken Men', showing that the progenitors of the Dalits had to carry on with embarrassing lives under the current social system. Accordingly, Ambedkar's long-lasting battle was to eradicate the caste to fabricate a populist Indian culture. But, for Dalits, caste abominations keep on being propagated against them, and the individuals of upper castes are as yet prejudiced against Dalit subjectivity.

With the origin and development of Dalit movement and Dalit writing all over states in India, Dalits began to become subject of consideration. They turned out to be increasingly coordinated and met up to claim their legitimate post in Indian social-culture. An early illustration of this was found in Maharashtra when Dalit activists met up in 1972 to dispatch a unified Dalit movement broadly known as the Dalit Panther movement. J. V. Pawar, Arjun Dangle, Namdeo Dhasal, and Raja Dhale were the pioneers and founder members of Dalit Panthers. With the emergence of Dalit Panthers, the term 'Dalit' turned out to be used to in the public domain, first in Maharashtra and later all over India.

Dalits are the "members of Scheduled Castes and Tribes, neo-Buddhists, the working people, the landless and the poor peasants, women and all those who are being exploited politically, economically and in the name of religion" (Joshi, 145). The Panthers envelops problems of caste, class, identity, sex, and minority groups across religions who are normally against upper class Hindu men, in the following way:

> The problem of untouchability of the Dalits is no more of mere mental slavery. Untouchability is the most violent form of exploitation on the face of earth, which survives the ever changing forms of the power structure. Today, it is necessary to seek its soil, its root causes. (Joshi, 141-142)

Gopal Guru, a social scientist, depicts how Dalits are victimised of cased-based humiliation:

> The ideology of purity-pollution helped the top of the twice born to transmute the human body as an aesthetic idea into a "filthy reality". Untouchables are forced to eat human excreta. This atrocious act seeks to reduce the Dalits to the levels of dogs, pigs, and cows that are considered wretched as these animals (not the pampered pets) also eat human excreta. The body of the Dalits is treated as if it is trapped into a septic tank even if it is a vibrant think tank. This is obnoxiously special to the Indian form of reduction (Guru, 213).

Sharankumar Limbale, who appreciates Guru's observation, remarks the rejection of Dalit subjectivity is "aimed at the unequal order which has exploited Dalits" (Limbale, 31).

Manoranjan Byapari, a Dalit Bengali writer, was born in 1950, in the district of Barisal, at present Bangladesh. As *namashudras*, the most reduced layer of the Dalit community, his family also had to face the trauma of partition. The Byaparis were driven by a truck, along with the members of thirty different families, and shipped to detention camps in West Bengal. Memories of that alarming displacement—being knock around in the vehicle under the scorching sunbeams, the air obscured with red dust of the road from the wheels, a child being born in transit, and an elderly person passing on the truck, were scorched into the psyche of the four-year-old Byapari. Refugees from the upper class were furnished a land to live after partition; however, Dalits were tossed into camps. Shiromonipur, in the district of Bankura, West Bengal, resembled a jail camp and lived on stinking rice received as ration. The evacuees were arbitrarily pushed into furnace-like tents. It was difficult for Byapari to forget the moaning of bereaved mothers and screams of starving children.

Manoranjan Byapari had to grab numerous queer occupations for his livelihood—as a sweeper, a cook, a porter, a guard, a rickshaw puller or whatever else came to his direction. Through these, he adhered relentlessly to his lone enthusiasm of composing. Byapari is one of those writers who expound on the conflict they have lived in. During the 1970s, following a tussle with the police who had identified him for being a Naxal for thrashing a so-called gentleman for harassing a lady, Byapari was arrested and shipped off Alipore Central Jail, Kolkata. It was during the 26 months of imprisonment there, Byapari started to read and write.

He particularly adored the literary works by Mahasweta Devi (1926-2016), another Bengali author and activist, whose notable works include *Hajar Churasir Maa* (*Mother of 1084*), who composed on the persecuted individuals, living on the periphery of society. A specific word she has written in one of her books, *jijibisa*, aroused his interest. He scrounged through dictionaries looking for the significance and meaning of this word, with no achievement. An unexpected chance of meeting with Mahasweta Devi, as she rode on Byapari's rickshaw in College Street, Kolkata, made a huge difference. In addition to the fact that he got the meaning of *jijivisa* (the will to live), he likewise discovered the will and inspiration to channel his conflict and disgust into something useful in the form of writing. She requested him to write a literary piece for *Bartika*, a journal edited and published by Mahasweta Devi. Her initiation and inspiration were a turning point in the life of Byapari as he was first published with his *Rickshaw Chalai* (*I Pull a Rickshaw*), and he discovered himself anew. Many of his books have been translated into English, among those *Interrogating My Chandal Life* (*Itibritte Chandal Jibon*), published in 2018, and *There's Gunpowder in the Air (Batase Baruder Gandha)* in 2019. His pen, absorbed the perspiration, blood, and anxiety of individuals who subsist as diminished, has earned him literary awards like the

Hindu Literary Prize in non-fiction in 2019 for the translation of his autobiography *Interrogating My Chandal Life.*

*Interrogating My Chandal Life: An Autobiography of a Dalit* (2018) by Manoranjan Byapari and translated by Sipra Mukherjee, is an autobiography of a Dalit of Bengali origin which was published originally in Bengali as *Itibritte Chandal Jivan* in 2014. It depicts the excursion of a poor, distressed soul as a victim of the caste system through socio-political topsy-turvydom and terrible disturbances. Belonging from the lower stratum of the society, as *Namashudra* or *Chandal*, Byapari tends to portray his suffering and trauma that become the factors in determining his appalling destiny at each and every steps of life, "I have lived my life as the ill-fated Dalit son of an ill-fated Dalit father, condemned to a life of bitterness" (Byapari, 4).

*Interrogating My Chandal Life* is divided into seventeen chapters after *Preface, Acknowledgements, A Note by the Translator* and followed by *Epilogue, Notes, Index* and *About the Author and the Translator.* Each of the chapters contains consistent clarifications, contentions and social realities and furnishes a chronological record of episodes in Byapari's day to day existence which drove him to encounter further embarrassment and exclusion.

*East Bengal, Partition and West Bengal*, the opening chapter of *Interrogating My Chandal Life* portrays the trauma of partition and identity crisis of a Dalit who is born in Byapari family that pertains to the "Namashuddurs of Kashyapgotra" (Byapari, 4). Byapari exhibits mythological and historical references to depict the caste system with minute references to Namas Muni, the Pala dynasty and the Sena dynasty and the scornful term 'Chandal' with which the British colonisers labelled the Namashudras. He also refers to the emergence of Guruchand Thakur, the pioneer of Matua religion and emancipation of Namashudra community across Bangladesh.

His father was an indentured labourer, subsequently he couldn't take care of his family. In his childhood his family continued attempting to have essential conveniences. In this section, he acquaints us with his caste which is Namashudra. The community he belongs to, is treated as the Chandals. Byapari says that his social rank has not been wiped out because of the steady sufferings, discriminations and difficulties that were enforced on them. Even the upper-caste stakeholders of the social framework stigmatised them as Chandals. We are additionally enlightened that the whole Namashudra community began to follow another religious doctrine called Matua which was established by Harichand Thakur. Because of consistent perturbation authorities had to rename the community from Chandals to Namashudra, but the frame of mind towards this community has not altered, according to Byapari, who also feels that the battle which went on for forty years went to no end. Byapari believes that it would have been one step ahead for them to abolish the orthodox four-fold *varna* system since it might have awarded them liberty, equality and privileges. He also perceives that they are manacled by and victim of such a caste system. Byapari expresses, "I do believe, in fact, that rather than seek to be included within the four varna system of the Hindus and offer servility to the varna Hindus, the Namashudras should have preferred to remain as the fifth varna. He or she was nobody's slave then" (Byapari 11).

In the second chapter entitled *Dandakaranya Rehabilitation Project, Food Riots and Calcutta,* Byapari recalls the ensuing establishment of rehabilitation camps on the peripheries of Calcutta for Dalit refugees who received lump sum cash as dole, however, that also puts to an end following a couple of months when restoration project begins. Byapari depicts the congestion, fatality and unhygienic condition of the camp where lethal infections like Cholera, Diarrhoea, and Malaria among the camp inhabitants are normal and death of individuals are an everyday occasion. Displacement from there to the Andaman Islands and

Dandakaranya, where detention camps were settled, make lives twice miserable. Byapari communicates the catastrophic circumstance and sufferings of the refugees in Chola-Doltala camp and Shiromanipur camp where "poverty, destitution, starvation and penury" (Byapari, 36) are the only truth of life. He additionally uncovers the humbug of the local political leaders who discriminate against the lower castes like Namo, Malo, Bagdi, Jele. Muchi and the Kaoras who are marginalised to only sub-human species, and the incident of Marichjhapi Massacre in 1979 that outcomes from the disdain of the government. His father started to sell kindlings and would do various other things to run a family of eight members. In any case, it was not adequate. Appetite was taking cost for each individual from the family. It was getting extreme for Manoranjan Byapari to choose to go out and accomplish some work. Byapari recollects, "I was developing and, with it, was developing my appetite. I was unable to bear the aches of that yearning. My eyes would diminish, my guts would feel as though they were being destroyed and my legs would tremble" (Byapari, 30).

The following four chapters *I Run Away from Home*, *My Lone Travels across East and North India*, *On the Road for Five Years* and *Return to Calcutta* portray the journey of a rootless, helpless kid named Jeeban, the fictitious counterpart of Byapari, who flees from his family and goes through the face of adversity to be exposed to realities, too hard to cope up. He embraces each odd and even kind of occupation like porter, dish-washer, and cook going ahead of his way in farther places like Assam, Siliguri, Jalpaiguri, and Darjeeling. Byapari uncovered the appalling faces of members of upper castes when he records the horrifying sexual tortures twice released on him by Amulya Thakur, the Brahmin head cook and the havildar, the cheating committed by Sashibabu and whipping for being of the lower caste and his sibling Chitta being beaten falsely accused of theft by political leaders Anil, Bilu and Basak. Destiny draws on each progression of his life and he does neither try nor able to stick to a particular place as he mentions: "Life has spread skittish mustard seeds under my feet" (Byapari, x).

After five years of perilous journey, Byapari chose to get back to his place, Bengal. These years of long stretches of difficult work and agonizing stay in various places didn't give Byapari anything. He left his place five years prior with the expectation of a handful of rice twice a day. At the point when Manoranjan Byapari returned, he came to know about a movement that found its cradle in the village of Naxalbari in north Bengal. The movement was driven by the down-trodden class. Byapari expresses, "I had heard the name of the Naxalbari village and the rumblings of a movement spearheaded by peasants, field labourers and adivasis who had declared war against the eternal oppression they had faced" (Byapari, 103). The agrarian revolution that erupted in the surroundings centering the village of Naxalbari in 1967 drew Byapari to the populist dream of Naxalite movement. They were trained in dealing with pipeguns and minor weapons. Their adversaries were small industrialists and capitalists. At some point as a Naxalite, when Byapari witnessed one of his nearest friends, who was slaughtered by Naxals, he became baffled. As a Naxalite, he came across Naxal leaders like Charu Majumder, Kanu Sanyal, Ashu Majumder, Mohit Barman, Khoka Chakraborty and many more. Byapari pens down such first-hand experiences and incidents of his life in the subsequent chapters: *My Entry into the Naxal Movement*, *To Dandakaranya and Back to Calcutta*, *Life on and around the Railway Station*, and *Bomb Explodes in Barddhaman*. The Naxalite period of his life found scope of vivid literary shape in his novel *There's Gunpowder in the Air* (2018) translated by Arunava Sinha from original Bengali text *Batashe Baruder Gondho* (2013).

Notwithstanding, the direction of the path of Byapari begins to turn as found in the rest of the chapters of *Interrogating My Chandal Life*. In these sections of the book, Byapari sheds light on the recoiling identity of Dalit caste *Chhotolok* into the liberation into a stature afresh among the *Bhadralok* through penetrating the universe of letters inside the prison and acquires stability of life by setting up his own family. He became acquainted with Shankar Guha Neogi and his 'Chhattisgarh Mukti Morcha' that caused him to revive the vision in legislative issues in the locale of Dalli, Rajhara, Bastar and Kanker and author Mahasweta Devi who protracts the self of an author in him by giving him a scope to publish his writing in a journal named *Bartika*, which she herself did edit, with the pen name of Madan Dutta, a rickshaw puller-cum-writer appear to make his daily routine worth experiencing. With various ceaseless endeavours to publish, Byapari first sends his articles in the pseudo-name *Jijibisha* to numerous periodicals such as *Runner, Vigyan, and Banga Barta*. From there on, he establishes his distinct social identity in literary circles.

The section *A Note by the Translator* lays the foundation of the book. Every single chapter of the book disseminates torment, trauma and opposition faced in the expedition of a hero who dispatches legions against the hypocrisy of the current social and political biasness. Strikingly, Byapari unwraps the attire of sentimentality and thoughts of past memory with firm realities in various periods of his life that cannot be more dull and grievous where his adolescence spends as "a bare-bodied goatherd running behind his cows and goats with a stick" (Byapari, ix), childhood in torn clothes with uncombed hair and messy, grimy appearance without any dream realm and youth as an agitator Naxalite with weapons and a hideaway from the police. In his words, "You've seen me a hundred times in a hundred ways. Yet if you insist that you do not recognize me, let me explain myself in a little greater detail, so you will not feel that way anymore. When the darkness of unfamiliarity lifts, you will feel, why, yes, I do know this person. I've seen this man" (Byapari, ix). Sipra Mukharjee, the translator, mentions "Bypari's narrative is packed with events, sweeping reader up with its speed and movement" (Byapari, xix).

Social Science, being a dynamic discourse of humanities, centres around essential social cycles like social change, social equity, and social turn of events. In any case, development and expansion create and recreate marginality and untouchability in the everyday existence of the individual and group in evolving circumstances. Byapari insists that none from the lower castes had voluntarily left their native place as displaced people and took shelter at the refugee camps. Such persons had escaped from their roots due to the dread of losing their lives, dignity, and identity. People of both the elite class and downtrodden class were removed. The greater part of the upper standing, with the assistance of the Hindus in West Bengal, figured out how to get a space inside or close to Kolkata in more than 150 resettlement camps. However, only Dalits were deprived of space, dignity and privilege. Byapari, who calls himself a *lekhowar* which means one who uses his pen as a weapon, always wears a *gamchha* (towel like piece of thin cotton cloth) round his neck as symbol of identity, has been elected as one of the members of West Bengal Legislative Assembly in 17th General Election, 2021, and proclaims as a victorious hero of his survival saga, which is absolutely of his own.

## Works Cited

Ambedkar, B. R. *The Untouchables: Who Were They and Why They Became Untouchables.* Bombay: The Education Department, Government of Maharashtra, 1990.

Byapari, Manoranjan, *Interrogating My Chandal Life: An Autobiography of a Dalit.* Trans. Sipra Mukherjee. SAGE Publications, 2018.

Guru, Gopal, ed. *Humiliation: Claims and Context.* New Delhi: Oxford U P, 2009.

Joshi, Barbara, ed. *Untouchable: Voices of the Dalit Liberation Movement.* New Delhi: Select Book Service Syndicate, 1986.

Limbale, Sharankumar. *Towards an Aesthetic of Dalit Literature: History, Controversies and Considerations.* Trans. Alok Mukherjee. New Delhi: Orient Longman, 2004.

Nirmal, Arvind P. *Heuristic Explorations.* Madras: CLS, 1990.

# 13

# Transforming Consciousness, Ushering Mobility: The Role of Education in Dalit Men's Autobiographies

*Sukriti Sobti*

## Introduction

Power and Knowledge are intimately linked. Michael Foucault in his interview 'Prison Talk' in 1975 states that "It is not possible for power to be exercised without knowledge" and "impossible for knowledge not to engender power" (51-52). Paulo Freire in his book *Pedagogy of the Oppressed* considers education as an instrument in the hands of the oppressor. He elucidates how education can be an "exercise of domination" (78) which aims to indoctrinate the oppressed and adapt them to the world of the oppressor. In the light of the above statements, it is clear that education is a powerful weapon which can be used by one group of people to suppress and overpower another group of people. When education is kept as a closely guarded terrain which is controlled and disseminated by one group of people and precluded to another; a wide gulf develops between these groups. This same system of control and hegemony can be seen in the case of Dalits, who were subjected to systemic discrimination since ages.

The 3500-year-old caste system of India ensured that Dalits were deprived of education for several centuries. While

Brahmins were believed to be the custodians of knowledge, Shudras were relegated to performing menial tasks. Traditional knowledge structures produced by Brahmins laid the foundation for indoctrination and internalisation of the caste system. Ancient religious texts such as the *Manusmriti* prescribed a series of injunctions against Shudras which proscribed the acquisition of knowledge to them. This is a clear example of Foucault's idea that forms of "power perpetually create knowledge" ('Prison Talk', 1975).

## A Historical Overview

It was with the advent of the British in India that education which was the sole preserve of the upper castes began to be made accessible to the castes lower down in the hierarchy. Apart from the British Government, Christian missionaries played an important role in imparting basic education to 'untouchables'. A major breakthrough occurred in the year 1858 when Jyotirao Phule established a school for the children of 'untouchables'. Later, his wife Savitri started a school for women.

Phule's campaign for education of the traditionally disenfranchised sections of the society was continued and carried forward by Dr B. R. Ambedkar. Ambedkar was highly educated himself. He had a PhD from Columbia University, a Doctorate in Science from London School of Economics and a Law degree from Gray's Inn, London. He strived to make it easier for other Dalits to get educated by providing hostels for 'untouchable' students and opportunities for earning while learning.

After India's independence, Ambedkar became the chief designer and planner of the Indian Constitution. As a result of his efforts, the Indian constitution today contains several provisions such as Article 14, 15 and 17 which are directed towards promoting the principles of equality and non-discrimination. However, despite so many provisions being made, Dalits continue to suffer from low levels of literacy.

According to the 2001 Population Census, the literacy rate among Dalits is 54.7% compared to 68.8% for others. Also, the national dropout rate for Dalit children is 36.6% at primary level of education, 59.4% at middle level and 73.1% at secondary level of education. These figures are a clear reflection of hurdles Dalits have had to face on their roadway to education. Dalit children are forced to discontinue their studies because of poverty and the discrimination they face from both students and teachers.

This paper examines Narendra Jadhav's *Outcaste: A Memoir* (2003) and Vasant Moon's *Growing up Untouchable in India: A Dalit Autobiography* (2001) as examples of Dalit writings that deconstruct the traditional knowledge structures propounded by the upper castes. The lead characters in these texts battle socio-economic hurdles impeding their pathway to education and challenge Brahminical epistemology. Through an analysis of these texts, I would argue that education ushers empowerment in the lives of Dalits and produces an alternative paradigm of humanisation.

## *Outcaste: A Memoir (2003)*

Written in the first person, Narendra Jadhav's *Outcaste* incorporates perspectives of his parents, his daughter and his own. It relates instances of discrimination against Dalits in educational institutions, which discourage them from pursuing education. Jadhav's father, Damu narrates his personal experience at the local village school where Dalit children sat on the floor, apart from other high-caste boys and girls. Damu's teacher Genu Master asked the Dalit children to bring good cow dung cakes and forced them to massage his back with the dried dung. This incident had such a negative impact on him that he stopped going to school.

It was during his time in Mumbai in the employment of an Englishman named Nearle that Damu learned the real value of education. His association with Missybab, Nearle's daughter, taught him a little English. He even accompanied her to school. On his first day at the school, Damu experienced myriad conflicting emotions. He felt "awkward, unsure and confused" (Jadhav, 94). He had never been to a school before. Here in the city school, he was treated on par with other students. He was not asked to sit on the floor apart from other students but sat on a chair, like other high-caste children. This was a turning point in Damu's life and a moment of reckoning for him.

> That was the moment, for the first time in my life, when I started to think for myself instead of merely obeying others. It was a queer and uneasy feeling knowing that I was the one who could decide what was right for me. At the same time, I felt that I could think for myself and find out what could go wrong. I felt strong and powerful. In that place, and at that moment, I almost discovered myself as a person who could think." (94-95)

Even though Damu was still a child, the change a little schooling brought in his level of understanding is significant. It enabled him to exercise his own intellect. Earlier, he had only been taught to conform to the upper castes' consciousness but education brought forth a transformation that taught him to make his own choices. Following the teachings of Ambedkar, he also vowed to get his children educated as that was a small step he could undertake at a personal, individual level.

> If Babasaheb was doing so much to improve the lot of all Dalits, the least I could do was uplift at least one family—my own. I vowed to give my children the best possible education and raise them with the spirit of public service. (146)

As a result of the transformation in Damu's consciousness, resulting from his involvement in the Ambedkar movement; Damu even starts teaching his wife, Sonu. He tells her the story of Phule's wife Savitri who started a school for women, faced fierce opposition but went on teaching undeterred. The story sparks Sonu's interest in learning and she learns about the importance of education as a means to attain equality.

Ambedkar remains an important influence on both Damu and Sonu throughout their lives. Even after Ambedkar's death, Damu and his family continued following the teachings of Ambedkar and vowed to "carry forth the torch of Babasaheb's dream: to have education for all, eradicate poverty, and create a just and equal society" (198).

Damu's conviction to get his children educated despite the monetary difficulties his family faced, bears fruit. While his eldest son becomes a civil servant; his youngest son, the author himself obtains a PhD from an American university and becomes an eminent banker and economist.

Jadhav attributes his success to Ambedkar and reminisces the day when he had met Ambedkar for the first time, along with his father. That day, Ambedkar persuaded his father to give his children a good education. When Damu reached home, he excitedly narrated the story of Ambedkar and how he had studied in a foreign university. Ambedkar's success story had such a great impact on Jadhav's mind as a child that he decided to "go to school and become like Dr Ambedkar...carry a briefcase like him...and drive a car like him" (200).

Once when the author scored high marks in Sanskrit, his father was overjoyed because he had mastered a supposedly divine language, which was "an exclusive preserve of the high castes for centuries" (206)... "The Brahmins never let us learn this language because it was the language of the gods. Now we have shown them..." (237). Damu's remark reflects how language is used as an instrument of dominion and mastering the language of the powerful gives a sense of power. The phrase 'we have shown them' indicates a euphoric sense of talking back to the oppressor.

Throughout the memoir *Outcaste*, Narendra Jadhav underscores the role of Ambedkar in exhorting Dalits to educate their children and through it, encouraging them to achieve social and political mobility. Ambedkar believed that education should be made accessible to each and every one, and it was lack of education that was the reason for the poor conditions of Dalits.

> The most profound way in which Babasaheb Ambedkar influenced my father's generation was to teach the importance of education. 'Educate, Unite and Agitate' did not remain a mere slogan; it became the vow of the entire Dalit community. (237)

Education gave Jadhav confidence to take the decision of marrying Vasundhara, a girl from a higher caste. But her mother vehemently opposed the match. Even when the girl protested that the Dalit boy she wanted to marry was well educated, settled and a good man, her mother was reluctant to accept the match on sole grounds of caste.

> Education has nothing to do with it. He may be good but he belongs to a low caste. If you marry him, our family's reputation and position in society will be reduced to nothing. (243)

This proves that even though education leads to emancipation of Dalits, it does not guarantee a change in societal attitudes towards them. The caste system is so ingrained in our psyche and implanted in our social consciousness that it is difficult to annihilate it in a single day. The realisation that caste does not matter and is a mere promoter of social discrimination dawns only gradually on Vasundhara's mother. After years of marriage, she finally accepts the author as her son-in-law and admits that "she was a victim of her ignorance, coupled with societal conditioning" (244).

The "Epilogue" of Jadhav's memoir is written from the perspective of his daughter Apoorva, who was born and brought up in the United States. Her epilogue is a testament to the change and mobility that education brings. Unlike her parents or grandparents, she has had no experience of discrimination on the basis of caste. She did not have to struggle for an education, like her parents did. She is not even completely aware of her identity as a Dalit. The first time she came to know that she was a Dalit was when a teacher asked her whether she was the daughter of the Dalit scholar—Narendra Jadhav.

Apoorva is aware of the price her ancestors paid and the sacrifices they made. But as part of the new generation of educated and privileged Dalits, she is ready to chart a new glorious terrain, rather than get bogged down by the baggage of the history of caste oppression.

> My ancestors carried the burden of being a Dalit and bowing down to demeaning tasks even after India's independence. I have the torch they have lit for me and nothing can stop me. (263)

Narendra Jadhav's *Outcaste* is a significant text in the history of Dalit Literature because it not only provides the perspectives of three different generations and the impact of caste on them, but also shows the difference in the conditions of the three generations. Education leads to upward mobility and smoothens the inequalities imposed by birth. Dileep Padgaonkar's essay "Look back in Languor" explains this point by remarking that "the emancipation of the Dalits, slow and partial though it might be, lies in the pursuit of academic excellence and efficacy of a high order in the upper echelons of decision making, whether in or out of government".

## *Growing Up Untouchable in India: A Dalit Autobiography* (2001)

Vasant Moon's *Growing up Untouchable in India* contains an autobiographical account of an untouchable boy living in conditions of extreme poverty in a slum in Nagpur. Despite his adverse circumstances, Moon completes his post graduate degree, rises to a position of eminence and climbs the social ladder.

Like Damu in Narendra Jadhav's *Outcaste* who encourages his children to study, Moon's grandfather Sadashiv is committed to the pursuit of education. He had grown up in the company of Europeans and taught Moon the English alphabet. His notion of education was derived from the Western concept of becoming a 'sahib'. And the idea of a sahib was derived from his observation of Europeans, who wore shirts and pants, and spoke immaculate English. Wishing his grandson to become a sahib; he would dress Moon in shorts and a shirt, put 'handsome socks' (Moon, 10) on his feet and canvas shoes over them, and put a small handkerchief in his pocket.

Moon was registered in the first grade at Sitabardi Normal School, a government school in the neighbourhood. Despite being the only Mahar at this school, he was fortunate enough not to face any caste discrimination as both the teachers and students were supportive. However, getting an education became increasingly difficult for him because of financial constraints. Moon's father had deserted his family at an early age and his mother barely managed to make both ends meet. When the results of Moon's fourth grade examination were declared, it was his uncle Hari who got him enrolled at the Patwardhan High School and paid his fees. This was considered to be the best school in all of the Central Provinces. Admission in this school was not on basis of caste reservation, but on pure merit.

Even though Moon had got enrolled at the school; he found it difficult to buy clothes, books or paintbrushes. Once, a scholarship scheme for 'Harijan' students was announced. But as followers of Ambedkar, all the Dalit students of his class refused to accept the demeaning and patronizing term 'Harijan' and rejected the scholarship. It was during this hour of need that members of the Samata Sainik Dal, an organisation founded by Ambedkar to protect the interests of the Dalits, extended a hand of help. They provided him food, clothes, books and notebooks and in turn, Moon participated in the activities of the Dal.

Discrimination by upper caste teachers towards Dalit children was common in educational institutions. Both Moon and his friends were at the receiving end of such discriminatory attitudes and practices. His English teacher had cursed him that he would never be able to learn English grammar and would not pass his matriculation exam even in ten years. Another teacher, Vaidya Master insulted him when he made a mistake in pronouncing some words. "Oh, you would garble the words of the Gayatri mantra itself!" (83). His friend Atmaram Varade also recounted a humiliating personal experience at the school where he would be given the 'horse' punishment and beaten up with a cane (83). Sandwiched between beatings from teachers and parents, Varade's school days came to an end as the violence and aggression made it impossible for learning of any kind.

A Study by Human Rights Watch and the Center for Human Rights and Global Justice unravels the reasons behind these discriminatory practices and states that the antagonism of the upper castes towards Dalits is "linked to their perception that Dalits are not meant to be educated, are incapable of being educated, or if educated, would pose a threat to hierarchies and power relations in society" ("Hidden Apartheid" n. pag.).

Shattering the expectations of his upper caste teachers who viewed him from a casteist lens, Moon successfully cleared his matriculation. After that, he joined Morris College and passed his BA exam. Immediately after this, Moon got employed at the office of the Deputy Account General, Post and Telegraph but left the job to pursue his masters in Marathi.

The decision to pursue masters was not an easy one for him. Resigning from his job meant that the entire burden of their livelihood fell on the shoulders of his mother. Even though his mother gave him the freedom to do what he wanted, Moon experienced a great deal of mental tension. Moon was not the only Mahar committed to the pursuit of education. At the office of Post and Telegraph where he worked earlier, there were other Mahar boys who wanted to continue their studies. They were "very dogged about education, would show up at work, finish the day's tasks in a short time, hang their coats on a chair, and go to the college to register their attendance". Many of them "studied for higher education and graduated while holding a job" (157).

The impact of education can be clearly seen in Vasant Moon's case. A person who used to be hesitant about learning and writing English as a little boy in high school went on to edit several collections of Ambedkar's writings.

> The English language, which gave me so much trouble in high school, was the language of the writings of Babasaheb Ambedkar, which I was given the opportunity to edit, and I successfully did so. I always had doubts lurking in the corner of my mind that I might have made some mistakes in English, but I am no longer afraid of that. (38)

Education also brought a transformation in the level of cultural consciousness. After his father died, Moon refused to get his head tonsured and rejected the validity of such rusted worn-out traditions. "What tonsure? I don't feel that my father's soul won't go to heaven if I have my hair" (140).

Like Moon, other youth of the Ambedkarite movement refused to believe in the sanctity of religious traditions and rejected age-old superstitions and rituals. Moon talks about a Godman Laldasbuwa, who would light the *holi* fire, without the use of a match. He would light up the *holi* fire through his chants. However, the young educated men and women involved in the Ambedkar movement unravelled the reality behind the Godman's 'miracle'.

> The youth of the Ambedkarite movement were not ready to sit quietly, and they exploded the tricks of the godmen. 'The godman puts some phosphorus in the tinder; his chants

> are only a show,' they said. And this worked. From then on Laldas Buwa only did *puja*, and the *holi* fire was ignited by the new youth. (42)

The ignition here is not just literal but metaphorical. The youth inspired by the Ambedkarite movement were ignited by the fire of education and this in turn led to a change in their mindset. Therefore, the traditional superstitious outlook was replaced by a rational, scientific bent of mind.

Vasant Moon's *Growing up Untouchable in India* therefore showcases how a Dalit can overcome despair, poverty and casteism through education and personal endurance in addition to the support of his community. Gary Tartakov in his review of the book accurately sums up Moon's story as "one of the untouchable activists who followed B. R. Ambedkar's lead out of the shadow of supposed—pollution, wished upon them by Brahmanical society, into the center of contemporary India's political stage' (Tartakov, 302).

## Conclusion

Education is a liberating and democratising force. It acts as a catalyst bringing forth social, political and economic empowerment to marginalised sections of the society. Both Phule and Ambedkar laid great stress on education as a means of ensuring the emancipation of Dalits. Phule believed that the main instrument for awareness and anti-caste consciousness among the people of the lower castes was education as all their sorrows sprang from one source-illiteracy (Phule, 44). Ambedkar, on the other hand, reiterated that there was no safe existence for Dalits without education. (Ambedkar, 62)

Both Narendra Jadhav's *Outcaste* and Vasant Moon's *Growing up Untouchable in India* exemplify that it is education which awakens the notion of change in Dalits by making them politically and socially aware of their condition and providing them confidence to change their situation. It is education which encourages Dalits to search for the 'beautiful swan inherently present in all mankind' and stimulates them to let that swan 'emerge in all its glory' (Jadhav, 227).

## Works Cited


Anonymous. "Hidden Apartheid: Caste Discrimination against India's Untouchables". *Human Rights Watch and the Center for Human Rights and Global Justice (CHRGJ).* New York University School of Law. Retrieved from://www.hrw.org/report/2007/02/12/hidden-apartheid/caste-discrimination-against-indias-untouchables.

Foucault, Michel. 'Prison Talk'. (Spring 1977). Retrieved from https://www.radicalphilosophy.com/interview/michel-foucault-prison-talk.

Freire, Paulo. *Pedagogy of the Oppressed.* New York: Continuum Publishing, 2000.

—. *Pedagogy of Hope: Reliving Pedagogy of the Oppressed.* New York: Continuum Publishing, 2004.

Jadhav, Narendra. *Outcaste- A Memoir.* New Delhi: Viking, Penguin Books, 2003.

—. "Empowerment of Dalits and Adivasis: Role of Education in the Emerging Economy." Retrieved from http://casi.ssc.upenn.edu/system/files/Empowerment+of+Dalits+%2526+Adivasis++Narendra+Jadhav+%28CASI+Working+Paper+%2526+Khemka+Lecture% 29_0.pdf. CASI. University of Pennsylvania.Philadelphia.3 Dec 2008.

Moon, Vasant. *Growing up Untouchable in India: A Dalit Autobiography.* Trans. Gail Omvedt. New Delhi: Vistaar Publications, 2001.

—. Ed. *Dr Babasaheb Ambedkar: Writings and Speeches.* Vol. 2 and Vol. 7. Bombay: Education Department, Govt. of Maharashtra, 1982 and 1990.

Padgaonkar, Dileep. "Look back in Languor." Rev. of *Outcaste.* Retrieved from http://drnarendrajadhav.info/drnjadhav_web_files/DrJadhav_Untouchable/DrJadhav_Untouchable_LookBackIn Languor.pdf.

Tartakov, Gary Michael. Review of *Growing up Untouchable in India. The Journal of Asian Studies.* Vol. 61, No. 1. (2002): 302-04. *JSTOR*. Web. 5 July 2011.

Vijapur, Abdul Rahim P. "Education of Ex-Untouchables (Dalits): Plight of Human Rights Education in Indian Schools". Retrieved from http://www.hurights.or.jp/archives/pdf/asia-s-ed/v10/15Education%20of%20Ex-Untouchables,%20Dalits.pdf.

# 14

# Exposing the Social Inequality and the Pursuit of Identity of Marginalised People in *Akkarmashi*: An Analysis

*N. Padmapriyadharshini*

There are many autobiographical works written by many writers around the world. The autobiographies mainly consist of the life struggles and the road which those writers opted for acquiring recognition and fame in the society. Hence, autobiographies are considered as the motivational and inspiring works of art. There are some autobiographies which constitute humiliation, mental struggle, oppression, suppression, exploitation, deprivation and discrimination and those are written by the writers who belong to the marginalised or the oppressed communities. In India, there is an unavoidable special place for Dalit Literature which speaks about the true face of the society and shows how conservative the citizen of this land. The discrimination and oppression made by the so-called "upper caste" people in this society has forced a particular group of people to live a marginalised life throughout their life and that continued for many generations and still continues. This makes it important for a Dalit writer to write his autobiography and project his pain to this world. Das rightly observes thus:

> Scholars defending the system always argued that the caste-system in its original form was not hereditary but based on

> psychological foundations; division of the society according to different occupational groups was in fact an exercise towards the recognition of the innate psychological inclinations of men. Some of them agreed that the complete stratification of the society, denying the lower groups any opportunity towards vertical mobility was unjust and inhuman. And some condemned it severely. But all writings on caste-inequality failed to create any significant impact until the movement against the system emerged from the oppressed themselves. (Das, 301)

Casteism in India has taken a great turn but there are huge dangerous discriminations made then and there on people who belong to the marginalised caste. There are many movements and constitutional acts which stood with these people but still they could not come out of this discrimination. Casteism is found only on community certificates in cities but in villages, there are serious practices which still make the oppressed people live a bad life. What is really pathetic is that, those discriminated people believe that they are 'low' and they should respect the 'upper caste' people. There are some villages where even tea was not provided to Dalit people in glasses in which the other community people drink. There are streets where the upper community people live, where the Dalit people are not allowed to walk with slippers or not carry any kind of towel on their neck. All these oppressions are realistically picturised in the autobiographies of Dalit writers and hence reading these autobiographies projects casteism as a terrible monster. Krishnaveer Ghurye writes:

> The caste system is classification of people into four hierarchically ranked castes called Varnas. They are classified according to occupation and determine access to wealth, power, and privilege. The Brahmans, usually priests and scholars, are at the top. Next are the Kshatriyas, or political rulers and soldiers. They are followed by the Vaishyas or

> merchants and the fourth are the Shudras, who are usually labourers, peasants, artisans, and servants. At the very bottom are those considered the untouchables. These individuals perform occupations that are considered unclean and polluting, such as scavenging and skinning dead animals and are considered outcastes. They are not considered to be included in the ranked castes. (Qtd. in Challa 7)

Though many technological developments happen, though humanity finds a way to live on Mars, though technology starts ruling us, this casteism could not be eradicated as it is in the deep roots of DNA in Indian people. There are many Dalit writers who presented their plights in their autobiographies. Among them Sharankumar Limbale was one the powerful writers who presented his life struggles in his autobiography *Akkarmashi*. Limbale is working as a professor in Yashavantrao Chavan Maharashtra Open University. His autobiography *Akkarmashi* was published in 1984. The main aim of Dalit Literature is to protest against the contaminated caste system by exposing the struggles of oppressed people. This aim was achieved by Limbale through his autobiography. The struggles he faced to achieve success in life was unimaginable. In the "Preface" of *Akkarmashi*, G. N. Devy writes the remarks of Limbale thus:

> Every time the dominant classes attack and exploit the weak, they violate their women. The several sexual exploits of the men among the wicked exploiters draw legitimacy from their authority, wealth, society, culture and religion. But what of the exploited woman? She has to carry the rape in her womb. The rape has to be borne, fed and reared. The rape acquires and lives a life. My autobiography holds in the agony of such a life. My experiences are my words. What will remain there if you take experiences are my words. What will remain there if you take experience away from a life? A living corpse? (Devy, xxiv)

These lines present the pain experienced by the writer in his life. The comparison made by the writer also proves Limbale's attitude towards women. The struggle of women could be understood only by other women and some men who really live with some humanity. He has presented many woman characters, the widows, childless women and his own mother who was cheated and exploited by many people in many situations. He never criticised or blamed women but stood with them as if he could feel the pain of those characters. This is only because he could understand the pain of exploitation and oppression. These oppressions created a sense of deep depression in his mind and that forced him to write this autobiography. Limbale in an interview writes that:

> Atrocities against Dalit made me to react. My writing is reaction against brutal and inhuman caste system. Equality, freedom, justice, democracy are streams of my blood. I never tolerate injustice against common man irrespective of his caste. I want to see a beautiful nation without exploitation, corruption and atrocities. From thousands of years Dalits are neglected. Now we are aware of our rights and power. Dalit Literature is a manifesto of our movement. My life is part and parcel of Dalit movement. Movement is my life. (Nawale, 125)

Limbale experienced double marginalisation. The community which he belongs to was considered as the untouchable among the marginalised. He deeply writes about that in his autobiography. Considering the meaning of the term 'Akkarmashi', 'the illegitimate child', Limbale's inner pain was exposed by him in a pathetic way. 'Akkarmashi' in Marathi means 'Eleven', which signifies one less from a dozen. This symbolically means his incompleteness. Sharankumar never had a life of selecting his love from people. He was not given a chance to select even his wife. He got his wife out of sympathy. He hated the traditional Hindu rituals as he hated the Hindu caste system. He opted for Buddhist marriage instead of Hindu one. His words are evidences for the real horror of the caste system in India. In an instance in his life, when he faced double marginalisation, he understood that even Dalits are internally divided by a hierarchy. He shares one such instance in his childhood thus:

> Once, in summer as usual I was playing with Arjya, a Mang. Thirsty, we entered my house and I drank water first before giving the cup Arjya. Santamai shouted, 'Why do you play with that boy? Is there no one in the whole village to play with? Don't give him water in that vessel. If he touches it he will defile it. Go away... Arjya and I kept walking towards the river... different part of the river are reserved for Mahar and Maang... Arjya and I drank water from the reservoir for the Maang. When I reached home Santamai hit me because I drank water meant for Maang. Ansamai too hit Arjya, because by allowing me to drink water from reservoir for Maang he was responsible for contaminating. (Limbale, 19-20)

Limbale has presented many instances like this in his book which includes even the humiliation made by his teachers in his classroom. When he and his friends belonging to the Dalit caste are forced to eat the leftovers in the class room, he ate it with greed as if he were starving. They ate the food when the other students laughed and mocked them. This particular incident created a deep scar in his mind. Limbale has starved many days and nights as he experienced poverty due to his low caste. Wearing chappals was also considered as the crime for Dalit people. When his grandmother gave him a pair of slippers, he wore it to school but he was teased and accused by his fellow students for wearing them in school. Limbale has faced the tea cup incident too in his life. This is the point where he hated the caste system totally. He says thus:

> Casteism made us bitter. There was a small tea shop in our village owned by Maangs, where a separate cup and saucer

> were kept for the Mahars and Maangs. I had seen the cup and saucer many times. We also had to move aside to make way for high-caste persons while passing on the road. (Limbale, 76)

A lot of physical and emotional violences took place in his life. All these were totally due to the caste he belongs. Fed up with this caste system, Limbale even decided to follow Buddhism leaving Hinduism. The cruelty of the caste system made people like him to ignore their own identity and go somewhere they could live freely without such discriminations. In his work *The Outcaste*, he presents various questions to the society to which none could answer. There are various such incidents which actually hurt someone who understands everything. Dalit writers like him would never write for the readers. They write to expose the sufferings and pain they experienced in their life. Though they faced discrimination in their childhood and early young age, they managed to study and create their own place in the society. Comparing with other writers and achievers, the Dalit writers are considerably strong as they faced many challenges than gaining knowledge. Their words truly throw light on the dark side of society. Thus, he concludes his book by posting some questions to the society asking who created such inequality and why? Though this book ended with the question, there is a clear answer to the question which tests the identity of the author.

## Works Cited

Challa, Krishnaveer, A. & Raghu Raj Yerra. *Dalit Literature in English Translation: A Critical Study*. New Delhi: Prestige Books International, 2016.

Das, Sasir Kumar. *A History of Indian Literature (1911-1956): Struggle for Freedom: Triumph and Tragedy*. New Delhi: South Asia Books, 1995.

Devy, G. N. "Introduction." *The Outcaste*. New Delhi: Sahitya Akademi. 2003.

Ghurye, G. *Caste, Class and Occupation*. Bombay: Popular Books, 1961.

Limbale, Sharankumar. *The Outcaste: Akkarmashi*. Trans. Santhosh Bhoomkar. New Delhi: Oxford U P, 2003.

—. *Towards Aesthetics of Dalit Literature: History, Controversies and Consideration*. New Delhi: Orient Longman, 2004.

Nawale, Arvind M. "A Literary Interview of Sharankumar Limbale." *Nation with Discrimination: Literary Voices from the Subalterns*. New Delhi: Access Publishing India, 2012.

# 15

# Mohandas Naimishray's *Apne Apne Pinjare*: A Groundbreaking Document of the Neglected

*Abdul Wahied Wani*

There may be several factors such as destitution, humiliation, suppression and ostracisation which may drive anyone at the fringe of the society. Dalits are those people who are undergoing all these factors for a long time. Not only this, they think that they are born to suffer and all this is happening with them due to their low caste. Dalit consciousness and proper education helped them a lot to improve their pitiable plight. Educated Dalit writers spill their pain on a piece of paper by writing their autobiographies, memoirs and personal narratives so that other also may be familiar with their pain. Bijender Singh writes about these texts, "Dalit personal narratives reveal the collective consciousness of the community which was repressed for a long time. Through individual memoirs, the writers presented before us documentation of a caste-tormented society" (Singh, 14). In the last few decades, many Dalit men and women writers have written their autobiographies in different languages. There are several Dalit autobiographies in Hindi Literature also. Heinz Werner Wessler writes, "Literature was an important medium of what is sometimes called colonial modernity. From the second half of the 19th century, Hindi literature was deeply concerned with issues of social reform" (Wessler, 2).

Among many famous Dalit writers, an important Dalit writer is Mohandas Naimishray who was born in Meerut on 5 September, 1949. He presently lives in Delhi and has written several books. Part 1 of *Apne Apne Pinjare*, his autobiography, was published in 1995. The second part of this autobiography was published in 2000 and the third part of his autobiography was published in 2019 by Vani Prakashan under a different title *Rang Kitne Sang Mere*. Mohandas was born in Meerut, Uttar Pradesh, in a poor Chamar family. The life of his family was very tough. He studied in Kumar Ashram in Meerut which was built by Lala Lajpat Rai for Dalits. Mohandas was so poor that he did not get proper clothes and shoes to wear. His family lived in a mud house in Meerut.

His autobiography *Apne Apne Pinjare* describes the experiences of his childhood and his struggle for life. Part one of this autobiography describes the writer's childhood in Meerut, his school experiences and the pitiable situation of his neighbourhood. There is a story behind his name. A neem tree was in the courtyard of his house. 'Naimi' stands for neem and 'shray' stands for 'courtyard'. As there was a neem tree in his courtyard, his surname was put 'Naimishray'. He describes how Chamars had to live in unhygienic conditions and other upper caste people were enjoying their life.

In this autobiography, he describes how he went to Mumbai. Naimishray's father was a retired soldier and he married again after the death of his first wife. Naimishray's uncle and aunt adopted him and that's why he did not have to suffer at the hands of his step-mother. His father lived in a three-storey house while his uncle and aunt lived in a mud house. Sometimes Naimishray would also think to sleep in his father's house but he could not realise his dream. He praises his *tai* in the following words, "There was milk in his *tai*'s breasts and a sea of affection in her heart" (Naimishray, 13). He was feeling sad at the death of his mother but his *tai* loved him so much that he forgot the absence of his mother. He writes, "His mother's death after a few months of his death was a great loss to him but the act of adoption by his *tai* was much comfortable to him" (Naimishray: 1995, 13). The village life was much different and the people were divided among different castes. Mohandas Naimishray writes about the caste system of his village:

> After all, the village was a village. There was nothing like a city—neither concrete roads nor cemented houses. There were small mud houses, but these houses were divided among the imperishable lines of casteism. I had understood about the structure of caste along with the geography of the village. (Naimishray: 1995, 7)

Naimishray would go to his school in another village by going fourteen kilometers on foot daily and completed his matriculation in 1940. The students of his school would call him "the son of a Chamar". He writes about the pain of his caste, "We were slaves for generations. As soon as a mother would give birth to her child, his caste was put on his forehead with his birth. He was made aware that he was born in a low caste" (Naimishray: 1995, 26). The author boy writes that their identity was linked only with their caste which is evident from the below quotation:

> Our school was called the school of Chamars by outsiders. Everything was related with their caste such as the well of Chamars, the hand pump of Chamars, the neem of Chamars, the street of Chamars, the panchayat of Chamars etc. Likewise their school was linked with their caste. The caste came earlier than the school. (Naimishray: 1995, 33)

Naimishray's caste becomes an obstacle in his love affair. He was in love with Raswanti but she belonged to an upper caste, that's why their marriage could not take place and he went to Mumbai with his uncle in frustration. The environment of Mumbai was not much better and there were many poor people but nobody was humiliating him there for his caste. He writes, "There was hunger and poverty in Mumbai but there was not any wall of caste between two men. He was never asked about his caste" (Naimishray: 1995, 136). Mohandas writes that a girl named Suji fell in love with him in Mumbai. Mohandas knew that this relationship has no future but he does not disappoint her outwardly. He narrates about this incident, "Suji extended her hand towards me and placed her palm on my lips and said emotionally, "Fill your breath in my fist. Till you come back, I will keep the smell of your breath. I'll wait for you" (Naimishray 2000: 140-41).

He was sent to school when he was seven years old. He did his graduation with English subject and did his MA and BEd. He prepared for the Public Service Commission and Indian Administrative Services also but he could not realise his dream. He did some odd jobs such as home-guard and clerk etc for his livelihood. He met with Mayawati and the agents of BAMCEF in Delhi and he resigned from his post of a token inspector. And became a lecturer in CAB College. He was so influenced by Mayawati that he resigned from his college post also and devoted himself for social welfare. He would consider job just like a slavery. He was so excited for the social service that he sacrificed everything. He writes, "I wanted to be liberated by all means. And wanted to meet people by travelling from one place to another and wanted to listen to their problems'' (Naimishray 2000: 147).

Mohandas faced problems at every step of his life. He was against the dowry system and wanted to believe in simple life. His father-in-law wanted to marry his daughter with great pump and show. Mohandas had to succumb. He writes that his brothers, cousins and relatives "were dancing, singing and enjoying and I was rankling" (Naimishray 2000: 114).

He writes that his wife Shakoon was not a jovial woman and she did not like the poverty of her husband's family. After some time, they settled in Haidarpur and Mohandas started working as a manager in his father-in-law's company. His wife was also working as a supervisor. They had three children. His son Manish died at a tender age due to lack of medication. His daughter did the diploma of an air hostess.

Naimishray was against the caste discrimination. He writes in his autobiography that the cook got angry in the mess when he touched the utensils in the kitchen. He had gone there for a week's training after becoming a home guard. He and his friends told the cook frankly that they are Chamars by caste. They sent him away and a low-caste cook was appointed in the kitchen.

Mohandas was against gender discrimination. He writes about the pitiable plight of Dalit women. He gives the example of a Dalit woman who was married but her husband had relationship with his aunt and that's why he did not touched his own wife. Other women also knew about the whole story but they were also helpless. Naimishray writes about it, "Women could feel her pain but what could they do? Their position was not better than a tethered cow or a buffalo" (Naimishray: 1995, 23).

Naimishray faces many problems due to his caste. When he married, he was doing a private job as a teacher and his salary was only two hundred rupees. He goes to take his wife to Delhi. When his wife comes to know about his salary, she humiliates him for his low income. Her father had a good income that's why she humiliates him. Naimishray takes different jobs for his livelihood. His family members and relatives were against his decision and they tried to persuade him for not resigning from his college job but he did not listen to anybody.

The second part of this autobiography describes the author's struggle in Mumbai and his literary career. He involved in Dalit activities and devoted himself for his writing. He came back to Meerut but the death of his son gave him a shock. He writes that the Dalit people were derived of their fundamental rights:

> Along with the crises, we were also victims of untouchability. There was no way to come out of those crises. Muktidwar was closed to us. We could only yearn, weep, weep. There were peculiar outcrops inside us. But who had time to listen to them? (Naimishray, 2000: 25)

Naimishray writes that most of the Dalit people were the blind followers of the rituals and traditions. They did not use any logic behind anything. They believed in their actions but were the slave of their fate. Only few people were so strong who had the courage to take a bold step to break the age-old traditions:

> Though education started coming among the Dalit castes, it was proving to be superficial. People did not want to leave the traditions and believed more in keeping them sticking to the chest. Kuldevata and gotra deity began to emerge among the Dalits. They were busy beating the left streaks of their fathers and grandfathers. Very few people had the courage to erase that line and draw a new line, who were struggling, struggling to do something new. (Naimishray, 2000: 46)

Mohandas writes that the seeds of discrimination were firm among the lower castes also as it is very common and can be easily found among other autobiographies also. The caste system of India is so rigid and complex that it becomes very difficult for the lower caste people to survive. Mohandas criticises it in the following words, "The example of the complex, well-organised and rigid caste system in India will not be found in any part of the world. In fact, when we think deeply, we find that it is found only in India and not elsewhere" (Naimishray, 2000: 45). Dr Sheoraj Singh Bechain also writes that the other Chamars who were financially strong would look down upon the poor people of their caste. The people of Mohandas' caste would exploit the people of other lower castes in hierarchy. He writes:

> There was a lack of dialogue among the Jatav and Valmiki castes among the Dalits as well as there was also an atmosphere of hatred and tension among themselves. Sometimes, there was also a fight. There was a sky difference between the occupation / living / food and religious traditions of both the castes. People of one caste used to eat pigs, people of another caste do not even want to see pig. (Naimishray, 2000: 67)

It is a common trend in Indian villages that their caste is people's identity. The people are called by their caste but the lower caste people feel it their humiliation if they are called by their caste. The same kind of pain is expressed by Omprakash Valmiki who is also called by his caste. In *Joothan*, Valmiki asserts, "Being born is not in the control of a person. If it were in one's control, then why would I have been born in a Bhangi household? Those who call themselves the standard-bearers of this country's great cultural heritage, did they decide which homes they would be born into?" (Valmiki, 133-34). Mohandas also writes about the same problem of Indian villages in his autobiography:

> Our caste houses also used to come with scavengers, who, like others, considered our greatness in calling Abe O Bhangi Ke, Ari O Bhangan ...... etc... etc. They used to be abused on talk. When the food of all the people was finished, they used to wait like beggars for crates, silver plates, glasses etc. (Naimishray, 2000: 67)

Mohandas writes that the people of his caste were superior from some other lower castes and untouchability was prevalent among the lower caste people. It was really a strange thing. It is a fact that the people who are sitting at any higher level do not think much about those people who live at the lower level. They blame those people whom they cannot compete with. They feel jealous of them and try to find fault with them. The same happens in this autobiography also. Mohandas Naimishray writes that the people of Valmiki caste would not sit with them due to inferiority complex and fear of humiliation:

> Till that time, no one from the Valmiki society dared to sit with us in the marriage of our caste. Nor did he dare to call them from our midst. There was also a lack of mutual harmony among the Dalit castes. There was more hatred and jealousy towards each other....From some settlements in Meerut, Valmiki families were getting involved in the Dalit movement... They were also making progress in education, business and politics, but they had a clue as to why Valmiki is behind the Jatavs. (Naimishray, 2000: 67-68)

Thus, Dalit autobiographies are the repertoire of pain, humiliation and oppression. Dalit autobiographies depict the pain of not only the respective writers but also the sufferings of their entire community. These autobiographies have opened new avenues for other Dalit writers so that they may also get inspired and may dare not to bear any oppression at the name of caste. V. Kavitha also writes in this context.

> The sufferings of the marginalised people will be understood in a better and suitable manner only when they are transported in written form by the Dalit writers. This process of writing provides a space for these marginalised writers to voice not only their victimisation by writing autobiographical works but also that of their entire community through the portrayal of the lives of both men and women in their fictional works. (Kavita, 221)

## Works Cited

Kavitha, V. "Sabaltern Autobiography: Challenging the Cannon." *Research Journal English Language and Literature (RJELAL)*. 2.1 (2014): 221-226.

Naimishray, Mohandas. *Apne Apne Pinjare. Part 1.* New Delhi: Vani Prakashan, 1995.

—. *Apne Apne Pinjare. Part 2.* New Delhi: Vani Prakashan, 2000.

—. *Rang Kitne Sang Mere.* New Delhi: Vani Prakashan, 2019.

Singh, Bijender, Ed. *Indian Dalit Literature: Marginalised Voices*. New Delhi, Authorspress, 2015.

Valmiki, Omprakash. *Joothan: A Dalit's Life*. New Delhi: Samya, 2003.

Wessler, Heinz Werner. "From Marginalisation to Rediscovery of Identity: Dalit and Adivasi Voices in Hindi Literature." *Studia Neophilologica*. 2020. 1-16.

# 16

# Deconstructing the Identity of a 'Dalit' in Bhanwar Meghwanshi's Memoir *I Could not be Hindu: The Story of a Dalit in the RSS*

*Guni Vats*

> I remember people wearing garlands, a saffron band tied around their heads, a blood red tika on the forehead, fists raised to chants of *Jai Shri Ram, Jai Jai Shri Ram*, their voices rending the sky. (Meghwanshi, 16)

*I Could not be Hindu: The story of a Dalit in the RSS* is the story of the disillusionment of Bhanwar Meghwanshi, a *karsevak* in the organisation that claims to be born of a dream of constructing a Hindu *Rashtra*. Meghwanshi, a spirited youth who dreamt of sacrificing his life to the noble cause of cleansing the nation of the 'other' is awakened of his caste identity in the process. 'Dalit' is a political idea of an untouchable who has existed in the history of the nation that boasts of a golden past. The organisation trying to reconstruct a Hindu identity opens its gates to all castes until they demand to be treated with dignity and respect. The systematic deconstruction of being a Dalit in the largest non-Government Organisation is a saga of the awakening of an untouchable. The reading of the text unveils RSS as a microcosm of the Hindu Nation that celebrates *Varnashram*. The careful division of labour and the art of designating befitting jobs according to one's caste identity is represented in the book. Bhanwar Meghwanshi is unaware of his social standing in the caste hierarchy until he is taught so by the men he looked up to. The dichotomy of caste is not limited to an assertion of hierarchy, but caste is hegemonically forced. The later chapters unfold how an entire repressive apparatus is applied to ensure censure of any dissent.

The memoir of Bhanwar Meghwanshi is unlike the Dalit autobiographies we are trained to read. It is not only a saga of caste-based oppression but a systematic deconstruction of an organisation that constructs the leaders of a nation. It is not the story of oppression, but a saga of rebellion. The very act of writing this book has liberated Meghwanshi of the obedience that was expected of his caste. He questions in the novel fights for his rights and then spearheads a campaign to challenge a mammoth organisation single-handedly. It is the saga of a Dalit who refuses to be bound in his caste identity and questions the system that labels him 'untouchable'. Meghwanshi had joined the cause of Hindu Rashtra and was willing to fight for his nationalism. Little did he know that the ideology constructed was a farce built on prejudices and hatred. Having picked naïve boys from school, the *Shakha* planned an hour's worth of intellectual and physical exercises that would etch their narrative of Hindu fanaticism in the vulnerable minds. If the organisation used men from lower castes only for the manual jobs, what was their representation in a Hindu world? Meghwanshi tackles the existence of a Dalit in a Hindu(tva) organisation and also questions if the face of a New India would accommodate Dalits, Adivasis, and women?

## Constructing an 'Other'

> How much longer were we to tolerate the presence of that structure of slavery in our own land. The land of Hindus, and at the very birthplace of our revered deity? (Meghwanshi, 17)

The invocation of demolishing a mosque at Ayodhya was not merely a political stance or a religious statement; it was an effort to save the home from outsiders. Meghwanshi recounts at many places throughout the novel that he hated the existence of a minority religion, even though he had never met one. The construction of 'us' and 'they' was a clever act of the Sangh. Once the Hindus had an enemy to fight against, they would almost always be intoxicated by hatred. It was this hatred that had united Hindus in the Sangh and not their mutual respect. The caste bias was hidden under layers of a mutually constructed sense of enmity directed at a minority religion. 'All differences among people had been erased—young and old, rich and poor, ordinary and privileged, we had become as one' (Meghwanshi, 17). The 'us' and 'they' were constructed and defined. 'Us' could stay in harmony only until they had an 'other' to fight against. The individual identities of all *swayamsevaks* were amalgamated in the bigger narrative of serving and protecting the nation. 'Karsevaks' was the term labelled on all the men who swore to work for the sangha voluntarily. Their identity as a sangha volunteer never mentioned their castes, but the inherent bias soon unveiled the ugliness of caste in the very foundations of Sangha.

An identity can be constructed only when a binary is supplied to the supposition of a character. Like Lacan explained how a child learns about his identity by looking at the mirror, a *karsevak*'s mirror became the sangha structure itself. The very development of identity involved rigorous techniques of constructing a narrative through literature, morning prayers, 'Sanskritised' sermons, and the inherent injection of the sangha values in the culture outside. The construction of the 'self' and the 'other' were continuous exercises in the *shakha* of the sangha. The Dalit identities remained hidden under new terminologies and all were labelled Hindu until the need for new definitions emerged. Meghwanshi was a devout follower of the ideals of Sangha until he was treated as an outsider, an untouchable, a man not worthy enough to be shared meals with. It was only after his personal awakening that he assumed the role of a dissenter. He tried to assert his voice staying in the structures of the sangha, but only after his letters left unheard did, he turn to abolish his beliefs and fight against the organisation that refused to accept him as a Dalit. He refused to stay confined in the suffocating milieu of racism and prejudices.

## Sangha as a Microcosm of *Varnashram*

Bhanwar Meghwanshi was injected with the Sangh ideology at his school itself. His Guruji would steer them away from science and towards religion. The impressionable minds slowly turned towards the workings of shakha. The well-divided hour was carefully allotted to physical exercises, games, intellectual inputs, and prayers. The curriculum was so impeccably defined that the students were spoon-fed (Hindutva) ideology under the garb of nationalism. The ideology was not limited to the hour of active participation but a passive assertion in the daily rituals of its volunteers. Hindutva was celebrated even through the festivals that Sangha celebrated, 'Sangh celebrated six main festivals—among these Diwali, Holi, Republic Day were *not* included. What we did celebrate was Varsha Pratipad, Vijayadashmi, Makar Sankranti, Hindu Empire Day, Rakshabandhan and Guru Poornima' (Meghwanshi, 31).

The image of the senior leaders of the sangha was designed so carefully that they would appear like Hindu monks. Their word was not merely an order of a mortal then, it was revered as the word of the Lord himself. 'Every caste has been allotted a particular kind of work, and they are good at it, perhaps this is why our ancestors allotted occupations by caste.' (Meghwanshi, 37). The microcosm of *Varnashram* in the Sangha made sure that labour was divided befit the caste identities. All the senior posts of the Sangha were occupied by the higher castes, 'so far six pracharaks have become sarsanghchalak, of whom five are Brahmin (Keshav Baliram Hedgewar, 'Guru-ji',

M.S. Golwalkar, Madhukar Dattatraya 'Balasaheb' Deoras, K.S. Sudarshan, Mohan Bhagwat) and one Kshatriya (Rajendra Singh, known as Rajju Bhaiyya). In the Sangh, posts are filled by nomination, not election (Meghwanshi, 43). While Brahmins mostly became the pracharaks, Baniyas were entrusted with the treasury, and often colloquially their caste identity would be invoked to justify them handling the money. While pracharaks were expected to lead a simple life, the Kshatriya pracharaks were allowed to eat meat. A section of the Hindu leaders believed that vegetarianism was the cause of the weakness of Hindus.

The list of office bearers suggests a gaping vacuum in the caste representation and the leadership roles. On the ground, the Sangha required lower castes for mass mobilisation, but they almost always preferred an upper caste for office. Dalits and Adivasis were involved in the Sangha to only carry out the menial jobs. They were stuffed into trains to Ayodhya, they are readily made available by the senior leaders whenever the threat from the 'other' arises. Thus, Dalits were required to only fight with the Muslims; they never made it to the table where decisions were made. There was no mechanism in place when a Dalit could even get his grievance heard. Meghwanshi, after being treated differently because of his caste identity, tried every official step to file his grievance, but he was never lent an ear. The very attitude of the Sangha unveils the imitation of Manuvadi Hindu Rashtra. They are attempting to recreate the ideals of Varnashram in the Hindu Rashtra they strive to construct. Meghwanshi then worries that since 'no Dalit or Adivasi has managed to reach the national level of the organisation. How then will Dalits and Adivasis be part of a Hindu Rashtra?' (Meghwanshi, 44).

## Women in RSS

The construction of a cultural identity remains incomplete until the other gender is also constructed, in passive relation to the masculine self. Women in RSS were constructed owing to similar patriarchal stereotypes. They were passive bystanders to the unfolding of the greatest initiative of constructing a Hindu Rashtra. The shakha's initiative was to construct brave men who could fight battles and secure the dream of a Hindu nation. What role did women have to play in the construction of a strong masculine nation was made clear by the 1936 initiation of inaugurating a women's organisation? Its leader Lakshmibai Kelkar (famously known as *mausi-ji*) organised a female counterpart to RSS, the Rashtriya Sevika Samiti because women could not have been part of the mainline RSS. Meghwanshi argues how the very terminology exposes the intent of introducing women to the Sangha, 'the word swayam (self) was missing from its name, thus making its members 'servants' of others rather than of the self. Swayamsevak denotes volunteering, an autonomous volition, while sevika evokes a menial position of waiting in others' (Meghwanshi, 45).

Women were to play the role of servants to the masculine warriors who were destined to actively fight for a Hindu nation. The terminology evidently did not irk other members of the Sangh. It was an organisation run on high levels of testosterone that believed that women were hindrances in the path of complete political gains. It was probably this reason that the highest office holders of the Sangh were not allowed to get married. It was also because of the prejudice against women that 'the seniors of the Sangh believed that doctor sahib (Hedgewar, the founder) did right by not permitting women into the Sangh, that it was a good strategic move because women in the Sangh would have by now ensured its destruction' (Meghwanshi, 45). The identity creation of volunteers of Sangh was not only prejudiced towards other religions but also the other gender. The 'othering' aimed at constructing a 'self', who would be blindly devoted to the cause of the Sangha.

## Intoxication of Nationalism

Tagore regarded Nationalism as 'one of the most powerful anaesthetics that man has invented' (Tagore, 133). Rashtriya Swayamsevak Sangha assured that the anaesthetic of Nationalism must never wear off its volunteers. During the act of training its volunteers, Sangha became synonymous with the nation. The prayers and Sanskrit verses constructed a milieu where the volunteers swore their loyalty to the nation, and an extension to the cause of the Sangha. Meghwanshi recalls how he was introduced to the idea of a nation for the first time in his life. 'It was in the shakha that I first beheld the portrait of Bharat Mata, Mother India, with the saffron flag in her hand. I wondered how it was that Bharat Mata held not the national tricolour but the Sangh's saffron flag' (Meghwanshi, 50). The construction of symbolism that defined the identity of Meghwanshi and many other volunteers like him involved the construction of the Nation as a vulnerable mother, always in need of protection. It was this need that led the swayamsevaks to believe that there was a need to not only militarise the project of Hinduism but also a 'Hinduisation of the military' (Meghwanshi, 50).

Sangha could be understood as the hegemony of power that constructs a vicious circle of oppression. The art of symbolisation helped them construct their office bearers as spiritual gurus, any dissent was considered treason. Sangha became equivalent to the image of the Nation itself, any discourse that challenged the narrative of sangha was labelled treacherous. The symbolisation of saffron colour as the colour of nation and Sangha was celebrated and ingrained sub-consciously to the conscience of its followers. Sangha had its literature and publishing houses that ensured that the ideology went beyond the active sessions of the shakha and etch in the general conscience of the people. 'It was the *Panchjanya* that made me an ideological and intellectual fanatic in the cause of this Hindu Rasthra' (Meghwanshi, 57). Sangha was thus not a mere organisation but a 'factory that built individual like me into cultured and patriotic young men' (Meghwanshi, 63). The culture and patriotism were subject to the constructed definitions of the Sangha and its leaders.

## Disillusionment of Caste

> What is my own identity? What am I? Who am I after all? A devotee of Ram, a Hindu karsevak, or a Shudra, an untouchable? One so impure that even the food from my home could not be touched by these flag-bearers of Hindu Rashtra! What was my identity? (Meghwanshi, 87)

The first instance when Meghwanshi realised his caste identity was when he had organised an event for the Sangha. He had made arrangements for dinner following the event. His father had asked him not to as he was well aware that the hypocrite Sanghis would never eat at the house of a lower caste man. Meghwanshi was fuelled with the Sanghi propaganda and believed in their idea of social harmony. He could never have believed that the leaders he always looked up to failed him and disgraced him. The food was requested to be packed on the pretext of a few members being uncomfortable at eating from the house of a lower caste. Promises were made that the food would be consumed at the other location, but it was all a farce. Meghwanshi learned through a friend that the food he had packed was lying at the sides of the road and scavengers were feasting on it. It was this incident that shook the Dalit consciousness in Meghwanshi. He realised that he was not only being pushed away from the authorial posts of the Sangha, but also that he was a mere pawn. He was a Dalit who was only good enough to be a part of the mob, but never to be given the dignity of sharing a meal.

> Later, I realised that in the Hindu caste system, I was lower than the Shudra, I was an untouchable; not one of the four varnas, but an outcaste, the fifth caste, avarna. I may well be a Swayamsevak, but I was not a Hindu all the way. (Meghwanshi, 87)

The awakening of Dalit consciousness questioned if Meghwanshi was ever even Hindu enough? He remembered how he was patronised to accept his fate that would never allow him to be a pracharak of the Sangh. He believed earlier that these incidents of discrimination were merely isolated incidents occurring to maintain the decorum of Sangha. It was only after he experienced the humiliation that he realised that Sangha was Casteist to its core. The shock jolted the very identity of Meghwanshi. He was not only alienated politically, but every iota of his existence was carefully dismantled. The belief he grew up with, the idols he looked up to, the aim of his life were all suspended in uncertainty. He started questioning his place in the Sangha that still follows the Varna system. He started doubting his relevance in the fight towards a Hindu nation. If the nation doesn't accept equality in castes, where will he stand in the nation that he fought to construct? 'Why am I working towards a Hindu Rashtra that will discriminate against me?' (Meghwanshi, 91). Meghwanshi learned more about his caste identity when he started living at The Gandhi Nagar Hostel. It was an Ambedkar Hostel and for the first time, he interacted with other men who shared his identity. The Sangha soon got him out of the hostel though, for the fear of his ideology getting corrupt. Though the Apparatus of the Sangha ensured no dissent, the realisation of caste identity and the interaction with co-sufferers of that identity introduced Meghwanshi to a whole new ideological universe.

## Deconstructing Beliefs

Sangha was saturated with the propaganda of building a Hindu Nation. Any other ideology was considered a hindrance and soon tackled. Meghwanshi had left the Ambedkar Hostel for the fear of corrupting his ideology, but the series of events led him to deconstruct the beliefs of the Sangha. While reciting the fanaticism of his beliefs, he unknowingly unveils the strategy of construction of a Hindu(tva) ideology in the Sangha.

He recites how he only knew about the *Manusmriti* being the social constitution and had no idea about the Constitution of India. While this may be surprising for an intellectual class to believe, but the tightly constructed social fabric does not allow for any other ideology to seep in. The kids were trained to believe in the *Manusmriti* and they never questioned the frivolity of it because they were not aware of another discourse. Meghwanshi remembers how the narratives taught to them were all biased. Only the literature that suited the Hindu narrative was advertised, and others were never really even mentioned.

> I sang the praises of Maharana Pratap but had never heard of Bhilu Rana Punja. I knew the songs of Mira but was not acquainted with Sant Ravidas. I was thrilled to the courage and valour of Rani Lakshmibai of Jhansi, but Jhalkari Bai, a Dalit warrior who played a key role in the Rani Jhansi's women's army in the 1857 rebellion, was unknown to me. (Meghwanshi, 69)

The texts were not only cleansed of any mention of a Muslim existence, but also of any narrative that would incite Dalits, Adivasis, or women. The narratives that were told were carefully manipulated. Only certain Dalits were chosen from mythology and history who were grateful to serve the savarna. The language became so inherently etched in the conscience of the mass that the words became symbols that in turn cemented themselves in the narrative of an organisation. The manipulated words and mythological examples replaced the truth and the people were forced to believe a fabricated narrative. It was not merely a scenario of a utopian post-truth existence; it was a calculated construction of manipulated identities. Narratives and leaders constructed an unquestioning mob who would be obliged to sacrifice their lives at a call for their religious assertion in Ayodhya or minor squabbles with the Muslims. The lower castes were not only designated menial work but were taught to accept it as their fate and bind them in a vicious circle of servitude.

> If I knew anything about communities like mine, it was about those who had loyally served upper caste idols—Shabari who fed Shri Ram with berries she innocently first tasted herself; of Eklavya who gave up his thumb as offering to his guru Dronacharya; Hanuman who tore open his chest to reveal Shri Ram enshrined in his heart. The dhobis made themselves useful by washing clothes, leather workers made shoes, others cleaned up after the higher orders; that is, the same ancient caste system and traditional, inherited menial work. (Meghwanshi, 70)

It was only after Meghwanshi was disillusioned with the caste identity that he realised that on the social hierarchy, Dalits and Muslims were almost similar. Both had been oppressed and subjected to undue violence. Servitude and obedience were expected from both of them, and neither could ascend the social hegemony without facing the repressive apparatuses of the State. The identity that had been carefully constructed by the Sangha and the biases injected was starting to wear off. The disillusionment of caste identity made Meghwanshi realise how he had always fought the wrong enemy. On the social hierarchy, Dalits and Muslims were similar. 'Those whom I thought dangerous and had been suspicious of, turned out to be people like me. Just like us, in their laughter, their tears, their anger; just as patriotic as us; as beset by difficult circumstances as we are' (Meghwanshi, 100). They have been manipulated to fight against themselves when they must be fighting together against the hegemony that has bound them in their minority identities and hinder their social development. 'The condition of Muslims and Dalits was equally bad, that our enemy was the same, and we should fight it together' (Meghwanshi, 101).

The awakening of a Dalit identity broke apart the Hindu consciousness in Meghwanshi. The realisation that he would never be treated as an equal only based on his birth shook the foundations of his belief in Hinduism. There came a brief time in his life when he wanted to convert his religion. His amateur urge to break free from his Hindu identity led him astray in the dingy lanes of conversion to Christianity. He never believed in Christianity as a religion he could adopt, for him it was just an escape from his Hindu identity. 'I was not seeking liberation, nor god. Nor did I have any questions. I wanted no answers. I had one objective and one alone—to expose the hypocrisy of the Sangh and its unethical politics' (Meghwanshi, 103). To his surprise, the churches would not let him convert because of his past associations with RSS. They thought of him as a spy. The hegemonic apparatus of the Sangha was not limited to the boundaries of their faith, it extended beyond. The Sangha that would not respect the existence of a Dalit would also not let them convert. Meghwanshi was not allowed to become a Christian and he was not willing to imitate a Brahmin. At the behest of a senior leader of the Sangha, he was misrepresented as a Kshatriya Brahmin at the house of a volunteer. When Meghwanshi objected to the Sangha, the leader remarked that he was 'a living proof people of lower castes have lower intelligence. Here I am, trying to make you a Brahmin, he went, and you prefer to crawl about in that dirty gutter' (Meghwanshi 109).

## The Rebellion

It took some time for Meghwanshi to accept his identity. He was neither a Christian convert nor a Hindu Dalit, he was a rebel. He wanted to dismantle every thread of the Casteist society that did not appreciate his existence. His story is not a recollection of a Dalit who has been wronged and he turns to voice his experiences. His novel is a saga of rebellion. He recalls his acts of speaking against the power and winning many battles against the organisation that discriminated against him. He launched a newspaper called *Dahakte Angaarey* to combat the propaganda literature that the Sangha circulated. It unashamedly talked about how the organisation denied identity to Dalits in their dream of a Hindu Nation. The awakening of his realisation of a Dalit identity led Meghwanshi to see beyond the garb of RSS's false claims at harmony. He could see their inner workings from a fresh perspective of an 'other'. He was at the receiving end of the insult he had unhesitatingly hurled at the Muslims for a long time. He now realised that his individual struggle was against a well-planned organisation that had been recruiting devout volunteers for decades now. He was adamant at exposing the true nature of RSS, 'How, through their claim of samrasata or harmony, they were subverting the possibility of equality, justice, and social transformation. And what the politics was behind naming Dalits as neglected (vanchit) and Adivasis as forest dwellers (vanvasi), denying us our own identity (Meghwanshi, 115).

Every act of rebellion involved unlearning everything that Sangha taught him. The sermons in Sanskrit that had mesmerised his youth lost their grip over him now. He could see beyond the façade of using a sophisticated language. It was the domain of Brahmins, not meant for the lower castes to use or exploit. Dalits and Adivasis were only meant to revere every phoneme wrapped in Sanskrit, the language of Gods, and never question it. He got a job at the primary school in Rajasthan but soon discovered that it was also tainted with the ideology of RSS. The teachers were all welcomed with a tika and tying a turban, the symbols of Hinduism being slowly etched in them. He did not only express his disdain at a religiously biased act in a secular nation but also threatened to complain to the authorities. It was at his insistence that morning prayer that followed the Sangha routine were repealed and the prescribed prayers were made a rule. The job for him was a further identification of him as an untouchable. The village had urged him to separate his water container from that of the students and when he refused, they just stopped drinking from the same container. Every time he would ride his bicycle through the village, he was warned and reminded that he is a lower caste and he need not proudly stride mocking the upper castes.

The acts of reminding him of his caste hierarchy only strengthened the vigour in Meghwanshi. He was not only adamant at questioning the Hindu propaganda of the Sangha but also wanted to dismantle the myths they had constructed around local gods. Sangha would manipulate stories about the past of a local god and replace the Dalit priests of the temple with Brahmins. Brahminism was thus not an empty narrative but a minutely constructed myth. Meghwanshi wrote scholarly articles on *Ramdev Pir* educating the local people that the story of *Pir* sacrificing his life-saving cows from Mughals was a false narrative constructed by the Sanghis to construct the Muslims as enemies. Meghwanshi also initiated a 'battle of the printed word' (Meghwanshi, 150) by launching *Diamond India*. A journal to counter the claims made by RSS mouthpiece *Pathey Kan*. It proved to provide an alternative opinion to what the Sangh had propagated. It soon became famous and the Sangh launched a full-blown war of words to soften the attack on their propaganda. The fights would soon leave Meghwanshi short of funds because RSS was a loaded organisation and had the money and muscle to tackle any attack. It would starve any contradictory opinion.

Meghwanshi recites the tale of Sawaibhoj Mandir and Qalandari Masjid in Asind which was on the verge of becoming another Ayodhya had the police not intervened. It was through this incident that the narrator questioned the religious acts of Sangha more keenly. The Brahmin priests had announced an *Ashwamedhayagna* to boast their victory. The Hindu ritual of revering the sacrificial fire proved an insult to Dalits. They were not allowed anywhere near the fires despite them having helped build the ashram for the priest. They had donated towards the preparation of this ritual and were asked to not pollute the holy act. Meghwanshi writes, Khandeshwari baba 'had an ashram here, which was built with voluntary labour from Dalits. Wood for the yagna was taken from Dalits, who also contributed financially. But when it came to making sacrificial offerings at the 108 fire pits, not one Dalit couple was permitted to participate' (Meghwanshi, 162). After protesting for their right to participate in the holy ritual, Dalits were compensated with separate fire pits for them but they could not have offered their prayer at the pits the upper castes were praying at. Dalits refused to bear the repeated insults and the *yagna* had to be cancelled. They were soon compared with *Rakshasas* (demons) who obstruct holy rites.

> We had to be purified by eating cowdung and drinking cow urine before we would be allowed to participate in the yagna. We were enraged and declared it inhuman to expect any self-respecting and intelligent human to eat the excreta of an animal. (Meghwanshi, 165)

## Of Animals and Dalits

Meghwanshi records at many places in his novel how Dalits were considered even lower than the animals in the social spectrum. An incident was recorded in 2001 at Chakwara, Rajasthan. At a pond where animals used to bathe, a Dalit man was slapped with a fine of fifty-one thousand rupees having dared to bathe in the public pond. He couldn't have polluted the upper castes, but he did pollute their animals. He goes further to document how the Dalit Sadbhavna Rally, organised in support of Dalits, proved to be a massive failure. The *Manuvaadis* refused to accept Dalits as human beings. Another incident was recorded from Jhajjar, Haryana where five Dalits were burnt alive on the suspicion of cow slaughtering in presence of the Police. The 2002 incident proved how the police were just a hegemonic extension of the dominant *Manuvaadi* thought process. Post the horrific incident, General Secretary of the VHP, Acharya Giriraj Kishore 'declared openly that the life of one cow is more valuable than the lives of five Dalits' (Meghwanshi, 195). The author could not believe that he had spent his youth trying to fight for a religion that respects the life of an animal more than that of a human being. He failed to understand how the men who labour are considered lower than those who eat off of the labour of others? Meghwanshi was alienated in his rebellion against the ideologies of RSS. His friends turned against him and sided with the Sangha. He was portrayed as an anti-Hindu nuisance to the Hindu volunteers.

> Most of my friends had ceased to be human and had become merely Hindu. Many started wearing the tilak on their foreheads. I was ostracised from society, called an enemy of Hinduism, an advocate of evil mullahs, even very close Hindu friends started avoiding me. I felt totally abandoned, even by my own shadow. (Meghwanshi, 205)

H.V. Sheshadri, RSS leader, in the pamphlet, *Dalit Andolanbanam Sangh Kaarya* published how he saw Dalit politics seeping into the social fabric. He blamed the Dalits for having been misguided the politics. He claimed how Dalits were demanding a change for them in the social strata and blamed it on the politics that was just a few years old. He wrote, 'The village had a temple to Maruti where they used to pray, content to receive prasad and observe the aarti from a distance, but now they had flung cow dung at temple itself.' (207) The Sangha was comfortable with the Dalits until they accepted their fate as 'untouchables' and did not question the oppression they were subjected to. They were accepted as part of the Hindu Nation only if they signed a social contract that confined them to the duties that were appropriated according to their caste identities. Any murmur of Caste oppression was blamed on the Muslims rather than the practice of casteism inherent in Hindus. Sangha had carefully woven together a narrative that celebrated the 'other' castes in their servitude. The Dalits who continued to serve with reverence and obedience were equated with the upper castes, all the others were mere 'untouchables.'

> From the victory of Valmiki, the supposed Dalit who wrote about the glories of Ram; to Sabari who innocently taste

> the berries she then fed to Ram; to Eklavya, the archer who gave up his thumb, and with it his skill, to his Brahmin teacher Drona as guru dakshina—all of them Dalits, Shudras and Adivasis who bowed humbly before their savarna lords. For years the RSS has been distorting the history of Dalits, trying to portray them as Kshatriya in disguise. (Meghwanshi, 222)

## Sangha Promoting Social Harmony

The continuous efforts of dissidents like Meghwanshi forced the Sangha to take notice of the cracks that were visible in its tightly woven structure. The continuous efforts made to change the narrative and question every act of oppression made the Sangha publish a list of changes that would make the organisation more inclusive. The first step for the Sangha was to invoke all the Dalit swayamsevaks to take the stage and preach how they were always treated equally in the sangha. The speakers acted more as the spokespeople of the organisation than representing their castes. Sangha found it necessary to re-write its literature. The narrative had to be freshened to match the present times and its language had to do justice to it. 'Job of writing caste histories that presented Hindu texts and the Brahminical system as noble and egalitarian, placing the entire responsibility for caste-based evils on Muslim invaders, thus obviating the need to amend religious texts in any way' (Meghwanshi, 226). The third step was to appropriate and taint the legacy of Ambedkar. Sangha not only manipulated and quoted Ambedkar out of context but also hailed him as a Sangha pracharak. They did not dare to accept the lower castes as equal but constructed new narratives to justify the caste bias. The fourth step aimed at tainting the image of any left-wing or progressive organisation. Any organisation that dared to differ in its ideology was labelled to be funded by the Christian Missionaries or Muslim patrons who always wanted to destabilise the harmony of Hindu Rashtra.

Meghwanshi's struggle was political, personal, and philanthropic. He did not only realise his caste identity but fought against all the propaganda that was subjected to make them 'untouchables'. He countered the narrative of Hindu Rashtra and questioned what space was designated for a Dalit in a nation that could not even eat with a lower caste man. His cry against injustice soon became a social cause and his never-tiring rigor has since been dedicated to unfolding any event of oppression against Dalits. Meghwanshi refused to contest in elections for he wanted to remain true to his cause and his courage was contagious. He met hundreds of people through his journey of rebellion, but he stood his ground for demanding his rights as a human being. The autobiography of a Dalit in RSS is not merely a story of Dalit oppression but a saga of well-documented political suppression of the untouchables. The ideology of Sangha seeps through the social fabric and has entered the veins of our nation. Meghwanshi's story inspires a change and demands an answer. He questions every Hindu and Non-Hindu. He commands to be heard and has created a social space for his ideology. The most pertinent question that he raises in his novel must be my concluding line, for it shakes a society out of its slumber of normalised oppression against Dalits.

> Far more painful and unbearable than bullets and bombs is the question, what is your caste, and the sudden change of behaviour upon learning it. This has to be *experienced* to be understood. Hearing or reading about it means nothing. (Meghwanshi, 179)

## Works Cited

Anderson, Benedict. *The Imagined Communities: Reflections on the Origin and Spread of Nationalism*. New York: Verso, 1983.

Gandhi, Mahatma. *What is Hinduism?* New Delhi: National Book Trust, 1994. pp. 1-11.

McAfee, Noelle. *Julia Kristeva*. London: Routledge, 2015. p. 33.

Meghwanshi, Bhanwar. *I Could Not Be Hindu: The Story of a Dalit in the RSS*. New Delhi: Navayana, 2020.

Savarkar, V.D. *Hindutva*. 5th ed. Mumbai: Veer Savarkar Prakashan, 1969.

Tagore, Rabindranath. *Nationalism*. New York: Macmillan, 1917.

# 17

# Unpleasant Childhood Memories Pertaining to Poverty and Untouchability in Aravind Malagatti's *Government Brahmana*

*Sanjay Kumar*

Multi-faceted phenomena of poverty, hunger, untouchability, and discrimination are rampant in Indian Dalit autobiographies. These autobiographies are called the capsules of agony and pain, and that's why being a Dalit is no longer considered a matter of shame for Dalits as they accept it the part of their destiny or they are helpless in front of the corrupt social system. Many profound issues are found in the Dalit personal narratives.

Dalit Literature always revolves around caste prejudices; the stigmatized bodies of caste-ridden society and untouchability remain the focal trope of Dalit writings. Many Dalit writers have focused on the dichotomy of caste and untouchability as projected by many Dalit writers.

Among such writers, Aravind Malagatti is one of the most significant figures of Kannada Literature. He has raised his voice against all kinds of discrimination against Dalits. He earned his popularity due to his vast contribution to creative writing. He has written his creative pieces in the form of poetry, essays, folklore study, plays, criticism, and autobiography. He won the most prestigious Ambedkar Fellowship Award for his autobiography *Government Brahmana*. It is the first Dalit autobiography in Kannada, which bagged him the Karnataka Sahitya Academi Award.

Aravind Malagatti was born on May 1, 1956 in a Maali caste in Holeya Community at Muddebhihal, a small town in the Bijapur district in Karnataka state. His father, Yallappa, was a teacher, while her mother, Basavva, was a homemaker. Aravind Malagatti, like many other Dalit writers, had to see the bad time even in his childhood. His father passed away by scorpion stinging when Malagatti was merely ten months old. It was his uncle who brought him and his two brothers, Ramasamy and Basavaraju. He was weak in his studies in his school time. He started taking an interest in his studies after being admitted to MGV College, Muddebhihal. He joined Karnataka University in 1987 and did his PhD in Folklore studies. Dr Malagatti has worked as a professor in the Kuvempu Institute of Kannada Studies and Director of Jayalakshmi Vilas Palace Museum in the University of Mysore. He was the director of the Publication Division of the University of Mysore.

He has published around forty-two books. Dr Keshava Sharma writes about his writings:

> His writings take up a social criticism in the process of searching for a human being. Therefore, his writings have become a social question rather than an expression of writing skill. Structurally this is the secret of the uniqueness of his works. (Sharma, 18)

Aravind Malagatti's *Government Brahmana* was published in 1994 and was translated into English by Dharani Devi Malagatti, Janet Vucinich, and N. Subramanya. He has written in the form of dialogues between writer and reader. He gives a prominent place to his readers; that's why he asks questions from readers so that he may know what his readers think about

Dalits' lives. His autobiography opens with the following lines: "I do not have any illusions of becoming Mahatma by presenting these few pages of my life story. I am quite ordinary" (Malagatti, 1). Like several other Dalit writers, he also thinks of himself as an ordinary person. In this autobiography, he gives a special place to his community because he believes that he is a part of that community. He describes the troubles and tribulations of his community and how they were forced to live in a spate settlement called Keri in Kannada.

They had the most prominent house in the Keri, and other people of his community would consider them rich, but they had to struggle to make both ends meet. The children of his community would become happy when they come to know about the news of a death in the upper caste family because the people would throw coins on the dead body, and the Dalits would pick up these coins. Aravind Malagatti narrates it in his autobiography:

> The coins were thrown such that they would roll through the feet of the corpse-bearer and the mourners who followed them...After everyone had walked on them, we had to pick up the coins. No sooner had they walked on the coins than the older ones among us scrambled for the loose change....Among the loose change they threw on the corpse, the highest denomination would be the five paisa coin. Coins with a hole in the center, one paisa, and two paisa coins were more in number. If the family was rich, then ten paisa coins would the highest denomination. The more their value, the lesser the number of coins that were thrown. When we got coins of higher denomination, our joy knew no bounds. (Malagatti, 8-9)

Aravind Malagatti describes the poverty of the whole community. There is a chapter in this autobiography entitled "Coins on the Corpse, and Wedding Feast" in which Malagatti describes a joyous occasion of marriage ceremony of Shetji's daughter in the village. The Dalits of the village wait for the grand feast. Malagatti writes about this memory:

> As we were used to eating roti and nuchchu...we considered even rice and saaru festival food. We had those items only once or twice a year, during Deepavali or Nagarapanchami. Dalits of surrounding village also attended Shetji's daughter marriage. Of course, for the meal. That day, the Dalit had outnumbered the others. (Malagatti, 9)

Aravind Malagatti describes how Dalit children had to support their family in their family professions. There is a chapter "Dead Sheep and Meat Heaps," in which Aravind has to attend the meat shop when his uncle has to go somewhere. He had to pour water while skinning the dead animals. The children of his community played games with the shit and intestines of sheep. He narrates about it:

> I was the owner if Maava was out. A big heap fetched eight annas and a small one four annas. The buyers were none other than the people of our lane. Most of our energy was spent driving away from the flies. Not one or two, but many! And so many varieties too! There were the blind flies, green flies- all flying in front of our eyes. Sometimes we were so fed up of chasing them away from that we killed them with our hands. (Malagatti, 33)

The people of his community did not have any substantial work to do. They worked once or twice a week, and on other days, they remained out of work. There were no facilities for a good house, pure water, electricity, and sanitation. He had to study in the light of kerosene or street light. He could not prepare well for his examinations. Aravind Malagatti describes it:

> My study would take a serious turn only when there was a month or two left for exams. Electric bulbs had just then made an entry into our village. But they had not yet

> entered any of the houses. I had hence made it a habit to study under the street lamp. Sometime even when there was no power, I would light a kerosene lamp and study under the same pole, waiting for the electricity to be restored. (Malagatti, 57)

The poverty conditions of her community were so bad that the women of her community had to resort to prostitution in order to earn money. The poor and helpless women had to adopt this profession, and every prostitute would have her own story, "Every prostitute in the colony had her own story. Some lived by tying a replica of goddess Yellamma's feet around their neck...some women had settled into it after being deserted by their husband and few others were simply continuing their traditional profession" (Malagatti, 55). Aravind, as a boy, wished to eat sweet, but due to his poverty, he could not purchase it. He would steal cotton so that he may eat sweets. The upper caste people to whom he would sell the cotton would encourage him for stealing more instead of guiding him that stealing is wrong:

> 'Get double of what you have brought just now. I will give it to you then.' He looked at another fellow sitting in his shop and giggled. 'What a boy you are! You should bring more cotton. Then people will appreciate you.' The other fellow, too, encouraged me, 'Go and bring a lot more; he will give you two undis.' I decided to collect double the cotton the next day. Usually, two or three of us would go together to steal cotton. (Malagatti, 40)

In *Government Brahmana*, Aravind Malagatti narrates different kinds of discrimination. The people of his community had to suffer at the hands of upper castes, and they were discriminated against based on caste. Aravind was humiliated and exploited due to his lower caste. He was getting stipend from the government, and that's why the upper caste students called him a "Government Brahmana" which is also the title of this autobiography:

> They teased me endlessly. Since I was getting the government's reservation policy benefits, they called me 'Government Brahmana'....When I went to college wearing the dress Appa had got stitched for me, they would question me, 'Is your dress a gift from Indramma?' Even then, I was unable to refute their words. There was every possibility of my answer leading to another taunt. So, I never attempted any justification. (Malagatti, 61)

Most of the students of his class belonged to upper castes, and there were only four low caste students. There were different seating arrangements for the upper and the lower caste students. Dalit students had to sit on a different section on the floor while the upper caste students would sit on wooden benches. Even after that they would make fun of Aravind, "Hey, it seems his chonna gets dirty. Wow! The great chonna!" (Malagatti, 15).

Aravind Malagatti was burning within himself to hear the above words, and he was deeply humiliated by this incident. Not only students but even the teachers would also show discriminatory attitudes toward Dalit students. They had to do all the menial work by coming earlier in the school. They would sweep the classrooms before going to morning prayers. Even there was the provision of severe punishment for them:

> Fold your hands in the style of a namaskar. Then interweave your finger together, okay? Now the fingers of your right hand are clutching your left hand, and the fingers of your left hand are clutching your right hand, aren't they? All right. Now hang yourself on a peg on wall, such that there is sufficient distance between the floor and your legs...the peg should be located between your braided fingers. Yes, that's right...when we hang in such a manner, we could not even loosen the grip of our fingers and fall on the ground. (Malagatti, 12)

Aravind Malagatti and the other lower-caste students had to bear different types of punishments in the school. Aravind writes that it was a kind of torture to them. He narrates about this incident, "One had to stand (half sit) in the posture of a chair, bending one's knees. It is impossible to maintain this position for long: after a while, one would inevitably sit down by folding the knees fully. To prevent us from doing so, two thick and slightly sharp pieces of wood were placed in the hollow behind the kneecaps" (Malagatti, 13). The students tried to humiliate Dalit children in different ways. They would write Aravind Malagatti's name differently on the blackboard. It was written as "Mala Katti" or "Katti" because the word 'Katti' means a donkey or an ass. Even his teacher punished him, taking the favour of the upper caste students. His teacher roared in anger, "So what if it is written as "Katti"? The bastard has just learnt to write and he already wants to correct what is written. A Katti is a Katti anyway. Can a donkey ever become a horse...?" (Malagatti, 16). His teacher kept beating him until Aravind took off his shirt and mopped the chair.

Aravind Malagatti speaks about some traditions in which he criticizes the upper caste people who would look at the other women with incestuous eyes. It was Okuli, a kind of festival in which women had to remove their blouses and wrap their saris to cover their heads and breasts. Men would splash coloured water on them, and women were expected to chase them and beat them or throw water on them. Aravind Malagatti narrates, "As the men splashed coloured water on the women repeatedly, the women chased them to take revenge, not bothering about their wet bodies and the loose end of their sari falling down from their heads. Their wet bodies, breasts, and thighs all bared to give free entertainment to the lecherous audience and the lustful players. The 34 red and yellow shades of colour that splashed on the women's bodies time and again gave the scene of effect of an Eastman colour movie" (Malagatti, 43). Only Dalit women were primarily engaged in that kind of practice, and the upper-caste women were exempted from this act. Dwaipayan Mitra writes about this tradition, "This dehumanizing game offered a sort of ribald entertainment for the audience and the real and yellow shades of colour gave the scene a flavour of a colour movie" (Mitra, 116). Aravind writes that both upper caste men and Dalit women had to perform a nude dance at Dharwad. He notes that programmes like 'feeding shit to Dalit' are still held in Savadatti.

The untouchability issue was serious among human beings; the upper caste people did not like it even in their pets. The chapter entitled "The She-Buffalo on Heat and the He-Buffalo after Her" exposes the stigma of untouchability even in domestic animals. The upper caste people did not give their he-buffalo to mate with the Dalits' she-buffalo. Aravind Malagatti provides another instance to substantiate the fact. A dog of a lower caste owner is brutally castrated just because it was trying to mate with his dog. Aravind pens down this incident in the following words, "Announcing that it is a dog belonging to the lower castes, he lashes its penis with a sickle" (Malagatti, 53). Smita Narula in a report entitled "Hidden Apartheid: Caste Discrimination against India's Untouchables" writes that Dalits are the most "vulnerable and exploited people in India" (Malagatti, 14). Apart from it, Dalit children were discriminated against in the school due to their caste. They had to sit separately and were forced to clean the school premises. Both the teachers and students humiliated them. Aravind Malagatti writes that his teachers would beat them more as compared to upper-caste students.

Thus, Aravind Malagatti's *Government Brahmana* chronicles the dynamics of caste discrimination, the utter poverty conditions of Dalits, and issues of untouchability. Dalit people were not given the status of human beings and were treated just like animals. Aravind Malagatti narrates, "If a Dalit happened to touch an upper caste person's vessel, it had to be smeared with cow dung and burnt in fire. It would then be immersed in a solution of tamarind and salt" (Malagatti, 102). R. Janani says that "Malagatti questions this denial of Dalits for ages and he has become the voice for his whole community whose struggle still continues" (Janani, 10). This autobiography presents the pictorial description of the lives of Dalits in the form of a criticism of caste discrimination in Aravind Malagatti's community. S. Johny writes in this context, "The title *Government Brahmana* might be intriguing to those who are familiar with Indian caste system outwardly. It might look like an irony" (Johny, 52).

## Works Cited

Janani, R. "Identity Crisis and Search for Self in Aravind Malagatti's Autobiography *Government Brahmana*." *Language in India*. 14.1 (2014): 1-11. January 21, 2014.

Johny, S. "Aravind Malagatti's *Government Brahmana*: A Discourse on Suppression and Survival." *Language in India*. www.languageinindia.com 16.08 (2016): 50-58.

Kanger, Kusum. "Problems of Maali Caste in Aravind Malagatti's Autobiography *Government Brahmana*." *Dalit Men's Autobiographies: A Critical Appraisal*. Ed. Bijender Singh. New Delhi: Kalpaz Publications, 2017. 123-128.

Malagatti, Aravind. *Government Brahmana*. Trans. Janet Vucinich, N. Subramanya and Dharani Devi Malagatti. Chennai: Orient Longman, 2007.

Mitra, Dwaipayan. *Indian Dalit Autobiographies: Marginalised Voices*. Ed. Singh, Bijender. New Delhi: Authorspress, 2015. 114-120.

Narula, Smita. "Hidden Apartheid: Caste Discrimination against India's Untouchables." *Human Rights Watch*. 2007. Web. January 8, 2014.

Sharma, Keshava. "Selected Writings of Prof. Aravind Malagatti." *Dalit India*, July 24, 2011. Web. June 9, 2013.

Singh, Bijender, (ed.). "Introduction." *Different Dimensions of Dalit Discourse*. New Delhi, Atlantic Publishers & Distributors, 2019. ix-xxiii.

# 18

# Writing Resistance: Journey from Marginality to Centrality in Surajpal Chauhan's *Tiraskrit* and *Santampt*

*Dr Avinash Kumar*

Literature and life are complementary to each other; neither life can be segregated from literature, nor literature from life. Autobiography remains very close to the authors because it occupies the personal experiences of their life. Readers find it very fascinating because it is an authentic record of a person's life. The readers feel happy to know the personal experiences of the life of their favourite authors. Literature can be called the criticism of life and Dalit Literature can be called the criticism of the people who sit at the best rank in the social hierarchy but think the worst and have a distorted mentality. Baburao Bagul writes about Dalit Literature:

> Dalit literature is not a literature of vengeance. Dalit Sahitya is not a literature which spread hatred. Dalit Sahitya first promotes man's greatness and man's freedom and for that reason it is an historic necessity. (Bagul, 56-57)

Surajpal Chauhan was born on 20th April 1955 in a Dalit family, in a village named Fusavali in Aligarh district of Uttar Pradesh. His father Roshanlal was a labourer and he would do whatever work he got. His mother Ashrafia worked in the houses of the Thakurs and Brahmins of the village. He had one younger brother. His family members were living their life in utter poverty as they don't have any agricultural land and they have a hut-like structure which they called their house.

Surajpal Chauhan started helping the poor and Dalit children in their studies just because he knew it well that he was very poor at one time and that is why he feels himself close to those children. Surajpal Chauhan was influenced by two persons in his life: Dr B. R. Ambedkar and Omprakash Valmiki. He received many awards, achievements and honour. He was featured in many magazines and TV programmes and established himself as a great Dalit poet, short story writer and an author. He was suffering from kidney failure and was put on dialysis. He took his last breath on 15 June, 2021.

Surajpal Chauhan's autobiographies have been written mainly about his personal experiences as a child and adult. Apart from it, he has also written about the hard work and humiliated life of his parents and community in his autobiographies. His mother was suffering from diabetes and back pain; still she had to work. Due to excessive working, her health deteriorated and ultimately, she died.

Surajpal Chauhan's father was an uneducated and highly conservative person who believes in the Hindu Gods and Goddesses. He was indulged in superstitious activities and also sacrificed cows, goats and pigs to please the Hindu deities. When Surajpal's mother was ill, he did not take her to a doctor, instead he rushed to the sorcerers, which was not a treatment at all. Ultimately, he took her to the doctors but he was too late.

This incident is quite similar with an incident of Sheoraj Singh Bechain's autobiography *My Childhood on My Shoulders* (2018). In the first chapter of his autobiography, he narrates how his father died just because he was not taken to doctors and once again sorcerers were approached for his treatment too. He also could not survive without treatment. It was the poverty which was a great curse just because they needed money for the treatment but being poor they could not pay doctor's fee. Moreover, the main reason behind it remained their ignorance. They did not know the importance of the medical science at that time. Many people die due to lack of proper treatment just because hospitals are not easily available and the poor people cannot afford it.

After his mother's death, Surajpal's father took him to Delhi near Khan Market where they made a hut but unfortunately it was demolished by the Municipal Corporation. His father worked as a loader at Hazrat Nizamuddin Railway Station, New Delhi. While working at the railway station, he came to know the value of education. He wanted that his son may get good education and stand on his own feet.

Surajpal has narrated one more incident of his life. His mother did sweeping work in the locality and Surajpal Chauhan also helped her a lot. He put the garbage in the bucket and she disposed it off. In this way, he helped his mother. One day his mother was ill and therefore she could not go to clean the garbage. After some time a Thakur named Pratap came and started abusing her and ordered her to clean their locality immediately. When she told him that she is not well, then the Thakur forced Surajpal Chauhan to work in lieu of mother until she gets back to work. Surajpal also described how one day Thakur Jaisingh tried to molest his mother:

> After some time I heard my mother's scream. I ran towards her. Thakur Jaisingh has embraced my mother tightly. My mother was moving her limbs and was crying. I was shocked to see my mother's miserable condition. My mother's *dupatta* was thrown away by him. I was merely a child but my eyes flared red with anger. I did not see anything nearby. But there was a broom besides me. Without any delay, I started hitting him at his back with my full strength....my mother hit at his vital organs. (*Santapt* 24-25)

When the people gathered there, they were talking in the favour of Thakur Jaisingh. Thakur Pratap also caught his mother by her hair and said, "*Saali Bhangin*, you don't feel shame on putting false accusation. Who will blemish his mouth with a *Bhangin*? He will be polluted even with your touch. If you want your favour, get lost from here immediately" (*Santapt*, 24-25). Even Thakur's wife also took her husband's side and said, "O my *Sautin Chuhri*, you are only a fairy queen in the whole village that my husband ..." (*Santapt*, 24-25). This scene is quite similar with one incident of Mulk Raj Anand's novel *Untouchable* in which Pundit Kali Nath tried to molest Bakha's sister Sohini when she came to his house to clean the toilets. When she cried and her brother Bakha reached there and, he lost his temper, "Son of a pig! . . . I will go and kill him" (*Untouchable*, 63). But all the upper caste people started taking the favour of Kali Nath. Bakha felt helpless as he could not do anything. He just said, "My poor sister! How can she show her face to the world after this? . . . why was she born a girl in our house?" (*Untouchable*, 65). Lalmingthani aptly observes, "We can see from reading Dalit literature that spends several decades, that the suffering of the untouchables is a never ending chain (Lalmingthani, 11).

Surajpal's childhood was full of struggles. He could not enjoy his life like others. He has suffering from the stigma of caste throughout his life, like Bakha in Mulk Raj Anand's *Untouchable* (1935). He had to wear old clothes and he would remain bare-foot. He describes how he brought a torn pair of shoes thrown by someone and his father got the shoes mended and gave him to wear. He would never go to the barber's saloon because barbers would not trim the hair of the *Bhangis* and Chamars at that time. That is why his mother brought scissors from the market and trimmed his hair at home.

Surajpal writes that his family was in so much poverty that the family members did not get the sufficient food to eat. He narrates an incident how he would eat the stale food thrown by a *dhaba* at night. Dogs would growl at him because he was taking the food of theirs. He narrates:

> My childhood was spent in great deprivation. I also craved for dry roti crumbs. The servants of the *dhabas* and restaurants of the Pandara Road Market used to throw the garbage at one place in the morning. Before dawn, I would choose and eat the small pieces of bread, while on the other hand, the dogs of the street would also eat that leftover. Sometimes the dogs would growl at me because I used to eat their share of food. (*Santapt*, 47)

Surajpal Chauhan had to massage a Russian woman, who worked in a circus. He was merely a boy at that time. She exploited him physically and mentally. His *tai* Santo and maternal uncle Munshi were behind all this. Thus, Surajpal's life remained full of challenges and he did not find the people who supported him at his worst time.

He has depicted many incidents of untouchability and caste discriminations in his autobiographies. He had a friend named Veeru who belonged to Thakur caste. One day he was playing with him and his father, Thakur Pratap noticed him playing with Surajpal. He immediately took him to the well and pulled a bucket full of water and poured water on Veeru. Being a child Veeru could not understand what was happening with him and he just asked why you are splashing water on me. His father slapped and told him that you were playing with a *Bhangi* child and still asking what has happened. This incident about untouchability has been described in the following words:

> Thakur dragged his son Veeru towards the well. I was looking at them with teary eyes fixed on the wall. Thakur drew a water bucket from the well and started sprinkling the neem twig in the water. Veeru said while crying, "Why are you pouring water on me?" His father replied, "O quiet, unworthy, you defiled himself by playing with the *Bhangi*

> and now you ask why you are splashing water. Thakur Pratap said while slapping Veeru's face. (*Tiraskrit*, 29-30)

Surajpal Chauhan was admitted in Deewana Chand Arya Higher Secondary School, Lodhi Road, New Delhi. He had to go to his school without shoes or slippers even in scorching heat. It was his responsibility to cook food and the school time was from 10 AM to 4 PM during winter. He would sometimes go empty stomach and would fall in the school due to malnutrition. He started wearing slippers in the sixth class.

Surajpal Chauhan was married with Vimala in 1975. Even after his marriage, he had to face many difficulties. His father was also not happy after Surajpal's marriage and started quarrelling with him because of his wife was less co-operative. His wife and her family members would taunt Surajpal for not getting a job and suggest him to do the work of a sweeper.

Surajpal's wife, Vimala had an affair with his nephew Jaiprakash. He openly shows his lust for Vimala. Chauhan mentioned about it in his work *Tiraskrit*:

> It was a matter of surprise that she did not oppose him. She has proved from her behaviour that she was prodding him. After few days Vimala proved through her actions that she had fallen in the deep mud with him. Once after falling, she kept on falling. She not only spoilt her and her husband's old age, she destroyed the life of his daughter Madhu and son Bhanu. (*Santapt*, 95)

She gave it in writing in the court that she did not want to live with him. After that day Surajpal's life became more problematic and he devoted himself to writing completely. Surajpal has depicted the extra-marital relationships in his autobiography. He had seen how the wife of a Thakur had illicit relationship with his uncle. He has written how upper caste women also exploited Dalit men.

However, life takes U-Turn and Surajpal got a job of Deputy-Manager and later he was promoted as a Manager. His financial freedom provides better education and lifestyle to his children. His prosperity was not liked by the upper-class people as they would say that he is on a reputed post and belongs to a good economic background so it is not justified to call him a Dalit:

> "Are, you have a car, a government house, have telephone etc all facilities. You are on a good government job of a Deputy-Manager. Your daughter is also doing you MSc. What sort of Dalit you are?" (*Tiraskrit,* 9)

Surajpal Chauhan first autobiography *Tiraskrit* was published in 2002 and his second autobiography *Santapt* was published after four years in 2006. Some people raised doubts, why he wrote two autobiographies being a single person. Surajpal Chauhan said defending himself that he has written those experiences in his second autobiography which he could not write in his previous book. In his autobiographies, he writes how the upper caste people did not want that Dalits may achieve success in their life. He writes how they would curse the Congress who has given equal right to Dalits and they did not like that Dalit people also reach at the top posts. Surajpal Chauhan has described all this in his autobiography *Triskrit,* "These *Saale* Chuhras and Chamars are moving ahead in life by reading and writing. Just look at Jagjivan Ram Chamar, he has reached the post of Defense Minister" (*Tiraskrit,* 17).

Surajpal feels very bad to hear such words. Surajpal Chauhan opposes it many times, but the upper caste boys would get united and would say considering him also an upper caste, "Chauhan, who do you get annoyed to see these talks regarding these Chuhras and Chamars? You are a Thakur. (*Tiraskrit,* 17)

Surajpal Chauhan describes his school experiences as a Dalit boy. There were total five Dalit boys in his class who sat separately under a *peepal* tree. They brought a sack from their house and sat on it. The upper caste teachers did not pay much attention to them. In fact, many of them did not like that these Dalit students may learn anything. They would think if these students become officers who will work for them. They had this type of mentality.

He has narrated the incident of his Sanskrit teacher Vedpal Sharma who was teaching him well but when he came to know that he is a Dalit, he started avoiding him. One day he asked a question from his teacher why Ekalavya gave his thumb as a *gurudakshina*? Instead of replying, he started beating him badly. Not only that day, his teacher would beat him without any rhyme and reason.

When he asked the question from Gupta teacher, he told him to study properly and he would automatically get the answers of his questions. Surajpal Chauhan has written in his autobiography that he was considered a Dalit even in Delhi. He was feeling so much frightened of his caste that he decided to hide his identity. He made few friends in the college. Among them Anupam Verma was one of his best friends during his college days. One day he saw Surajpal's name in the list of Dalit students. He was shocked and immediately asked Surajpal whether he was a Dalit. Surajpal was feeling numb and humiliated, and he was not able to utter a single word. While going Anupam said more humiliating words that now *Chuhras* and Chamars have also started writing their surname as Chauhan. It was the most shocking incident of Surajpal's life.

Chauhan was a real voice of Dalit writing who always fought for the social equality for the stereotype society. He belonged to the Dalit caste but he never felt untouchable from inside. He established himself as Chauhan. Actually the surname Chauhan represents the upper caste Rajput community, so he put his surname Chauhan to became voice of voiceless. Through his charismatic writing he gives new dimension to Dalit writing.

Thus, Surajpal Chauhan's both the autobiographies *Tiraskrit* and *Santapt* are full of pain and humiliation. Surajpal Chauhan's early days remained full of miseries and struggles. His childhood days, like many other Dalit writers, were full of challenge as the upper caste people exploited them. His writing stands unparalleled and consummate which seems to be the voice of every voiceless i.e. Dalit. Arjun Dangle writes about Dalit Literature:

> Dalit literature is not simply literature; it is associated with the movement to bring about change. It represents the hopes and ambitions of a new society and new people. (Dangle, 266)

## Works Cited

Anand, Mulk Raj. *Untouchable* (1935). London: Penguin, 1985.

Bagul, Baburao. "Dalit Sahitya: Man's Greatness, Man's Freedom." *Asmitadarsh*, Vol. I, (1973): 56-57.

Chauhan, Surajpal. *Santapt*. New Delhi: Anubhav Publication, 2006.

—. *Tiraskrit*. New Delhi: Vani Prakashan, 2002.

Dangle, Arjun. *Poisoned Bread: Translations from Modern Marathi Dalit Literature*. Hyderabad: Orient Longman, 1992.

Iyengar, K. R. Srinivasa. *Indian Writing in English*. New Delhi: Sterling, 1984.

# 19

# Traumatic Experiences amid Struggle for Education: A Study of D. R. Jatava's Autobiography *A Silent Soldier*

*Dr Vinod K. Chopra*

India—a country with rich history, culture, and heritage—has equally been infamous across the globe for a special type of social stratification in the form of castes resulting in untouchability. J. Webster rightly asserts in his *Dalit Christians* that untouchability is the age-old social problem in Indian history since the later Vedic Period between 600 B.C. and A.D. 200 (Manna, 358). The word, *Varna* clearly refers to the colour of skin and hair of the people of two different races: the Aryan Varna and the Krishna Varna in the *Rigveda*. The Aryan considered themselves superior whereas non-Aryans were treated as non-humans or *amanushya*. Though the evidence of caste is to be found in many parts of the world, but the most perfect and detestable instance is the one that is still pervasive in India. It is perhaps the world's largest surviving social hierarchy, which encompasses a complex ordering of social groups on the basis of ritual purity. A person is considered a member of the caste into which he or she is born and remains within that cast until death. Further difference in status is traditionally justified by religious doctrine of *Karma*, a belief that one's place in life is determined by one's deeds in previous lifetime. A.R. Desai has rightly asserted that "Hallowed with tradition and sanctified by religion, it continued to exist in all its barbarous vigor for centuries." (268)

Primarily, the evaluation of the caste system was meant to accommodate diverse racial elements into a meaningful whole, assigning duties and functions among communities. It was supposed to avoid conflict and competition. Unfortunately, this caste system has proved to be a black spot on the Indian culture. This caste system gave birth to untouchability and classified some groups as untouchable and unsociable. Mahatma Gandhi described untouchability as "the hatefullest expression of caste" (Hutton, 97). Indian caste system has been attacked from various quarters from time to time and has been attributed numerous evils from which society has been suffering. However, it still thrives in spite of all these attacks. A.R. Naronaker rightly avers, "Despite several forcing invasions, racial reform movements, the caste system has remained unaltered like Himalayas" (1). Throughout India, there are a number of Dalit castes like Mahars of Maharashtra, Parihas of Tamil Nadu, Hari, Dom, and many others in other parts of India are not only humiliated but also exploited and treated with inequality. It is not only the problem of a group itself but it is a problem of the society as a whole. Ambedkar was right to mention in his *Writing and Speeches*, "Untouchability is an indirect form of slavery.... It is enslavement without making the untouchables conscious of their enslavement" (Mishra, 46). To Ambedkar it is impossible to institute as well as pre-suppose an era of equality, liberty and fraternity so long as we ostracise each other, excommunicate each other, exclude each other, segment each other, stigmatise each other, hierarchise each other and segregate each other on caste grounds.

It is all owing to its prestigious nature and racial foundation that the institution of untouchability being an offshoot of the caste system in India has proved to be unique. No person in the world with a sense of humanism and same amount of civilisation could justify or defend this heinous and inhuman institution of untouchability (Naronaker, 81). Of late, untouchable word is seldom used as the use of the term untouchable is not appropriate since the day untouchability has been prohibited by law.

Untouchables are named in diverse terms. Mahatma Gandhi called them *Harijan*—children of God, though considered a derogatory term. They are called *Shudras* as per the religious books of the Hindus. Ambedkar called them "Depressed Classes". The term 'Dalit' has extensively been used since 1970. It was Mahatma Jotirao Phule, a 19th cen-tury social reformer who used this Marathi word 'Dalit'—"broken people"—for untouchables or lower caste people. He was the harbinger of a movement for the upliftment of untouchables. Officially, they are designated as the Scheduled Castes.

So much injustice and systematic discrimination has been done to Dalits for centuries. Curiously, the bases of this discrimination, as is the case with other countries, were not religion, language, sex or colour. Rather it was "caste" or "birth", which is unique.

In fact, untouchability is a stigma and ignominy on the glorious culture of India. The institution of untouchability was based on the consideration of defilement, pollution, racial discrimination and mixture of blood and beastly deeds. The untouchables were outside the *Chaturvarna* system and assigned such lower duties as those of scavengers—to clean and to remove dead cattle. They were socially and legally debarred from any other profession. They had no right to study or enter a temple. They had to live in a separate area in a village or town and had no freedom to use public wells and tanks which the caste Hindu used (Ambedkar, 100). For centuries, they have been struggling to achieve an equal status in society.

It is really a great matter of concern and that even after more than 70 years of Indian Independence and a plethora of legislative laws that disallow discrimination against Dalits, they are still oppressed and discriminated against in the name of caste. The present paper studies D. R. Jatava's autobiography *A Silent Soldier* to focus on the author's struggle for education. The way Jatava has penned down his trauma and bitter experiences at school does not limit his experiences to himself; rather he becomes a mouthpiece of others like him who also suffer the same way he has suffered. Not on a single point it seems that he is giving a subjective account of his personal life that is full of pain, humiliation, discrimination and oppression. The account of D. R. Jatava's life as articulated in his autobiography is as real as that of Omprakash Valmiki's life in *Joothan* and Laxman Gaikwad's life in *The Branded*. All of them represent their communities of Dalits in a very lucid style. After going through these autobiographies, one's heart-aches with pain and one wonders if anything has changed for Dalits after Independence.

Although untouchability is abolished under Article 17 of the Indian Constitution, Dalits are still the victims of this caste hierarchy. Their caste tag has brought them so much pain, suffering, humiliation and discriminations that their life history has become a traumatic experience for them. Article 15 of Indian Constitution prohibits discrimination against any citizen in any matter at the disposal of the State on any of the specified grounds, namely, religion, race, caste, sex or place of birth (Basu, 90). D. R. Jatava expresses the oppressed status of his forefathers:

> ...my forefathers were nonentities in the vast history of mankind. However, it would be enough to say, they were mere ciphers on the level of human existence. Why do I say so? For they belonged to the lot of unfortunate persons of the Hindu society, which was treated as despicable, and was known as the community of the untouchables of slave India. As untouchables, the forefathers were the poorest of the poor, whose mere touch, shadow or sight, was sufficient to pollute the people of the upper strata of society. They were deprived of all the roads leading towards education and

> enlightenment. In fact, they experienced the darkness of illiteracy, poverty and drudgery. They could not move freely, wear proper clothes; nor could they eat food of their choice and liking; they were actually engaged in forced labour or menial jobs. No rights, no amenities, doing all the filthy work since morning till the late evening, was their destiny. (1)

Their caste has become their destiny, because for being a Dalit they are forced to do menial jobs and simultaneously they are debarred from basic human rights. It is a fact that this notion of caste and destiny is sanctioned by the religion. (Bemal, 20). Religion calls it the doctrine of *Karma*. It is not for nothing that B. R. Ambedkar appealed to the community of untouchables to convert to other religions. He was forced by circumstances only when he found out that untouchables were neither allowed to enter temples nor were they allowed to participate in Hindu festivals:

> Religion if for man; man if not for religion
>
> If you want to gain self-respect, change your religion.
>
> If you want to create a cooperating society, change your religion.
>
> If you want power, change your religion.
>
> If you want equality, change your religion.
>
> If you want independence, change your religion.
>
> If you want to make the world in which you live happy, change your religion. (Zelliot, 192)

Actually, Ambedkar has positive plea in these lines, because he does not want to change the whole religion, he just wants to change the false notion of *karma* which debarred Dalits from their basic human rights. This is the reason that D. R. Jatava has written that his forefathers were the unfortunate persons of Hindu Society, who get in inheritance only untouchability and suffering. In childhood when D. R. Jatava listens to the painful incidents of their lives, his innocent heart starts cramping. But he consoles himself with the thought that these were the things of the past, now India has got independence and such incidents can never happen in free India, but it proves deceitful for him. His experience with untouchability starts in primary school "where things were harsh and hostile for an untouchable boy" (Jatava, 11). He remembers with pain, "The majority of boys and girls belonged to the upper strata of society; most of them being well-off, regarded themselves as superior. I was always cautious of their mischievous conduct. The caste feelings were rampant in the school, and I had to sit in an outside corner of the room, almost alienated from the other school-mates" (11).

Jatava's fate is not different from that of Omprakash Valmiki who expresses the same distressed fate, "I had to sit away from the others in the class, that too on the floor. The mat ran out before reaching the spot I sat on. Sometimes I would have to sit away behind everybody, right near the door. And the letters on the board from there seemed faded" (2-3). Both Jatava and Valmiki happened to join schools after independence. To them independence brought with it more sufferings, oppression, exploitation and discrimination, sadly, at the hands of their own countrymen. But soon children like Jatava and Valmiki adapted to these painful situations and kept going to school. Jatava is often looked down upon by the upper strata, and he also becomes the subject of humiliation and misconduct at the hands of teachers. His pain is expressed clearly in the following words:

> One Brahmin teacher was very cruel; he often beat us with a long stick of Babul or Neem trees; and he also asked us at times to become cocks. It was the worst type of punishment that any teacher could give to a student for the non-compliance of his wishes. We were not weak at our studies, but the caste discrimination had dominated that teacher's mind. It was but natural in a society, where things, thought

and behaviour, moved at the behest and volume of caste system. (11)

It is really a sad state of affairs that even after decades of independence the depressed classes are still at the mercy of those from upper castes who enjoy the power. In this context, we can give the reference of the report submitted on 17th September, 1996 in its forty-ninth session by the Committee on the Elimination of Racial Discrimination submitted by States Parties under Article 9 of the convention:

> It is noted that although constitutional provisions and legal texts exist to abolish untouchability and to protect the members of the scheduled castes and tribes, and although social and educational policies have been adopted to improve the situation of members of scheduled castes and tribes and to protect them from abuses, widespread discrimination against them and the relative impunity of those who abuse them point to the limited effect of these measures. The Committee is particularly concerned at reports that people belonging to the scheduled castes and tribes are often prevented from using public wells or from entering cafes or restaurants and that their children are sometimes separated from other children in schools, in violation of Article 5 (f) of the convention. (Web)

Isn't it more pathetic on the part of the Dalits that even today they are victimized in the name of caste and what would be more shameful for a country whose committee presents this bitter truth? Even today there are news of Dalit oppression and humiliation at the hands of upper caste people. It was on 6th October 2020 that the BBC Indian Correspondent, Soutik Biswas reported, under the headlines 'Hathras case: Dalit women are among the most oppressed in the world...', what a Dalit woman told researcher, Jayshree Mangubhai some years ago, "We are victims of violence because we are poor, lower caste and women, so looked down upon by all" (www. bbc.com).

Not only this, there are news of Dalit women allegedly gang raped by the group of upper caste men. Even today in schools one can witness discrimination on the basis of caste. Caste discrimination was reported in a government primary school in Uttar Pradesh's Ballia district where some students did not have their midday meals alongside Dalit schoolmates (Rashid n.pag.). Jatava somehow passed his matriculation in a life of penury. He had to suffer at the hands of upper caste students when he joined a college in Agra. He reminisces rather desperately:

> I faced the Chaube students. They not only discriminated against and alienated me, along with other scheduled caste hostellers, but also hated us. We were only five scheduled caste hostellers among the rest of the Chaubes of Mathura. They did not allow us to join the hostel mess. We had to go to Dhabas for our meals. We were allowed to use bath-rooms and toilets after all of them had finished their turns. They were always hostile and never exchanged talks. They openly practiced caste discrimination and showed all contempt to us because of our being untouchables. (22)

Sadly enough, even the Principal did not pay heed to their complaints and the Vice-Chancellor rebuked them for making such grievances against the Chaubes. Jatava had to struggle hard to get his PhD degree as one of the examiners appointed to evaluate his thesis was so rude that he humiliated him during the viva-voce and gave him shocking-treatment only because Jatava was an untouchable who worked on Ambedkar's philosophy. This was very hard to bear for an upper caste teacher to believe that Ambedkar had any philosophy. Jatava's viva-voce was taken time and again just to dawdle the final result.

It is not that Jatava belonged to a poor family and had to suffer humiliation at school and college for being an untouchable. Even Ambedkar who belonged to a well-off family had to undergo the same fate. He writes poignantly in his *Waiting for Visa:*

> The incident has a very important place in my life. I was a boy of nine when it happened. But it has left an indelible impression on my mind. Before this incident occurred, I knew that I was an untouchable and that untouchables were subjected to certain indignities and discriminations. For instance, I knew that in the school I could not sit in the midst of my class students according to my rank but that I was to sit in a corner by myself. I knew that in the school I was to have a separate piece of gunny cloth for me to squat on and the servant employed to clean the school would not touch my gunny bag used by me.... I could not touch the tap and unless it was opened for it by a touchable person, it was not possible for me to quench my thirst. (15-16)

D. R. Jatava bears all humiliation and misconduct as a silent soldier because he realises the truth that being an untouchable he must need courage to cope with obstructive circumstances in life. Here the title *A Silent Soldier* becomes suggestive, as the humiliating attitude of people around him has made him immune to the pain and harassment he is made to face. It is very clear that Jatava does not adopt the defeatist and pessimistic attitude in his struggle for education and to achieve social status in life. In his journey towards the achievement he ventures more bravely. He must have in his mind that only education can help him achieve respect in society as is clear in Savitribai Phule's "Haunted by 'The Gods on Earth'":

> For two thousand years,
> The perpetual service of the Brahmins,
> Became the plight of the Shudras
> Looking at their condition,
> The heart screams its protest,
> The mind blanks out,
> Struggling to find a way out
> Education is the path,

For the Shudras to walk,
For education grants humanity
Freeing one from an animal-like existence. (Sutradhar, 2167-68)

Ambedkar viewed education as a means for enlightenment that would provide a base for resistance to oppression. He championed the cause of Dalits and stood for their emancipation. He also thought that education was a primary factor to achieve it. Similarly, Jotirao Phule who worked for the upliftment of Dalits put special emphasis on education of Dalits so that they might win a respectable place in society. He has rightly asserted, "Ignorance, caste discrimination and discrimination based on language are the bane of this country. When everyone is sad, the question often arises of whom to help....it is better to help those for whom the suffering is the most....They can only overcome this suffering through knowledge. So, I first started work for them" (Sundararaman, 11).

Thus, it is clear after going through the autobiography of D. R. Jatava that caste system segregated the Dalits from the rest of the society to such an extent that they were denied even the basic human rights that one must enjoy in order to ensure one's bare existence. There is no use of bringing laws to protect Dalits from discrimination and oppression. One has to change the age-old feudal mindset as caste is the fixed notion in the mind of every Hindu. Ambedkar is right when he emphasises, "All reform consists in a change in the notion, sentiment and mental attitudes of the people towards men and things..." (Bhagat, 6). We cannot boast of having the largest democracy in the world until or unless people of upper caste change their notion of caste that is deep rooted in their mind. It is high time we in India acted like Australian reconciliation groups that asked aboriginals for apology. We must build solidarity with Dalits and act judiciously by extending love and care and must shun all ill-will and notion of humiliation and discrimination against them as they belong to us. Only then the healing will begin.

## Works Cited

Ambedkar, B. R. *Castes in India*. New Delhi: Samyak Prakashan, 2018.

—. *Waiting for Visa*. New Delhi: Samyak Prakashan, 2018.

—. *Writings & Speeches Vol. 5*. New Delhi: Dr Ambedkar Foundation, Ministry of Social Justice & Empowerment, Govt. of India, 1989.

Basu, D. D. *Introduction to the Constitution of India*. New Delhi: Printice-Hall of India Private Limited, 1992.

Bemal, Tofan. "Dr B. R. Ambedkar Crusador against Caste and Untouchability of Hindu Social Order.www.orisaagovt .in/e-magazine/arissareview/2008.

Bhagat, M. G. "Foreword". B. R. Ambedkar. *Castes in India*. New Delhi: Samyak Prakashan, 2018.

"Committee on the Elimination of Racial Discrimination Concluding Observations on Caste-broken People: Caste Violence Against..." https://www.hrw.org/reports/1999/india/994- 20.htm

Desai, A. R. *Social Background of India*. Bombay: Nationalism Book Depot, 1959.

"Hathras Case: Dalit Women are among the Most Oppressed in the World..." https://www.google.com/amp/s/www.bbc.com/news/world-asia-india-544418513.amp

Hutton, J.H. *Caste in India*. London: Oxford University Press, 1963.

Jatava, D. R. *A Silent Soldier: An Autobiography*. Jaipur: Samata Sahitya Sadan, 2000.

Manna, Samita. "The Sahish: A Stigma of Untouchability Devising Strategies for Their Survival." R. M. Sarkar. Ed. *Dalit in India*. New Delhi: Serial Publications, 2006.

Mishra, Bikram Keshari. "Dalits and Social Discrimination: Re-examining the Caste System in 21st Century." R.M. Sarkar. Ed. *Dalit in India*. New Delhi: Serial Publications, 2006.

Naronakar, A.R. *Untouchability and Caste System in India*. Delhi: Anmol Publications, 2003.

Rashid, Omar. "Schoolmates Shun Dalits during Midday Meal in UP's Primary School..." www.thehindu.com

Sundararaman, T. *Savitribai Phule*. New Delhi: NCERT, 2008.

Sutradhar, Ruman. "Dalit Struggle for Education: With Special Reference to Barak Valley". *International Journal of Science and Research (IJSR)*. Volume 3 Issue 12, December 2014. www.ijsr.net

Valmiki, Omprakrash. *Joothan: A Dalit's Life*. trans. Arun Prabha Mukherjee. Kolkata: Samya and New York: Columbia University Press, 2007.

Zelliot, Eleanor. *From Untouchable to Dalit: Essays on the Ambedkar Movement* (1992). New Delhi: Manohar Publisher & Distributors, rpt. 2005.

# 20

# Refugee Dalits and the Fight for Survival: A Study of *Surviving in My World* by Manohar Mouli Biswas

*Dr Tamanna*

> In these autobiographies, relating to different periods of time and set in different levels of society, we see varying facets of Dalit movement, the struggle for survival, the emotional universe of Dalit life; the man-woman relationship; the experiencing of humiliation and atrocities; at times, abject submission, at other times, rebellion. (Dangle, 1992: ix)

There is a long list of Indian Dalit writers but all of them are not equal in their writing style and reputation, but some of them have touched the pinnacle of their popularity due to their dedication to work. These writers have written their real life experiences in their autobiographies. Dalit discourse has become totally caste-based in the present context. Primarily it attempts to give voice to the sufferings, pains and struggles of those people who belong to the lower stratum of society and are not the part of the mainstream in the ancient four-fold social system of India and the present day caste-ridden society.

Caste gives a unique identity to a person in India. If a person is born is a low caste, he is not given the same place in the hearts of the upper caste people as he deserves. Indian social system has been based on the *varna* system since time immemorial. Initially it was based on the *karmas* (works) of people but later it was linked with the caste. The people, who adopted the work according to their skills, got their identity accordingly. A person who dealt in gold was called a goldsmith, a person who took agriculture as a profession was called a farmer, a person who engaged in leather work was known as Chamar, a person who started doing the work of cleaning was called a sweeper, and so on. The work of some people was of a low level and that was the reason that the people started maintaining distance from the calling them untouchables and in this way untouchability came into practice. Some Shudras who started doing the most inferior work were kept segregated by the upper caste society and they were the poorest people in the society and they were deprived of their fundamental rights also.

Dalit discourse can be better understood through the study of Dalit autobiographies because these autobiographies are the real and an authentic record of their oppression and exploitation. Among these Dalit writers, a prominent figure Manohar Mouli Biswas' contribution cannot be forgotten because he devoted himself for the service of Dalit literature. He is a bilingual poet, writer and essayist from Bengal. He was born in into Namasudra caste at Dakshin Matiargati, Khulna in East Bengal (now Bangladesh) in 1943. It was born in utter poverty but he continued his education and gradually established himself as a successful Dalit writer. It was the time when Dalit children usually did not go to school for getting education in India and only few parents paid attention towards it. Both Omprakash Valmiki and Laxman Gaikwad were the first members of their family who took admission in the school. They did not pay much attention to those students and teachers who made fun of them due to their low caste. Manohar Mouli Biswas faced all the obstacles and got his education. Currently he is the President of Bangla Dalit Sahitya Sanstha and is the editor of a bi-monthly literary magazine *Dalit Mirror* in English for more than a decade.

He has written four volumes of poems, one collection of short story, seven books of essays. He write his autobiography entitled *Amar Bhubaney Ami Benche Thaki* (2013) in Bangla and it was translated by Angana Dutta and Jaydeep Sarangi and was published in 2015 as *Surviving in My World : Growing Up Dalit in Bengal*. This autobiography has been prescribed in the syllabus of different universities in India. His poems also have been translated from Bangla to English and other languages. This autobiography depicts the saga of survival of Dalit people during the India-Bangladesh partition. He and his family had to move from the East Bengal to the West Bengal and these diasporic experiences, problems and fight for survival remain the dominant themes in this autobiography. Humayun S.K. writes that "Biswas' autobiography, *Surviving in My World*, has described the heavy burden of another kind of imposed identity of his Namashudra community" (175).

This is the main concern of all the Dalit autobiographies that there is somebody who inspired these Dalit writers when they were a child. In this autobiography also, the writer's father said, "The children must get educated" (Biswas, i). Manohar Mouli Biswas has depicted how he and his family have to face many problems as refugees after the partition from Bangladesh. He writes:

> My world is of great pain, one of being pitied by others...this world of mine is the Dalits' world of illiteracy, the Dalits' world of poverty, the world of keeping the Dalits powerless, the Dalits' world of sickness, the world of spending childhood in malnutrition the world of being unwanted, the world of jealousy-violence-hatred-abuse, the world of the multitudes staying alive, gasping. (xix)

Manohar Mouli Biswas knew that his children will get out of the clutches of casteism only after getting education. Mouli Biswas' grandfather also held the same opinion and he was also keen that the future generation should get education. He said,

"I do not know how to read and write. I could not make you all literate, but does it mean that even your children will remain as mukku, illiterate as this old man?" (Biswas, 2). There were very bad conditions of schools at that time and his school was set in a cowshed only when the cows would go for grazing. After some time the school building was constructed and the students started getting their education in school. His teacher was very cooperative and he would inspire his students to study well. Manohar Mouli Biswas recounts about this incident, "After we had stepped into school, hearing us speak, Amulya Master said, 'Forget the language you learned in the womb. The faster you can forget the faster you can learn the language of the books. The path of education will become smooth" (Biswas, 3).

Mouli Biswas writes about the ignorance of his parents. His parents were very poor and Manohar also had to help his family in the fields, and that's why his studies were getting affected. He writes, "I had to help Baba and Jetha on the land to such an extent that I could not concentrate on my studies" (Biswas, 6). He narrates an incident how his uncle ordered him to do some help in fishing. Biswas gets irritated to hear the orders of his uncle and he started ruminating as what sort of family I belong to that does not know the importance of education. He was solving a sum and Jetha ordered him to help him in his work. When Jetha came in the afternoon he noticed that Biswas was not reading and was writing something but his brother scolded him saying, "Who in your lineage ever became a pandit? I'll teach you a lesson for trying to become one!' Shouting these words, he raised a bamboo staff to hit me" (Biswas, 7-8).

It is really a challenge for a student to continue his studies smoothly when the members of his family are not aware about the value of education and fail to give time to the children. Sheoraj Singh also faced the same problem when his step-father quarrelled with Sheoraj's mother Mukhi and tells her to leave the children in their maternal-granduncle's house just because he could not afford the kerosene oil when Sheoraj would study at night. Biswas got inspiration from his teachers who encouraged him to study.

Manohar Mouli Biswas writes about the problem of untouchability in this autobiography. He narrates how his teacher Roychowdry appointed a boy of Kayastha caste as an office attendant showing nepotism. The people of his village had to face the wrath of nature sometimes in the form of famine and sometimes in the form of floods. The students would face the problem of going to school under such circumstances. The school was flooded with water in the rainy seasons and students would use boats to reach their school. The students were so poor that they did not get shoes to wear:

> The custom of wearing shoes was not yet prevalent. We walked barefoot to school. The condition was the same, be it sun or rain. Since we did not have umbrella's at home, its necessity never played in our minds. The years in which there would be heavy rain and the paths got submerged in water, we used to go to school climbing on boats like a donga or shalti, made by cutting a betel nut tree. (24)

Manohar Biswas was so poor that he had no money to buy the books when he took admission in college. He writes, "Now I had to arrange to buy my books, pay college fees, monthly hostel fees—tough time, loomed over my head" (25). He was very studious and would burn midnight oil. He writes about the days of his struggle in his autobiography:

> Every year during annual examinations, a great stress weighed down on me because I usually stood first in the class. This stress was generated due to the sole struggle for holding onto my position. Throughout the year I used to stay up late at night and study. I never limited myself to the books of the classroom. Everything of the world was unknown to me then. The innumerable things to be known of this unknown world raced behind me, almost touching me. I read and completed whatever book I could get hold

> of. Learning beforehand from the solved examples of the Maths book, I worked out Maths problems. Taking private tuition was not prevalent then. (26)

His family did not want to migrate to West Bengal during partition. Their condition became more critical after coming to West Bengal because they had no money in their pocket, no food to eat and no house to live in. Manohar Biswas had to travel without ticket in train just because he had no money to buy a ticket. He had to depend on the mercy of the ticket checker. He was sometimes allowed to travel by the ticket checker out of pity and sometimes he was thrown out of the train at some unknown station. He had to beg some food from a stranger's house when he was very hungry.

Manohar Biswas finds himself a foreigner in India. When he tried to get admission in a college in Uttar Pradesh, he was denied for it just because he had a foreign identity. After that he went to West Bengal by train without a ticket and took shelter in one of the distant relatives' house there. He took a loan of twenty thousand rupees from a distant uncle and took admission in a college. He was denied from the fellowship being a foreigner. Thus, he had to suffer a lot due to his refugee status. He compares himself with a hanging pendulum who does not find a fix place for it. He writes, "Yes, I become a vagabond refugee in India" (Biswas, 93). Thus, he suffered double marginalisation being a Dalit and a foreigner. S. Johny also writes that "Even though that double marginalisation was an excruciating experience, Biswas has successfully turned that experience into an autobiography that triggers empathy in readers" (Johny, 47).

Thus, this autobiography present the most painful experiences of a foreign Dalit refugee who is not well-accepted by the Indians. His identity as a foreigner brings the most difficult time for him. The complex dynamics of caste discrimination and diasporic identity crisis have been narrated in this autobiography. This autobiography throws light on the hurdles faced by a Dalit refugees and his family. Sutadripa Dutta Choudhury writes that this autobiography is about:

> Biswas's travel from the margin to the center against the oppressive hegemonic mechanism of power, caste, and tradition that intends to subdue the voice of the marginalised people under the monopoly of the ideology of mainstream Bengali 'bhodrolok' culture and society. It will serve as a reflection of our society where caste creates barriers within our hearts, our love, and ourselves....Dalits have been subject to oppression regardless of time and Manohar Mouli Biswas quite justly has mirrored his sufferings as a Dalit in his work, *Surviving in My World*. (48)

## Works Cited

Biswas, Manohar Mouli. *Surviving in My World: Growing Up Dalit in Bengal.* Trans Angana Dutta and Jaydeep Sarangi. Kolkata: Stree Samya, 2015.

Johny, S. "Voices of a Subaltern Diaspora: A Reading of Manohar Mouli Biswas' *Surviving in My World*". *Research Journal of English Language and Literature (RJELAL).* 5.2 (April-June 2017). 44-47.

SK, Humayun. "The Narrative of Imposed Identity and Epistemic Violence: A Comparative Study of Laxman Gaikwad's "The Branded Uchalya" and M.M. Biswas's "Surviving in My World". *The literary Hreald: An International Refereed English e-Journal in English.* 2.2 (September 2016). 170-180.

Choudhury, Sutadripa Dutta. "Societal Shallowness Compelling Manohar Mouli Biswas to Delineate his Own World of Suffering in *Surviving in My World*: Growing up Dalit in Bengal. "*International Journal of English Literature and Social Sciences.* 6.2 (Mar-Apr 2021) 47-53.

# 21

# Voicing the Miseries of Dalit Lives: Rereading Omprakash Valmiki's *Joothan: A Dalit's Life*

*Dr Budhanath Pratihast*

Omprakash Valmiki is one of the prominent figures of Hindi Dalit Literature whose contribution is so great that it will not be an exaggeration to say that Valmiki laid the foundation of Hindi Dalit Literature. Among the other works, his autobiography *Joothan: A Dalit's Life* got much publicity. It got so famous that it was translated into English by Arun Prabha Mukherjee. "Dalit Literature and books written by such writings as Valmiki enabled them greatly to develop their education (Magdum, 11). Dr A.P. Pandey writes that, "Dalit Literature looks at the things from the Dalit's point of view" (Pande, 10). Omprakash Valmiki writes in the preface of the autobiography that "Dalit life is excruciatingly painful, charred by experiences. Experiences that did not manage to find room in literary creations" (Valmiki, vii).

Omprakash Valmiki born on 30th June 1950 at Barla, District Muzaffarnagar in Uttar Pradesh. He was the only person of his family who had ever gone to school. *Joothan: A Dalit's Life* is a pictorial description of his life and his community. He describes that he was the first person in his family who attended school for the first time. His father puts him in the primary school of his village in 1956. It was the time when Dalit children were not entertained in schools. All the teachers of his school would address him not by his name but by his caste. His autobiography was first published as *Joothan* in Hindi in 1997 and later it was translated into English by Arun Prabha Mukherjee in 2003. Omprakash was very frank in the depiction of reality. Valmiki is a caste which is also known as 'chuhra' in derogatory terms. The people of his village would call him, "Oe Chuhre" or "Abey Chuhre" just to humiliate him, "if a person were older, then he would be called "Oe Chuhre". If the person were younger, or of the same age, then "Abey Chuhre" was used" (Valmiki, 2).

It is the irony in Indian context that even after more than many decades of independence, the lower caste people are deprived of their rights and they are not given the equal status in the society however people claim that the country's constitution is to safeguard their rights. The people of Valmiki's community would sweep the roads, clean the floor, dispose of dead animals and would do all kinds of labour. Valmiki thinks, "Why are Dalits treated worse than animals. This was the unanswerable question which was hidden in his conscious till his death" (11).

His community lived separately from the upper caste people and a pond would separate their houses from the village. All the women of their community would go to shit in the wide open just because there were no latrines in their houses. All the women of the village, young girls, older women, even the newly married brides would sit in the open space behind these homes at the edge of the pond to take a shit. (Valmiki, 1). He narrates, "Our family lived in this *Chuhra* basti, five brothers, one sisters, two chachas, one tau and his family" (Valmiki, 1). Not only this, the major problem was of untouchability in his village because the upper caste people would look down upon them. Valmiki narrates about it:

> Untouchability was so rampant that while it was considered all right to touch dogs and cats or cows and buffaloes, if one happened to touch a Chuhra, one got contaminated or polluted. The Chuhras were not seen as human. (Valmiki, 2)

Omprakash was humiliated by the upper caste boys. They would laugh at his clothes which were not much far better than rags. Even his teachers would not show any sympathetic attitude towards him and they would take the task of sweeping their homes and school. It was a government run school in Barla village. The author boy was forced to sweep the school by his headmaster's orders. It was a general trend in the school that's why other Dalit people would not send their children in school. When Omprakash's father told other low caste people to send their children in school, they showed pessimistic attitude. They even criticised his father for sending Omprakash to school. They said, "What is the point of sending him to school? When has a crow became a swan?"(Valmiki, 6).

Omprakash showed keen interest in his studies and he showed good results that's why he became the leader of the class and he was also shifted from the back to front seat in his class. Most of the students and teachers belonged to the Tyagi community who showed discriminatory attitude towards Dalits students. Valmiki narrates about it, "During the examinations we could not drink water from the glass when thirsty. To drink water, we had to cup our hands. The peon would pour water from way high up, lest our hands touch the glass" (Valmiki, 16).

The writer tells about the title of the autobiography 'Joothan' which means leftover remnants of food especially from weddings, feasts and other special occasions in which food is served. The people of his community were so poor that they would eat this leftover food. Omprakash Valmiki feels fed up with this life, "What sort of a life was that? After working hard day and night, the price of our sweat was just joothan"

(Valmiki, 10). Omprakash Valmiki had to face different kinds of discriminatory attitudes in his school. One day his teacher abused him and told him to sweep the whole school. The task of sweeping was taken by him by his headmaster in the school and one day, his father saw him sweeping the school and he started quarrelling with the headmaster. The headmaster humiliated his father also publically. Valmiki had to face this kind of humiliation in his life. He narrates his anguish in these words:

> I was kept out of extracurricular activities. On such occasions, I stood on the margins like a spectator. During the annual functions of the school, when rehearsals were on for the play, I too wished for a role, but I always had to stand outside the door. The so-called descendents of the Gods cannot understand the anguish of standing outside the door. (Valmiki, 16)

When Omprakash Valmiki reached in tenth standard, he decided to obtain good marks so that he may take admission in the inter-college. In Uttar Pradesh, students are admitted in inter-colleges after tenth class. He was forced to sow sugarcane even on the eve of his mathematics examination by his Tyagi teacher. Omprakash was fuming with anger that day but he was helpless, "My mind was set aflame by his swearing. A fire had engulfed my inwards that day. The memories of these crimes of the Tyagis continue to smoulder deep inside me, emitting red hot heat" (57). He was offered proffered *rotis* to eat but he refused to eat their food just because he thought that if he ate this food, he would be forced for another manual labour. His refusal infuriates Tyagi and he wanted to beat Valmiki but he escaped somehow.

Valmiki's father was very supportive to him and he would always think that his education would change the course of his son's life, that's why he inspires his son to study well. Omprakash writes that his father did not know that the education cannot be change the attitude of the upper caste people's attitude towards lower caste people, "He did not know that 'caste' cannot be improved by education. It can only be improved by taking birth in the right caste" (Valmiki, 58).

Being poor, Omprakash had to face many problems in his studies. Due to lack of electricity, he had to study in the light of lamps and lanterns. Moreover, he could not concentrate due to noises in his neighbourhood but his neighbours were indifferent to his interest in studies just because they were feeling jealous of him and they would also want him to drop his school and adopt some menial job which was befitted for the people of their caste. Valmiki passed his high school examination with good marks and it was time to celebrate in his community because he was the first boy to pass this examination in his community. Chamanlal Tyagi came in person to congratulate him and it boosted Valmiki's confidence that education can give him respect and dignity. He read religious books like the *Bhagavad Gita*, the *Ramayana*, *etc.* and developed his interest in Hindi literature and read some prominent writers of Hindi Literature.

Omprakash Valmiki took science as an optional subject for higher education. His teacher Omdatta Tyagi would insult the low caste students. Dr R.P. Singh comments in his book about this autobiography, "This belongingness of the experiences of insult and indignity strikes the readers in this autobiography" (8).

His Mathematics teacher also showed discriminatory attitude towards him. Even after getting admission in inter-college, his Mathematics teacher would not drink water from Valmiki's hand. His Chemistry teacher Brajpal did not give him good marks in his practical examinations and he would keep him out of the lab so that he may not go ahead in his career, "I felt that whenever I went to the lab for practicals, Brajpal would keep me out on some pretext or the other" (65). Consequently, he got passed in all other subjects but failed in

Chemistry. Narendra S. Tayade, and Umesh G. Tayade write, "His upward social mobility underlined a message that birth in a typical society never affects the talent one possesses but many talents had been wiped out by the caste system in India" (Tayade *et al.* 4). Omprakash lost all hopes from this failure. He writes about it, "I no longer felt interested in studying. I couldn't make up my mind as to what to do next. I felt surrounded by darkness" (Valmiki, 66).

It was Valmiki's elder brother Jasbir, working in Dehradun, who inspired him to study further. He says to him, "Come on, let this village go to hell. Come to Dehradun and study there. I will get you admitted to DAV College. Why are you worrying? You will definitely pass next year" (Valmiki, 66). Thus, Omprakash joined DAV College in Dehradun. He was influenced by Ambedkar there and he started taking interest in various activities of the college. His uncle showed reluctance to give him accommodation in his house in Dehradun due to his late working hours where his brother Jasbir lived. Valmiki did not want to miss his opportunity of studying there and he obeyed his uncle's orders in order to stay in Dehradun.

Valmiki got a job as an apprentice in an ordnance factory and left his college education. When he told his father that he has got a job, his father became very happy to know about it. He encouraged him saying, "At last you have escaped 'caste'" (Valmiki, 78). But the writer knew it well that it is not so easy to escape the intricate labyrinths of caste that's why he writes, "One can somehow get past poverty and deprivation, but it is impossible to get past caste" (Valmiki, 7) and he writes at another place of this autobiography, "Caste follows one right up to one's death" (Valmiki, 78). Valmiki was getting a monthly stipend of one hundred and seven rupees a month during his apprenticeship. During this time also, he kept reading books which gave him much courage. He proclaims, "Books were my greatest friends. They kept up my morale" (Valmiki, 79). After one year work in the ordnance factory, the writer appeared in a competitive examination and fortunately, he got his selection there. He was sent to Jabalpur for his training. It was a wonderful experience for a low caste boy who did not see anything except discrimination in his life. He writes:

> The new surroundings and the new environment gave me new experiences. The hostel was huge, large enough to accommodate up to five hundred students. The rooms were very large and ten to twelve students shared a room. The students had come from different parts of the country. (Valmiki, 84)

The new atmosphere of Jabalpur helped him develop his interest in Marxist ideals. He read Maxim Gorky's novel *Mother*. He thought that it was the right platform to change his life. He was totally transformed in Jabalpur. He writes how he started taking part in seminars and cultural functions:

> Jabalpur changed me. My speech patterns changed. My manners also changed. I made friends who were deeply interested in contemporary issues and constantly argued about them. I took part in seminars and cultural functions. I became involved in Jabalpur's literary life. I also began to develop my own views on literature. (Valmiki 85)

Jabalpur provided him a platform for his development and at that time, the Ordnance Factory Training Institute in Bombay invited applications for draftsman training. Omprakash applied there and luckily, he got this opportunity also. He was immensely helped by Mr Thomas, a senior lecturer in the institute. Valmiki started reading the books of renowned English writers in the hostel library in Mumbai. He read the works of Rabindranath Tagore and Kalidasa there. He was inspired by many Marathi Dalit writers such as Daya Pawar, Gangadhar Pantavane, Baburao Bagul, Nemdev Dhasal, Vaman Nimbalkar and Narayan Surve. He found that the environment of Mumbai was much better than his village because he thinks how untouchability was unbridled in his village:

> My village was divided along lines of touchability and untouchability. The situation was very bad in Dehradun and in Uttar Pradesh in general. At times when I saw well-educated people in a metropolitan city like Bombay indulging in such behaviour, I felt a fountain of hot lava erupting within me. (Valmiki, 95).

It is a place that defines a person's value. Though Omprakash was now living in Mumbai yet his caste followed him there also. He mentions in his autobiography how he came close to a Kulkarni family as this family took him as a Brahmin. Kulkarni's daughter Savita fell in love with him but when she came to learn that he is Dalit, she broke her relationship with him. This incident left an indelible scar on his psyche. He left this place when he was appointed at the Ordnance Factory in Chandrapur where he became engrossed in Dalit Movement. He remarks:

> It was in this part of the country I came across the marvelous glow of Dalit consciousness. The self-fulfillment that I experienced in connecting with the Dalit Movement was a truly unique experience for me. The deeper my involvement became with the movement, the further many of my friends moved away from me. In their eyes, I had wandered away from the right path and was bent on destroying my talent and creativity. (Valmiki, 100)

His marriage with Chanda brings some new challenges in his life. He was not allotted any accommodation in the government quarters. He faced many problems in the initial days of his marriage. He devoted himself for Dalit movement and Dalit consciousness. His caste was becoming a severe problem in his life. He writes it is impossible to get rid of the caste discrimination in the rigid Indian society:

> 'Caste' is a very important element of Indian society. As soon as a person is born, 'caste' determines his or her destiny. Being born is not in the control of a person. If it were in one's control, then why would I have been born in a Bhangi

household? Those who call themselves the standard-bearers of this country's great cultural heritage, did they decide which homes they would be born into? Albeit they turn to scriptures to justify their position, the scriptures that establish feudal instead of promoting equality and freedom. (Valmiki, 134)

Thus, Dalit autobiographies are the strong testimonios to showcase the concerns of the lower caste writers. The events have been narrated in a pictorial manner and are the voices of revolt and pain. According to Prof. Waman Nimbalkar "The autobiographies in the Dalit Literature are records of Dalit Cultural Revolution" (Nimbalkar, 15) and Omprakash Valmiki's *Joothan: A Dalit's Life* is not an exception. Dr Kusum Kanger also avers, "Omprakash Valmiki's autobiography *Joothan* depicts the hellish life of the Dalits whom have to face the cancer of caste since their birth" (Kanger, 6).

## Works Cited

Kanger, Kusum. "A Study of Hellish Life in Omprakash Valmiki's *Joothan: A Dalit's Life.*" *The Expression: An International Multi Disciplinary e-Journal.* 1.4 (August 2015). 1-6.

Nimbalkar, Wamanan. "Dalit Autobiographies: Graph of Pain." *Journal of Literature and Aesthetics* 9 (2009): 15-19.

Singh, R. P. *The Subaltern Speaks and Asserts: The Autobiographies of Narendra Jadhav, Omprakash Valmiki, and Sharankumar Limbale.* New Delhi: Authorpress, 2013.

Tayade, Narendra S., and Umesh G. Tayade. *Pune Research: An International Journal in English.* 3.4 (2017). 1-5.

Valmiki, Omprakash. *Joothan: A Dalit's Life.* Trans. Arun Prabha Mukherjee. Kolkata: Samya, 2003.

# 22

# Combating Caste Discrimination through Education: A Study of Y. B. Satyanarayana's *My Father Baliah*

*Dr Ritika Agnihotri*

Education provides the required impetus for the social and economic development of the impoverished groups. With education comes the awareness of identifying one's self and to give voice to one's life stories. Whenever it comes to the strengthening of the various marginalised sections of the society, education has always been seen as an important player in turning the tables. Be it women's emancipation or the elimination of the evils of caste system, education has evidently brought about awareness and assertion of rights to the weaker sections of the society. In different situations, it has formed the basis for the struggle and victory of the oppressed. "Education expands the knowledge of possibility to poor individuals, and is often a necessary factor in providing incentive to escape poverty and social oppression" (Fraser n. pag.).

Throughout the world, education has led to an upliftment of the lower sections of the society. George Psacharopoulos in his article "Education and Development: A Review" published in *The World Bank Research Observer* asserts, "About 17.2% of economic growth in Africa and 11.1% in Asia between the 1950s and 1960s have been credited to the increase in education" (102).

In the Indian context, the spread of education was greatly influenced by the social factors which largely discriminated people on the basis of caste. The caste system in India was originally based on occupation. The society was hierarchically divided into the Brahmins (teachers and priests), the Kshatriyas (warriors), the Vaishyas (the merchants) and the Shudras (the labourers). The lowest caste also comprised of people who did menial jobs for the upper classes because of which they were treated as slaves and often called untouchables. This group has also been referred to as 'Dalits'.

Though education became an important pillar of the Indian society with the education policies of the British, the native caste system offered a step motherly treatment to the lower castes. They were even denied right to basic education. They continued to suffer on account of illiteracy and lack of awareness. The dark lives that they led were rampant with low self-esteem and superstitious beliefs. These two drawbacks had become a way of life for them.

Initially it was the foray of only the upper castes (Brahmins) or kingly classes who could receive education and use it for their betterment. With time, people from other castes also acknowledged the significance of education and came forward for their rights. Today, there is no existence of caste bias when it comes to education as the Constitution of India provides the basic right of education to all its citizens.

But if the ground reality is considered, education was not served on a platter to the lower castes. In the twentieth century pre-independence India, it was near to impossible for a Dalit to even dream of receiving formal or informal education. The Dalits were kept out of the domain of education. The guilt of belonging to the Dalit class loomed large in their minds. Their mindsets had been structured in a way that they were superstitious about any attempt to get education. The upper castes had a hegemonic control over them and preached them that if they ever tried their hands on education; it would be calamitous for humanity and would invite the wrath of the deities. They never even dared to reach out to the scriptures because of the same reason. "It was a sin for untouchables to read and write!" (Satyanarayana, 64). Their minds were greatly under the control of untouchability which made them believe in their worthlessness.

Dr B. R. Ambedkar, the renowned Dalit rights activist, in the twentieth century raised his voice for various fundamental rights for the Dalits and stood for their upliftment. In the "Foreword" to *My Father Baliah* authored by Dr Y. B. Satyanarayana, S. R. Sankaran writes:

> In its social potential, education becomes a process of transmitting a specific consciousness to particular social groups. Babasaheb Ambedkar too saw education not just as a means for livelihood but as a powerful tool to liberate Dalits and strengthen their fight against injustice and humiliation. (Satyanarayana, xvi)

In 1945, Ambedkar founded the People's Education Society to assert the right to education for the Dalits. Despite innumerable efforts of various social reformers and activists, Dalits in India suffered a poor literacy rate owing to the class discrimination. Hence the Dalit community required a sense of awakening and a realisation of the fact that education could liberate them from the shackles of untouchability.

To support this cause, many writers from this community came forward to share their experiences through their writings and contributed to this revolutionary movement of caste annihilation. In the latter half of the twentieth century, many Marathi writers came up with Dalit writings and it was soon followed by writers in other languages like Bangla, Kannada, Tamil, Hindi, Punjabi and many more. Today, Dalit Literature occupies an important critical space in Indian literature. Social reformers like Sree Narayana Guru, Jyotibha Phule and

Bhimrao Ramji Ambedkar and their successors may be given the credit for the establishment of Dalit writings as a distinct literary genre. Some famous writers of Dalit Literature are Arun Krushnaji Kamble, Daya Pawar, Laxman Mane, Sharankumar Limbale, Narendra Jadhav and Urmila Pawar to name a few.

Dalit writings problematise the structure of the social worlds created by the so-called upper classes. *My Father Baliah* (2011) by Dr Y. B. Satyanarayana is one such work which highlights the role of education in the elimination of the biases of the caste system. Satyanarayana belongs to a poor Dalit family in Telangana and is the sixth of eleven children born to Baliah (Yelukati Ramaswamy) and Narsamma. He holds a doctorate degree in Chemistry and after a long teaching career, retired as the Principal of Dharmavant College of Science and Commerce, Hyderabad. In spite of being from science background, he started taking interest in Dalit Literature. Currently, he holds the position of President of the Centre for Dalit Studies, Hyderabad.

In the memoir, *My Father Baliah*, the writer Y. B. Satyanarayana narrates the experiences of three generations of the Yelukatis belonging to the Madiga clan of a Dalit community in Telangana. Hence, it may also be referred to as a 'family biography'. It particularly encapsulates the efforts of the writer's father, Baliah who may be seen as a link between the pre-independence and post-independence Dalit conditions.

Yelukati Ramaswamy, better known as Baliah had been a witness to the injustices faced by his previous generations, that of his father and grandfather in the name of caste. Even their shadow or the air around the untouchables was considered to be polluted. They were not allowed to touch anything that belonged to the upper castes. They were seen as "untouchables" or "landless Dalits" (Satyanarayana, 15). His father even had to surrender the land gifted to his grandfather by the Nizam himself because of the reason that "being an untouchable, he was not supposed to hold land" (Satyanarayana, 15). They were poorly paid for the difficult jobs they were made to do. The language used for them was also derogatory.

> ... the way the untouchables were addressed ... reflects the deep societal bias against them. A caste Hindu whose name is Malliah remains Malliah, but if he belongs to the untouchable community, he is called Malligadu; the suffix 'iah' is respectable whereas 'gadu' is contemptible. So too among women. (Satyanarayana, 18)

As a child, when he expressed his desire to go to school like the other children in his society, he was introduced to the reason of all the bias that he witnessed throughout his life. His father told him that they were "Harijans" and "untouchables" and could never be taught at school (Satyanarayana, 22). Still he contradicted his father, Narsiah who had no answer to his argument. But that deprivation that he suffered left an indelible mark on his mind which made him hungry for education for his next generation. Thus, against all odds, he fought for educating his large family. He also thought about women's education which was still a taboo amongst the untouchables. Satyanarayana, in his memoir, observes his father's regret for not insisting on the education of his daughter. He reminisces, "My parents were unhappy... They had made Bachamma discontinue school after sixth standard: my mother had always discouraged her from going to school. My father bitterly regretted that decision now" (Satyanarayana, 132). Many other Dalit writers have also focused on the role of education in the upliftment of untouchables. The role of Omprakash Valmiki in this context cannot be overlooked. In his autobiography *Joothan*, in which he has described his life as an untouchable, he has elucidated the importance of getting education. Education brought an awareness which enabled him to "raise his voice against all the atrocities which were inflicted on them" (Valmiki, 84).

*My Father Baliah* is not merely a personal document but is also indicative of the vices of caste system which lay at the very roots of the Indian society. Like the other Dalit writers, Y. B. Satyanarayana has also put forward the resistance offered to the evils of caste system. E. V. Ramakrishnan has rightly observed, "The discourse of Dalit autobiography is anchored in the social context of resistance and affirmation" (67). The author has traced the journey of subservience to emancipation over three generations which was supported by the pillars of education. The author's father Baliah identified education as an important tool towards development and was able to do much by imparting education to his children. Factually speaking:

> The decade 1970-79 brought a lot of change in the identities of the individual families. Studying in convent schools, the children, the second generation learners, were at par with any middle-class family. ... they had no Dalit identity as far as their school life was concerned. They competed with higher-caste students without knowing what caste was. (Satyanarayana, 192)

The narrative is written in a simple language and rises above the elitist style of English writings. In its very form, it is indicative of the lived reality of the writer who takes pride in being an individual who rises above the stagnant mentality of the Dalits and identifies himself as any normal human being capable of immense potential. His father's inspirational ideology motivated him to never let his caste come in the way of his success. Satyanarayana confesses that many times, he had to hide his Dalit identity in order to claim award and appreciation for his efforts.

> My brother had suggested that I keep my caste a secret... Untouchability was still prevalent and strictly followed in villages....Had the villagers known my real caste, at best, they would have driven me out of the village with contempt. (Satyanarayana, 173)

In this way, he was able to escape the bias which pushed the Dalit communities to the margins.

It is noteworthy that this memoir does not attempt at portraying the Dalit community as a marginalised community, rather it demands an end to all such attempts. In his life he had never seen his father, Baliah reach out to the benefits showered upon the Dalits. He stood up for the rights of the Dalits even before Dr B. R. Ambedkar had put forward his policies for the Dalit community. In a way, he can be said to be a pre-Ambedkarite. Y. B. Satyanarayana notes:

> Though he had not heard of Dr Ambedkar, the saviour and champion of untouchables and a towering personality of the last century, he broke traditions and entrenched customs, ... My father was a visionary and a great man, greater than many intellectuals who claim to be Ambedkarites. (Satyanarayana, 185)

He had a lot of similarities with Ambedkar. He had his own principles which guided him to take his children to great heights and respectable positions in the society. Baliah perceived education to be the only way by which he could make his children climb the ladder of success. He fought against circumstances like poverty, lack of resources and others but never gave up.

His approach towards the emancipation of Dalits has been holistic. He deemed it important to learn about and relate to the historical circumstances in order to understand the Dalit issues and their criticality from a broader perspective. The memoir also highlights how class hierarchy works not just at the larger level but it operates within castes as well. It is evident from the fact that in his narrative, the Shudras were preferred over the untouchables to assist the upper castes and perform odd jobs for them. "The power structure in the caste and sub-caste systems did not allow the individual subject to recognise oneself as a human subject" (Ramakrishnan, 184).

Even after reaching the desired heights and attaining requisite qualifications, his children had to face the hatred of the upper castes over the Dalits. But being educated they had the strength to face all this discrimination. One incident the author has described is when once during his teaching career, he witnessed his fellow Dalit worker facing stark discrimination at the hands of a Reddy, an upper caste man. However, he consoled his friend with the following words:

> 'Friend, do not take this seriously'... After all, in this caste-ridden society, antagonism and intolerance by the higher castes does remain. And he is a Reddy; he expects us to remain at his feet. But now, we have a strong weapon: education. Let us use it. (Satyanarayana, 195)

The role of the railway culture in shaping the ideology of Baliah cannot be overlooked. Despite the class discrimination prevalent in the society in general, people in the railway colonies outlived the class structures. They followed only the hierarchy of rank. People of higher ranks were bestowed more benefits and respect irrespective of the social or religious class they belonged to. In railway colonies, they practised a secular mindset and lived like one big family.

> The untouchables who lived in the railway colony enjoyed the same freedom as the higher castes. There wasn't any social restriction here. In colonial times, cantonment areas and railway colonies were 'free zones' for untouchables, where they could aspire for better social lives, and earn their livelihoods like caste Hindus. The economic opportunities were similar for both the touchables and untouchables. (Satyanarayana, 68)

This had a great impact on the mind of Baliah. As a result, when he went to live with his son and observed domination by some families of higher castes, he was audacious enough to be vocal about the injustice on the basis of caste. The Dalits were prohibited to collect water from the common tap before the Brahmins had done it in the morning. But Baliah showed courage to be the first one to fill water one morning and this act of his was enough to teach a lesson to the Brahmins. They did not dare to oppose or stop him.

> He looked at the people who had gathered around, and not having the courage to fight my father, he quickly left the scene. It was a victory for the people living in the lane. They were jubilant that the imposed rule had been broken. (Satyanarayana, 109)

This gave Baliah more courage as he believed that subordination was only in the minds of the Dalits. It indicates the silent violence faced by the very existence of the low caste people in a hierarchical society. The social descriptions in such works highlight the injustices and hegemonic dominance of the upper castes over the Dalits.

Thus, by embedding individual stories across three generations, Y. B. Satyanarayana has been able to weave a narrative of the long journey of the Dalit community towards emancipation and the consequent empowerment. He has modelled it on the life of his father, Yelukati Baliah who emerges as an icon of perseverance and struggle for the identity of the Dalits. He was an inspiration to all the Dalit families around him and his hard work bore fruit when all his children were finally educated and could overcome the challenges of caste discrimination with the help of their strong weapon named education.

## Works Cited

Fraser, Eric. "The Dalits of India: Education and Development". *E-InternationalRelations.* June 2010. <https://www.e-ir.info/2010/06/23/the-dalits-of-india-education-and-development> May, 2021. Web.

Psacharopoulos, George. "Education and Development: A Review". *The World Bank Research Observer* 3.1 (1988): 99-116.

Ramakrishnan, E.V. *Locating Indian Culture: Texts, Traditions and Translations.* New Delhi: Orient Blackswan, 2011.

Satyanarayana, Y. B. *My Father Baliah*. New Delhi: Harper Collins, 2011.

Valmiki, Omprakash. *Joothan: A Dalit's Life*. Kolkata: Samya, 2003.

# 23

# Daya Pawar's *Baluta*: An Armature of Humiliations of Dalit's Existence in Shinning India

*Dr Parul Aggarwal*

In today's world, when we feel proud to talk about progress, development, freedom and equality in all spheres of life but the issues of caste and class discrimination in society make us compelled to think once again about the entire system of progressive India. As we all know that literature is the mirror of society so every aspect of social issues is presented by the writers in their literary works. Dalit Literature or marginalised literature written by the authors who themselves come from that particular section and background of society in India needs no introduction now as the Indian English writers have been given an authentic voice to their own experiences in the form of their literary work since the beginning of the 19th century which regularly sensitise all its readers about the real life experiences of the plight and pain of such weaker sections of Indian society even in 21st century also where we all claim ourselves to be a proud citizen of Independent nation having a democratic structure of society. Indian English Literature has become a potent and powerful way of expression for the social discrimination and economic marginalisation of Dalit communities based on caste identity which still exist deep into our Indian social structure. In contemporary Indian English

Literature, there are various authors who exhibit the pain of being Dalit or marginalised in their literary works projecting the themes of oppression, exploitation, and humiliation on the cultural, political, social and religious grounds.

*Baluta*, the book written by the Marathi language author and poet Daya Pawar in 1978, is one of the first Dalit autobiography in India. This book is a remarkable collection of memories that the writer, Daya Pawar, share with his readers to make them aware about the act of untouchability faced by the Mahar community in Maharashtra reflecting all the troubles and tribulations which his community keep fighting for. Daya Pawar, born on September 15, 1935, is known for his remarkable contributions to Dalit Literature needs no introduction as he is a remarkable poet, short story writer and a literary critic but in 1978, it was his book *Baluta* in the form of autobiography which gave him an everlasting name and fame in literary world. *Baluta*, considered to be one of the first Dalit autobiography was an authentic work meant to communicate the exploitation and subjugation of lower and working class, disregard of women of deprived sections of society in the era of globalisation with a loud voice as a clear refusal to tolerate the humiliations anymore. Written in Marathi language by Daya Pawar and translated in English by Jerry Pinto in 2015, *Baluta* won the Maharashtra Government Award for literature in the same year of its publication, three years later it won a Ford Foundation Award, between 1981 to 1992, it was translated into Hindi, German, French and Italian languages. The work *Baluta*, a record of anxiety, oppression and struggle of the writer himself who lived in the village Kawakhana, running parallel between Mumbai and Dhamangaon, shocked its upper caste readers with its graphic account of the community's sub-human existence in the rural interiors presenting an entirely different world of scavenging women, alcoholic men, sex and death in the collective pain and struggle of a community, Mahar community whose members were made to spend their whole life living on the outer side of the village named Maharwada where they were considered as untouchables and were used as peonage by the rich upper-caste community and were assigned the works such as the skinning of dead cattle and in return for their labour, the Mahars received baluta—their share in the village produce and the only means of survival. This work was indeed a daring step of a downtrodden in the literature for the first time to raise his voice to live like others and to show the unseen side of Indian social structure—the side which is so dark and the inhumane. The voice of Daya Pawar is not only his own voice; in fact, he is the mouthpiece of the oppressed community who has been denied the basic rights of being human only because of their caste. *Baluta* caught the attention of the readers for its true portrayal of the social, cultural and political life of the writer who was in search of his identity in a caste-ridden society, seeking himself through words, having derived a sense of being an alien in the land of his birth.

*Baluta*—the title of the work in itself evokes the feeling of humiliation and dirt as it is the identification with the "leftovers", Pawar writes, "We played music day and night at festivals and welcomed new bridegrooms at the village borders on their wedding days. For all this, what did we get? Baluta, our share of the village harvest" (Pawar, 2015: 66). This leftover after the celebrations was the thing for which all the Dalits waited for long and with it they received free violent abusive taunts as Pawar narrates, "Mother-fuckers, always first in the line to get your share (Pawar, 2015: 66). This work exposes the underlying reality of caste conflict Indian society where the sourness of cast practices are everyday reality of Dalit existence even in the free democratic nation, India. Pawar has tried his best to show the dark authentic side of the shinning India where Dalits in particular bear the brunt of untouchability in all spheres of life. In real sense, *Baluta* is not only about the plight and miserable life of the writer Pawar but a universal cry of all those who are the victim of the horrible phenomena of caste and category system of Indian social structure as Pawar has attempted to expose the brutal reality of human psychology that how sick it is as he writes:

> The restaurants had different cups for different castes; there were Mahar cups and Chambhar cups, Mang cups and so on. Our cups were very often without handles and ant-infested. We had to rinse them ourselves before ordering tea. We sat separately; either on the verandah or on a bench behind the restaurant (Pawar, 2015: 42).

The book *Baluta* is a life history of the Mahar community which always feels alienated and humiliated as in a society where caste plays a dominant role in deciding the present as well as future of a person, the people belonging to Mahar community faced a mental trauma by being suppressed at the hands of the upper caste people. Pawar states, "During the immersion of Ganpati, there was a fight to make sure that the Mahar Ganpati did not take precedence over the upper-caste Ganpati. Or the Mahars would take out a procession for the book Pandavpratap and the upper caste would object" (Pawar, 2015: 147). In this autobiography, the author has exposed all the unfavourable social, political, economic as well as cultural factors exploring the marginalisation of Dalits by the upper-caste section of Indian social structure as Pawar has given voice to each and every minute detail of everyday life of Mahar community. As the Mahars are considered pollutant so the other castes always maintain a distance from them even in giving water too. Pawar fills his readers' heart with utmost pity when he writes, "If we were thirsty, there was no water for us at school; we had to go back to the Maharwada to drink. The Chabharwada was close by but they too would not give us water" (Pawar, 2015: 45). Undoubtedly this book is a live picture of social discrimination of Dalits at the hands of upper caste community as the book has numerous day to day incidents of Mahar people's life which make the readers realise the pain and agony of Dalits in the framework of Indian social structure. Pawar draws a very live image of the troubles of Dalits when he writes, "The Mahar well was to the west of the village. To fetch water, we had to cross the village, and walk past the Maruti temple too. The villagers' well was below the village. The local Board has a notice there: 'This well is open to people of all castes and creeds.' Be that as it may, no Mahar was ever seen there (70). These lines clearly exhibit the discrimination of Dalits regarding them untouchables as they were not allowed even to come to the well to get water. *Baluta* is not only a literary work by Pawar but it is his mouthpiece to raise issues related to identity, meaning and social status of these under-privileged sections of the Hindu society. Such autobiographies are undoubtedly bold effort to show the imbalance in social ecology due to the complexities in human behaviour, human action and human life. The incidents that Pawar shares with the readers in this work are indeed sensitive economic and cultural degradation and environmental politics as regard caste blindness. As the narrative runs, "We made the proclamations announcing funerals from village to village. We dragged away the carcasses of dead animals. We chopped firewood" (66).

The anger of the writer comes from his own experiences as a Dalit man who saw the discrimination on the basis of caste in each and every sphere of life from his own childhood as he shares that he grew up in the social and political milieu reverberating with the angry rebellion of the Dalit Panther Movement in Maharashtra. Through his father and his associates, he had an immediate exposure the issue with the demand to rename the Marathwada University after Babasaheb Ambedkar. The anger which he felt around him became a part of his own being as he experienced all the happenings related to Mahar community and that inspired him to express those unheard voices of the suppressed marginalised people through his pen to raise voice of protest as well as awareness for the coming Mahar generation not to experience multiple layers of victimisation and discrimination at the hands of the upper-class section of Indian society.

In this work, the readers see how the basic rights of the poor Mahar people had been snatched away by upper-caste community as the experience of the writer himself speaks a lot about the humiliation faced by his own people when he narrates the experience of one morning quoting, "Mahar women polluting the Maruti temple when their shadows fell on it as they passed up and down to fetch water. So they closed the road. The other route to our well went past the lake, a mile-long struggle against sludge and slime" (71). In fact, the purpose of writing this autobiography was meant to give a loud and clear expression to all those agony and sufferings of Dalit community with a direct refusal to tolerate this pain of suppression anymore. In Marathi Dalit Literature, *Baluta*, the autobiography, has its own significant place as this book remains the authentic voice of everyday humiliation of the downtrodden at the name of caste and creed.

> The quest of identity by a Dalit person in the established world of the upper-caste people was not easy nut to crack but Pawar as a writer proved his potential of expression when he narrates every minute incident of his humiliated life to with courage and truthfulness, so straightforward in his approach, so honest in his conception that the readers feel themselves to be dragged in that brutal world of discriminated society. Pawar's experience says about the living condition of Mahar community in such a way that the readers feel pity about their miserable life as he writes, "Wooden boxes acted as partitions. But they were more than that: we stuffed our lives into those boxes. At night, temporary walls would come up, made of rags hanging from ropes. (7)

This book is a remarkable analysis of the everyday issues related to status and identity of Dalits of the Hindu society exploring the continuous exploitation of socially, economically, ethically and politically deprived section of society. The literary expression of Dalits in the book *Baluta* demand a new social order to get justice, identity and self-respect seeking humane conditions to live their life as a human being—not as an under-privileged one. Pawar has given a very clear expression to all those day to day exploitation of the Mahar's life which were unsaid and unexpressed -with a hope that this book will pave the wave for the liberty and freedom from the clutches of rooted casteism in Indian social structure and no need to say that *Baluta* has proved to be a milestone in Indian Dalit Literature.

## Works Cited

Limbale, Sharankumar. *Towards an Aesthetic of Dalit Literature: History, Controversies and Considerations*. Translated by Alok Mukherjee. Orient Blackswan, 2010.

Meherutru, Assefa, et al. "Concepts in Social and Spatial Marginality." Development of Settlements, vol. 82, no. 2, 2000, pp. 89-101. JSTOR, www.jstor.org/stable/491067.

Naik, C. D. *Buddhism and Dalits: Social Philosophy and Traditions*. Kalpaz Publications, 2010.

Nayar, Pramod K. *Contemporary Literary and Cultural Theory: From Structuralism to Ecocriticism*. Dorling Kindersely (India), License of Pearson Education in South Asia, 2008.

Pawar, Daya. *Baluta*. Translated by Jerry Pinto. Speaking Tiger, 2015.

"Who are dalits? & What is Untouchability?" National Campaign on Dalit Human. Rights.www.ncdhr.org.in/dalits-untouchability. Accessed on 15 May, 2021.

# 24

# Deep Wounds on Heart in B. Kesharshivam's Autobiography *The Whole Truth and Nothing but the Truth: A Dalit's Life*

*Harish Mangalam*

Dalit Literature is written almost in all the regional languages of India and has been unfurled all over the literary world. It is cultivated in all literary genres profoundly. The great social reformers like, Mahatma Jyotiba Phule, E. V. Ramasamy Periyar and Dr B. R. Ambedkar are the real pioneers for germination of Dalit Literature. They are the chief beacons for social awareness. Their social reformative movements sprouted radical thoughts and Dalit consciousness in Maharashtra and then disseminated in all the regional languages. Dalit Literature was first started in Marathi and then spread in other regional languages. Before that Dalit Literature was written but not termed as Dalit Literature. After Dalit movement, it was termed as Dalit Literature. It is an indispensable to take an earnest note of 'Dalit Panther' movement started in 1972 by the activists-cum-writers, like Namdev Dhasal, J.V. Pavar, Raja Dhale, Ramdas Sorte, Latif Kantek, Avinash Mahatekar, Prahlad Chendavkar, Arjun Dangle, Bhai Sangle, Anil Kamble, Arun Kamble, *etc.* Marathi Dalit Literature stimulated writers of other regions to write Dalit Literature and educated youth came out with a great force and revolutionary activity against age-old slavery, untouchability, ostracisation, discrimination, low and high divisions, religious related blind faith, holy and unholy beliefs, exploitation of women and unprivileged class, mental and physical atrocities, inhumanity, injustice and ultimately a furious struggle for equality, liberty, brotherhood to attain dignity, self-respect for the downtrodden communities. Marathi Dalit writer Tarachandra Khandekar highlights the significance of 'Man' in Dalit Literature and writes:

> Man is the centrifugal force in the philosophy of Dalit Literature. Man is supreme. He is above all God, sacred books and science. It is man who can make and unmake anything. Dalit Literature believes that nothing is permanent. Everything is subjected to decay. With every decay there is resurgence, new creation. It, therefore, does not accept the maxim 'Satyam, Shivam, Sundaram'. On the other hand, it proclaims that nothing is true which is not applicable for man's sublime freedom, nothing is good if it is not useful for man's welfare. Nothing is beautiful which is not useful for beautification of mankind. (6).

'Dalit' word for the first time was used in 1894 by Savitribai Phule in one of her poems, see:

> Accorded own wells for untouchables
>
> Showed the humanity—path to all
>
> Exhorted Dalits to get education
>
> Don't forget the wonderful done by Jyotiba. (32)

But 'Dalit Literature' term for the first was used in 1958 in conference of Maharashtra Dalit Sahitya Society. Today, Marathi Dalit Literature has been established as mainstream literature in Maharashtra. Some noteworthy and astounding autobiographies have been published in Marathi language and translated into many languages abroad and regional languages too. In comparison to other Dalit literary genre, Marathi Dalit autobiographies have drawn the attention of the whole literary world. Not merely in numbers, but in effective expression also are remarkable. Some extraordinary autobiographies are, *Baluta*, translated into 14 languages (Daya Pawar, 1978), *Upara*, translated into English as *An Outsider* (Laxman Mane, 1980), *Uchalya* translated into English as *The Branded* (Laxman Gaikwad, 1987), *Akkarmashi,* translated into English as *Outcaste* (Sharankumar Limbale, 1988), *Chhora Kolhatika* (Kishore Shantabai Kale, 1994), *etc.*

The first Tamil autobiography entitled *Jeeviya Sarithira Surukkam* (1938) by Rettamalai Srinivasan was translated into English as *A Brief History of My Life* by Meera Rajgopalan. Diwan Bahadur Rettamalai (1860-1945) was a Schedule Caste activist and politician from the then Madras Presidency of British India. (now Tamil Nadu). He was a Dalit icon and was a close associate of Mahatma Gandhi and Dr B. R. Ambedkar. He fought for the fundamental rights of *Pariayar* Schedule Caste people in Tamil Nadu. His autobiography should be admitted in the history of Dalit Literature as an imperative tool to re-write our history.

Directly influenced by the Marathi *Dalit Panther* movement, *Dalit Panther* movement started in Gujarat State with emergence of Gujarati Dalit Literature. Though Gujarati Dalit Literature is cultivated in all the Dalit literary genres powerfully, it is pertinent to note that due to lack of translation works into other prominent languages, it has not come in light on an extensive scale. It is true that in comparison to Marathi Dalit autobiographies, Gujarati Dalit autobiographies are a few in numbers and creatively also not up to the mark but other literary genres like poems, short stories and novels are powerful in Gujarati Dalit Literature. Till the day, scarcely nine to ten autobiographies are written in Gujarati Dalit Literature: *Autobiography* (Lalit Parmar, 1997), *Jivan Sangharsh: Ek Adarsh Krantikatha* (Dahyabhai R. Dinbandhu, 2001), *Poorn Satya* (B. Kesharshivam, 2002), *Thornu Fool Part-I to IV* (P.K. Valera, 2007, 2010, 2012 & 2014), *Bajta Jaye Ek Tara* (Vitthalray Shrimali,

2009), *Vadfaliyu* (Manilal Ranveriya, 2015) and autobiographical novel *Aganzal, Part-I* (Harish Mangalam, 2008), *etc.*

*Poorn Satya*, Gujarati Dalit autobiography by B. Kesharshivam, has been translated into English by Gita Chaudhary as *The Whole Truth and Nothing but the Truth*, published by Samya Publication, Kolkata in 2008. The pen name 'B. Kesharshivam' is coined from first letter/s of his original name, 'B' stands for 'Bhikha', 'Keshar' for 'Kesharben—his mother's name and 'Shivam' for 'Shiva' his father's name. Thus, his original colloquial name is Bhikha Shiva Jadav.

In *Poorn Satya*, he has delineated pungent reality of his life experiences from his birth (1940) to his retirement from the government service. (1998). It is divided in two parts. In the first part, he has covered the period up to College education and in the second part, he has covered the various bitter experiences during his government service period. It is the period of his becoming Mamlatdar-cum-Executive Magistrate of Dholka Town (District Ahmedabad), and thereafter, his various promotions to higher cadre, like Managing Director, Director-cum-Dy. Secretary IREP, Dy. Development Commissioner, Joint Director, Executive Director and Comptroller of Households to the Governor of Gujarat, *etc.*

B. Kesharshivam was born on 28th November, 1940 in Dalit *Moholla* of Kalol Town (North Gujarat). He narrates his self-portraiture:

> In the year of 1940, thunders and explosions of the third world war were continued in the whole world. There was an upsurge in our nation. Dr Babasaheb Ambedkar was fighting hard for the social independence for the unprivileged society first than political independence. A torch of revolution was travelling in each and every corner of the nation. At that time, Jean Paul Sartre believed a word as a pistol. He has written: *The author is like a word-loaded pistol. If he speaks, pistol fires.* At that moment, I was in an embryo

> of my mother. I would have uttered my first word—'Unva, Unva' (noise of first cry) from my mouth on 28th November, 1940. I don't know, whether pistol would have fired or not and sound would have aired or not because at that time I was not author. (206)

B. Kesharshivam's life was not so easy. With his birth, he starts facing problems which are nothing but natural for an untouchable like him. Still he was optimistic that the time will change for the people like him:

> On my birth, not one but 'two' fetters were ready there for me: First, politically our nation was slave but non-Dalits were considered as higher caste whereas the Dalits of the slave nation were untouchables and simultaneously, they were untouchables, means doubly slave who could not be touched—a slave like me! My condition was severely gruesome in comparison to non-Dalits' slavery. In our own country human being like me was born with an utter curse! It was under the direct influence of consciousness of Gandhiji and Arvind, though the great poet 'Sundaram' had sung: *Being human, be humane, that's all.* My grandfather, great grandfather had been baked, roasted and exploited in fire and departed from this world. Their strong bones might have dissolved in the dust of an earth. That song: *Phir Subah Hogi—after frightful night, there would be a dawn, however the night is so terrible, morning would be there...* Upon hearing this song, generations to generations had been pushed into the canyon of death before me. Awaiting of such morning, my grandfather, grandfather's father, grandmother have been liquefied in the deep earth. Therefore, my parents had constantly been longing for that morning and they also died in waiting for that sunrise. I have also since been waiting for that dawn. Now, in the latter life, I get twilight of that early morning but that morning has not yet appeared... How many generations would pass away for want of that morning? (206-207).

During his schooling period, he faced untouchability as his parents, grandfather and great grandfather faced. Even in our independent nation, frequently he has to suffer severely like a *Shambook-killing*. He exerts very hard for his education. All the social pollutions of discriminations prevalent even in education institutions as well as teachers too! The author highlights very efficiently that how Indian *Dronacharyas* created and spread the filth in education institutions. Please see some apparent examples:

> All had habit to drink water in *Khobo* (cavity formed by putting the two hands side by side hollowing the palms) outside their *Moholla* as and when they become thirsty.
>
> Always, they had to drink water in *Khobo*. In the School, I used to drink water in *Khobo* as if *Khobo* was my glass! (209).
>
> In the school, I could not drink water from the water-hut with other students. So that I was compelled to drink water from house...after releasing from the school and reaching at home every day in evening, I used to drink a *loto* (kind of metal pot) full of water. Once I became very thirsty and nobody was there in the water-hut of the school. So, slowly-slowly and silently, I entered the water-hut. I drank water using mine second hand palm. At that time, water-woman came and suddenly up-roared. I was beaten up by the young boys. (209).

In the high school, a clerk used to taunt: 'Welcome, son-in-law of government!'

> When I was in P.J. Vakhariya high school in 8th standard, the school had arranged a picnic party in *Mahadev Temple* of *Pavathi*. After finishing meal, everybody went to dispose of their *patrala* (plates made of leaves). I also went outside to throw out *patrala* and disposed of it as other thrown in the nearby pit. Some beggars were collecting

> leftover food from the *patrala* and some children of beggars were eating, standing there. Upon seeing me, one beggar-girl recognised me and immediately she thrown away the *patrala* as if she were shocked with an electric current and started grumbling: 'Alas! alas...! he is *Dhe...*' (210).

B. Kesharshivam was astonished and with his wide-opened eyes, he was staring at her constantly! At the moment, it made him to feel the worst experience of his life that his social status is lower even than a beggar-girl! He reveals very strange animosity of Hindu social system of *Varnavyavstha* based untouchability. Even beggars belong to Hindu religion who are not untouchables implement untouchability with the Dalits of India. However, Dalits may be of higher status officer, intellectuals, entrepreneurs or politicians too!! Even as on today, Dalits of India are being regarded very bad and low than an animal. Further, he brings into light:

> In some villages, Dalits were prohibited to take water from lakes and troughs, perhaps cattle would have become impure! A trough would have become unholy! (51).

The autobiographer snapshots of a disgusting event of a caste-tormented society which is haplessness and creates an earthquake in the minds of genius readers. No one would find such cruel untouchability on the part of *Chaturvarna* in the whole world. Hindu social system is rotten and wide-spreading stink everywhere, see:

> Once, Harima with loud laughing was talking about her own experience to other women of *Moholla*: Harima had gone to forest for plucking woods with other women. It was a summer day afternoon. She was thirsty but from where to drink water? She saw around but nowhere water was available. If field owners see landless labourers, they would not have allowed to enter the fields and would have taken away the baskets from the women! Over and above, they would have beaten up mercilessly and abused them.

> Harima's throat was drying-up. At a juncture, Harima saw a cow urinating. Immediately she ran there and made *Khobo* of her two palms with both hands and had drunk urine! Thus, cow-mother had satiated Harima! (52)

During his childhood, Bhikha Shiva Jadav being a Dalit boy, he had to labour strenuously in bone mill, cotter mill and carried on head the heavy baskets full of coal, even though was craving for a piece of *rotlo* (cake thicker than *rotli* done by patting dough with the hands). He had to suffer from penury as well as cruel, unjust and inhuman treatment given by the hegemonic castes. The barbaric and diabolic malediction wounded him deeply in his heart which would never be healed. Temple entry for the Dalits was impossible and today also it is prohibited. One day, Bhikha Shiva Jadav was passing by nearer to *Navratri Garbi*, (First nine nights preceding *Dussehra* festival and song in particular mode of music sung by women) though he was severely beaten up.

The autobiographer passed examination of Class-I & II conducted by Gujarat Public Service Commission and his first posting was Mamalatdar-cum-Executive Magistrate of Dholka Taluka (District Ahmedabad). Some people tried to cancel his order because they didn't desire posting of Dalit officer on such important key-post. However, his order was not cancelled by the state government so the present Mamlatdar Mr Mehta was compelled to hand over the charge to him. After taking over the charge of Mamlatdar-cum-Executive Magistrate, Dholka, the other problem of accommodation cropped up. Nobody was ready to give him house on rent. Though Hindus consider Dalits as Hindus, yet they don't give their house on rent due to untouchability! (How ludicrous it is!) Ultimately, one Muslim gives his house to him on rent. Dr Babasaheb Ambedkar also faced the same problem of house when he went to Vadodara to resume his duty in the state of Sayajirao Gaikwad. Giving false name, he got the house of one Parsi but when they came to know that he belonged to Schedule Caste, he was forced to vacate the house. *Varnavyavstha* based untouchability is deathless demon in Hindu society which quivers in violent passion under influence of evil spirit. Crores of gods and goddesses are related to Hindu religion, and unscientific approach of folks has been seized in suspicious traditions with blind faith.

The autobiographer of *Poorn Satya* (*Total Truth*), is well aware and conscious of the ideology of Dr Babasaheb Ambedkar to emancipate the Dalit community from the centuries-old slavery. So, during the period of his service as Mamlatdar, Dholka Taluka, he gives lands from herbages and surplus lands to the landless labourers—the untouchables of the villages, namely, Sahij, Dumali and other villagers, shouldering all the risks including life-venture too. Some casteist people threw crude oil, inedible and putrid food in the wells of Dalit ghettos of the villages, Kharanti, Vataman, Rajoda, *etc.* In Bavla village, untouchability was so prevalent that the Dalits suffered for the want of potable water. All the Schedule Caste MLAs from all over the Gujarat State were compelled to observe fasting *Satyagrah* (insistence on truth) against anathema. In such a severe condition of monstrous atrocities on the Dalits, B. Kesharshivam fights valiantly against inhuman injustice. Wounds on his heart were oozing continuously.

B. Kesharshivam was posted as Comptroller of Households to the Governor of Gujarat office, Gandhinagar where he had to make all arrangements for VIP guests as host. On 26th January and 15th August, both the national days, he had to prepare for a grand party and make all the arrangements of dining for round about 1500 to 2000 guests. B. Kesharshivam showcases contradictions occurred in between his destitution days of childhood and the days of the comptroller to the Governor office, enjoying healthy and lavish nutritious food in his own life:

> ... perhaps it must have written on my forehead to live contradictory life. In childhood, I was yearning for a piece of *rotlo* (cake thicker than *rotli* done by patting dough with the hand), and wallowing in poverty and socio-political-

> education darkness. Whereas in the Governor's house, I used to purchase the recipe books for cooking food. Each book costing about Rs. 200 to 250 and as per these books, I had to get food prepared by cooks and butlers. The cooks were separate for vegetarian and non-vegetarian food. The cook-mates and butler's staff were cooking and serving.... (37)

Very famous Dalit writer and critique, P.K. Valera who was IAS officer in Gujarat government has offered very apt analyses, "*Poorn Satya* autobiography will inspire all the Dalit and non-Dalit honest officers and whole Dalit community with its fragrance of flowers and make them powerful"(502). Focusing critical opinion, Dr Kanti Malsatar has analysed that:

> The compilation work of the various events in the autobiography is not arranged in a proper sequence and it has been an obvious circumscription in *Poorn Satya* a autobiography. Over and above, many incidents have been repeated! In part-I of *Poorn Satya*, B. Kesharshivam has given an appropriate title of the chapter related to the particular incident but the author has given more importance to irrelevant matters in depiction rather than what is relevant with the title. As per example, in the *Bhavai* (farcical dramatic show) chapter, the author has described the marriage ceremony instead *Bhavai*! In the chapter 'Anger of Bitch', more importance is given to *Makarsankranti* (kite-flying day) rather than the 'Bitch!' (144).

Over and above, the autobiographer has exposed corruption, tendencies, mentality, wiles and tricks in transfers and promotions of field officers done by the heads of the State government departments. He also asserts and describes caste-biased experiences under the guise of the two anti-reservation stirs started in Gujarat State and other day-to-day ruthless atrocities with animosity against the Dalits, but we fail to trace out any furious voice, protest, resistance or direct participation in revolutionary actions either by the autobiographer or Dalit community as a whole, in *Poorn Satya*.

The autobiographer brings into light the various types of incidents of untouchability based ostracisation, atrocities, disrespect, inhuman and unjust treatment, exploitation, poverty, wishes-longings, sufferings, pains, hellish conditions and anguish of the whole Dalit society. Its language is very simple and even a layman can understand. Making obvious, Dr Shivaji D. Sargar emphasises:

> However, it should be taken into consideration that Dalit writers have been using Literature as one of the means of social transformation. Literature for these writers is more a social than an aesthetic activity as it helps them to fulfil their aim of making the world aware of the socio-cultural realities of Dalit lives and bring in some positive changes in them. (186)

Thus, *Poorn Satya* is a transparent document of the unprivileged society. It is included in the curriculum of York University, Toronto (Canada). It is noteworthy for the Gujarati Dalit literary world that its translation works into Marathi and Hindi is under pipeline.

## Works Cited

Khandekar, Tarachandra. "Literature of Revolt and Resurgence." Bojja Tharakam (ed.) *The First All India Dalit Writers Conference: A Commemorative Volume*. Hyderabad: Dr B. R. Ambedkar Memorial Trust, 1994.

Kesharshivam, B. *The Whole Truth and Nothing but the Truth: A Dalit's Life*. Ahmedabad: Navbharat Sahitya Mandir, 2002.

Malsatar, Dr Kanti. '*Bharatiya Dalit Atmakatha*'. Ahmedabad: Gujarati Dalit Sahitya Akademy, 2019.

Ransubhe, Dr Suryanarayan. "*Savitribai Phule: Vyaktitvakekutchunchhuye Aayam.*" *Dalit Asmita*. Issue. 26. Delhi: Indian Institute of Dalit Studies, March 2017. (Trans. Mine)

Sargar, Dr Shivaji D. *Aesthetics of Subaltern Literature: Protest in African American and Dalit Autobiography*. Kanpur: Shubham Publications, 2018.

# 25

# A Study of the Untouchables in Subaltern Literature with Special Reference to K.A. Gunasekaran's Autobiography *The Scar*: A Clarion Call for Dalit Assertion and Emancipation

*Dr V. Brinda Shree*

The literature of the oppressed has surpassed the records of history and has also acquired a transition into a socio-political tool that symbolises the wretchedness of the poverty, predicament and injustice that was administered to the Untouchables in India. In this genre, the autobiography of the Dalit writers emerged as a weapon for Dalit to assert their identity, individuality and made them challenge the social order and protest against the oppression for centuries.

Dr Babasaheb Ambedkar and Rettaimalai Srinivasan are considered as the "Founding Fathers of Dalit Autobiography" in India. The former's autobiography illustrates untouchability that happened in the year 1939. According to Dr Gangadhar Patnavane, Marathi Dalit writer, "Only Babasaheb Ambedkar is the first Dalit autobiographer" (Translation Mine) (Prabodhan: Jan-Feb, 2009: 11). One can see the most brutal, barbaric and sub-human aspects of untouchability in Dalit autobiographies and therefore it can be proclaimed that these autobiographies sparked the movement against untouchability. According to Ambedkar:

> Foreigners do know that the stigma called untouchability is in vogue in India. But they do not know how gruesome it is. Ambedkar further observed, a Dalit in a village does not socialise with others nor is the welfare of these people is not without self-interest; and also to make clear the fact that this community of people have achieved whatever they have by their own struggle. (*Annihilation of Caste*, 95)

There are many genuine Dalit autobiographical narratives written by contemporary Dalit authors. One such Dalit autobiography named *The Scar* (*Vadu*) was written by K.A. Gunasekaran who hails from the Dalit community and which was formerly considered as 'Untouchables' in India. Born into a Dalit family of Elayankudi, in the Ramanathapuram district of Tamil Nadu, K.A. Gunasekaran is considered to be the first Dalit playwright. His play *Bali Adugal* (*Sacrificial Goat*) was a forerunner and marked the inception of Dalit theatre in Tamil Nadu. He has contributed immensely for the Tamil literary sphere through his plays *Sathya Sothanai*, *Thodu*, *Mazhi*, *Varaivu Kadavuthal* and *Kanthan Valli*. His conceptualisation of the theatre of the oppressed was a huge attempt in innovating, revolutionising and experimenting the Dalit theatre.

The exorbitant levels of discrimination and exploitation experienced by Gunasekaran were both psychological and physical, but he used his education, self-motivation and self-determination to overcome all forms of prejudice and wrestled with life to experience an existence which was beyond the boundaries and limitations imposed on him by his social class.

In the 1990s, Gunasekaran became the anthem of the Dalit Movement of Tamil Nadu. He has done substantial research on urban folklore and as a folk singer; he has published many books and research articles. Apart from being a Folk artist, Gunasekaran was also the former professor and reader (Drama

& Theatre Arts) of Pondicherry University. He was correlated with the Progressive Writers' Movement. Gunasekaran has received the Dalit Isai Kurisil Award from the Tamil Association of Canada and last but not least, was the recipient of the Kalaimamani Award by the Government of Tamil Nadu and Puducherry. He died at his residence in Puducherry in 2016 at the age of 60 after a brief illness.

Amongst the many autobiographies written by Dalit writers, *The Scar* (*Vadu*) by K.A. Gunasekaran, goes beyond self-expression and signals the exploitation of Tamil Dalit's life. V. Kadambari translated this autobiography from Tamil into English. V. Kadambari, in the autobiography's translator's note, states that this book was to him a " ... quest for understanding human nature and search for methods of societal change, at a time when caste and discrimination seem to be more crude now than ever before" (*The Scar*, xix).

The memoir *The Scar* is a quest of the oppressed class to reclaim their identity and ascertain their individual rights and also portrays their fight for freedom and liberty from the oppressors. Translation of Indian Vernacular Writings into English gives high recognition, acclamation and commendation to the author and also the translator. Translation to English from any of the many Indian languages is a very complicated job. According to Parvathi:

> Particularly to find equivalents in an alien language like English needs a lot of knowledge, efficiency and scholarship. Unless the translator is able to elicit the implicated meaning between the lines, he/she cannot render it successfully, in the target language. (Aital, 141)

*The Scar (Vadu)* is an accosting narrative of Gunasekaran's life experience of being born in an aboriginal agricultural Dalit community in Elyankusi village in Ramanathapuram district, Tamil Nadu. The novel begins with Gunasekaran's recollection of his homeland and the neighbouring upper class Islamist living in Elyankudi and it evokes a mixed culture of Hinduism, Christianity and Islam. Elyankudi, which was mostly populated by the Arya Vysyas, had a Shiva Temple which was restricted to Dalit and Gunasekaran has not been inside this temple even until his death. V. Kadambari states that:

> We understand from this autobiography that at the economically lower rung of society, religions like Islam, Christianity and Hinduism merges, losing their identities in a very natural manner. Especially now, when identities are frozen and differences are brought into sharp focus such efforts to lay open the reality are the need of the hour. Gunasekaran does not do it by displaying his political correctness. But just by laying his life, he has achieved this task. (*The Scar*, xiv)

Gunasekhar's father was a school teacher in Salaiyur and so was respected and given special access into the Muslim homes and the Masjids. His father was a great inspiratory person in his life, "Because he brought us up by paying attention to arts, literature, politics and education, we too developed an interest in all these things" (*The Scar*, 83). His mother was educated up to eighth grade through the sponsorship from a local Church. His father has over half a dozen children from his first wife and later it was revealed that he had a second wife from whom he had begotten a son and daughter in Marandai. So it was always difficult for his father to manage such a large family through his humble salary and more than often a quarrel would crop up between him and his wife due to poverty.

The Dalits or the Paraya lived in deplorable conditions in Elyankudi village of Tamil Nadu. They were forced to live in filthy enclaves, away from the main land and were excluded from the upper-caste residents. It was in school days, that Gunasekaran, for the first time in his life, experienced the humility of caste-stratification. Often, the school clerk would visit every class to list out the number of Parayars, Chakiliyas and Pallars and instruct them to fill the scholarship forms available in the school office within a speculated time.

> 'How many in this class are Parayars?' He would ask, 'Put up your hands! How many are Pallars? Stand up, I will count. Look, all of you should come to the office after class to pick up your scholarship forms which should be filled up within a week's time'. . . .They would reinforce caste identities by labelling us Pallar, Parayars and Chakiliyars. (5)

The Dalit could rarely eat an adequate meal. Frequently, his grandmother used to take him to hunt for snails and snugs for their meal in a nearby irrigation tank. All through his childhood, Gunasekaran worked in farms of the upper class people to earn money. Once, his grandmother sent him to a nearby village called Keeranoor to purchase some oil. While walking through the fields, Gunasekaran saw an upper caste man coming from the other side of the narrow bund and so made way for him by lifting his foot. After passing by, the man got offended by the acts of Gunasekharan and slapped him.

> 'Look at the cheek of the Paraya boy!' the man spat out, and then went on his way. It took me five minutes to come out of my state of shock. I put the box down and sat on the bund crying....
>
> ... I started walking back home. I had too many questions with myself. 'Why did that man beat me? What mistake did I do? Why did he call me a Paraya?' I didn't get any answer....
>
> The moment she heard the entire story she said, 'See we belong to a Paraya household, and they are Maravars. When we see men and women of high caste come, we need to stand at least eight feet away from them. We ought to step aside to give them way. That is why the man has beaten you' (43).

This incident left a massive psychological and physical backlash on him and thus, he understood untouchability and discrimination very early in life.

Gunasekaran had to go into exile after an agonizing incident, when the Konar people issued a warning to leave his birth place Elyangudi. It happened when Gunasekaran started a gift scheme shop near a village school. One day, an upper class boy bought something and when Gunasekaran asked for money, he refused to pay and ran away shouting, "Get lost Paraya!" Gunasekaran managed to chase him to his house and complained to his parents. This event had such a repercussion that the same evening many upper caste people took offence and marched to his aunt's house and made his relatives fall at their feet and beg for forgiveness and mercy. Neither Gunasekaran nor his relatives could resist the upper class people from barging into the Dalit colony due to their immense compliant and passive nature.

> When upper-caste people enter the colony of Dalits, they do not offer any resistance. Rather, the Dalits are immensely passive and obedient. On a warning issued by the Konar people, Gunasekaran was forced to leave Elyangudi.
>
> 'Ayya, he is my younger sister's son and is brought up in a town. He does not know anything about our village ways.' The men kept asking, 'How can a fellow from your caste enter the upper caste street? And worse, how dare he enter our house?'...'If the fellow had entered our house without knowing the limitations of his caste, then he must really be very arrogant. Where is he? Let's tie up his feet and hands, and carry him away', they shouted. I was panic-stricken (104).

Maduraiveeran and Balu were the two friends of Gunasekaran. Whenever a death happened in the village, these three used to go to report it from village to village " ... carrying news from the grief stricken households to places which were within eight kilometre distance ... (29), and in return for this favour, they were given paddy which these three exchanged them in nearby shops for eatables.

Once in Marandai, the birthplace of Gunasekaran, a young boy was seen chopping a tree. Since the tree was near Gunasekaran's house, he questioned him saying "Dei! Why are you cutting away the flowers and the tender fruits of our tree?" (51). As soon as he says this, the boy hits Gunasekaran and runs away. Later the boy brings his people to beat Gunasekaran threatening him saying ...

> Do you know whom you have addressed as 'Dei'? We will cut your tongue. Are you aware of the difference between your caste and ours? You've lost your mind having made friends with the Elayankudi Muslim fellows. Be careful and know your caste before you speak. (51)

It was Gunasekaran's grandfather who comes in the nick of time to beg for mercy from those upper class people and rescues him. Later, when they all leave after getting apologised, he makes Gunasekaran understand that as per the rule of the village, the upper class alone have the rights to address them by their names and they have to respect them even though they are much younger than him.

Every year, in the month of February, a ritual of a bull taming contest was usually conducted in the temple of Muniayya at a village called Chakiliyar. It was believed that they would be blessed with health, wealth and prosperity if they make their bull participate in this contest. The bounty was usually awarded to the brave person who was capable of taming the wild bull. During one such contest, Muniya's sister gets accidentally attacked by the bull and the villagers take her to Elayankudi hospital. Since her condition was critical, she gets shifted to the Madurai hospital but unfortunately she dies within a week and Gunasekaran feels that she would be alive and kicking happily now had it not been to the indifference of the Doctors of the Madurai Government Hospital and regrets of not been able to admit her in a private hospital due to lack of funds.

> After four or five days she died. We didn't expect it. I still believe it was because of the indifference of the government

> doctors that she died: if they had been attentive her stomach could have been stitched up and she could have been saved. If we had had money we would have admitted her in a private hospital. (32)

It was Gunasekaran's cousin named Muniyandi Machan who teached him singing and music while they walked through the lush green fields of Munirandi. He himself acknowledges that, "It is this practice that Machan gave me at home and on the fields and grounds that has made me known to the people as a singer" (63). Muniyandi Machan's colleague, T. R. Mahalingam, who was an actor as well as a singer, also taught him music. Once Gunasekaran gets a chance to sing a folk song which the All India Radio broadcasted all over Trichy. This was listened by the people of his native village over Panchayat Radio " ... after working in the fields the whole day, would listen to it on the Panchayat radio" (52). And every time before and after the song was played in the radio, they would announce his name as Elayankudi K.A. Gunasekaran which made his people proud of him.

During his college days, Gunasekaran participated in a singing competition and the upper caste students start booing him down but he continued to sing after the encouragement from the judges and suddenly everyone in the audience gets carried away by the charm in his voice and becomes silent. When the singing ends, many people from the audience praise him and he even gets an apology letter asking him to forgive his conservative behaviour. Later, Gunasekaran goes on to win the first prize in a district level music competition which was conducted in Ramanathapuram. It was in his college days that, for the first time in history and also for the first time in his life, Gunasekaran, a Dalit, gets appointed as the secretary of the Bharati Club and also the cultural secretary of the N.S.S. Unit. Gunasekaran developed a unique relationship with his Professor named Meera.

> Until this time, no student belonging to the oppressed class had held such posts in the history of the college. Despite knowing that I belonged to the Dalit community, Professor Meera took me to his house and offered me food. (69)

It was also through Professor Meera's help that he gets introduced to many Tamil writers and also Reviewers. It was also Professor Meera who recommended Gunasekaran to learn Saiva Siddhanta, a subject which he despised, after getting admitted to Masters in Tamil. Gunasekaran's parent's poverty made them incapable to fund for his Master Degree and so during his vacations he joined the folk artists in his village and started to learn and perform 'Karagattam', a type of rural dance of Tamil Nadu in the course of celebrations at temples.

Undeterred and regardless of all the uncountable prejudices and injustices meted out to the Dalits of Elayankudi, Gunasekaran, like a phoenix rising from the ashes, emerges strong, both mentally and physically, and realises his inherent talents of acting, singing and also completes his Masters of Arts successfully. He also learns folk arts such as karagattam and kavadi and goes on to perform it during the Republic Day celebrations at Delhi in the year 1981. The then Prime Minister of India Mrs Indira Gandhi invited all the folk artists who performed at the occasion of the Republic Day to her residence for dinner. She also shook hands with him and suggested that he should pursue his research on Folk Arts which he eventually does and gets recognition not only in Tamil Nadu, but also internationally. The photograph of his handshake with the Prime Minister of India is in the Madurai newspapers and he becomes a starry sensation throughout India.

The title of the autobiography *The Scar* or "Vadu" in Tamil signifies not only the mark or the sore left on the skin that has not healed completely but it symbolises the painful mark left on an individual psyche and signifies the total destruction of the individuality of that person. Gunasekaran's life which was full of ugly scars is portrayed nakedly in this autobiography. It gives a graphic narrative of the life of an untouchable in India and also projects how the oppressions and discrimination have denied the basic human rights of the Dalits whose lives are controlled by the so-called upper caste people. Thus, the Dalit autobiography breaks all the limitations, boundaries and hurdles of discrimination based on caste, creed and religion. Gunasekharan's *The Scar* has emerged as the manifestation of the unbreakable spirit of a human to rise higher and touch greater heights and celebrates the reconstruction of a broken society.

## Works Cited

Aital, Parvati. *Studies in Comparative Literature: Translation and Beyond.* Mumbai: Prestige Books International, 2017.

Ambedkar, B. R. *The Annihilation of Caste*. Columbia: Columbia U P, 2014.

Azhagarasan, R., and Ravikumar. *The Oxford India Anthology of Tamil Dalit Writing*. Oxford U P, 2012.

Das, Bijay Kumar. *A Handbook of Translation Studies*. 3rd ed., Atlantic Publishers and Distributors, 2018.

Gunasekaran, K. A. *The Scar*. Kadambari, V., translator. New Delhi: Orient BlackSwan, 2012.

Prabodha, Ed. Waman Nimbalkar. Nagpur: Jan-Feb 2009.

Prasad, Vijay. *Untouchable Freedom: A Social History of a Dalit Community*. New Delhi, Oxford U P, 2000.

# 26

# Intertextuality of Self and Indigenous Society in Narendra Jadhav's *Outcaste: A Memoir*

*Dr B. Manivannan*

Dalit Literature emerges as an alternative to the high-brow literature. And, among the Dalit Writings, autobiographies are endorsed as a unique genre that receives huge popularity and is academically acclaimed today. Attributing the identity of Dalit to such autobiographies is structured and evolved as socio-political movement in post-independent India. Narendra Jadhav's *Outcaste: A Memoir* is not only a discourse of self, elaborating the author's personal experiences connected with his family but also it reveals his social self, marked with protest voicing for social justice as outcasted in an Indian context. This article aims at redefining this kind of interpersonal split as self and social self, which is of indigenous society, and this complex entity has been analysed in terms of Julia Kristeva's 'intertextuality' considering this autobiographical text a text of many texts, interchangeably composed.

Narendra Jadhav, born in 1953, hailed from a Mahar family of Maharashtrian village, Ozar in Nashik district. He might have been born as Dalit but has emerged with an incomparable emancipation as his profile shows great evidences ranging from a doctorate in Economics, bestowed with many titles and awards, as highly admired economist serving in Planning Commission of India, Member of Rajyasabha to a prolific writer in Marathi, Hindi and English. His text, *Outcaste: A Memoir*, first published in 2003, originally titled as *Amaca bapaanamhi* and later found an alternative title, *Untouchables: My Family's Triumphant Journey out of the Caste System in Modern India*, in 2005. The present text is, in fact, an intertext comprising both autobiography and biography, narrating the story of Jadhav's individual self on the one hand and on the other, all about his father and mother Damu and Sonu respectively. It is in the foreground a success story of Jadhav, an individual but in the background a deprived history of the subaltern community. The positive note underlying the narrative well motivates the younger generation.

The conceptual frame drawn from the post-structuralist theory of intertextuality may well be applied to Jadhav's life narrative, *Outcaste* or *Untouchables*, as Allen defines:

> The theory of text, therefore, involves a theory of intertextuality, since the text not only sets going a plurality of meanings but is also woven out of numerous discourses and spun from already existent meaning. The text's plurality is neither wholly an inside nor an outside, since the text itself is not unified, isolated object upon which an inside and an outside can be fixed. (67)

In this context, Jadhav's self is interchangeable with Ambedkar's intellectual personality; for, Ambedkar's influence on him is obvious as he has delivered seminal speeches and critiques on the architect of Indian Constitution incessantly. It can be substantiated by Barthe's view: "A text is made up of multiple writings, drawn from many cultures and entering into mutual relations of dialogue, parody, contestation, but there is one place where this multiplicity is focused and that place is the reader ..." (148) and, for instance, an autobiography is a literary text as well as a social document; it may be because of the 'readers' response' that brings out its multi-layered texture. But, it cannot be ignored that subjectivity of an author exists in such self-narrative, which is author specific. Eagleton's assessment on intertexuality is:

> All literary texts are woven out of other literary texts, not in the conventional sense that they bear the traces of 'influence' but in the more radical sense that every word, phrase or segment is a reworking of other writings which precede or surround the individual work. There is no such thing as literary 'originality', no such thing as the 'first' literary work: all literature is 'intertextual' (119).

Of course, "all literature is intertextual", and autobiography or biography cannot be exceptional. Jadhav's text is family specific on the surface level. The reader could find a trajectory that starts from his reading of author's self, curving over the family setting, touching the rural base of the Mahar community and reaching to review Dalit in Indian context, as the text criticising the *Manusmriti* and voicing for Ekalaiva who represents depressed class so was depicted in the *Mahabharata* text. Also, Jadhav brings out the drastic difference between village and urban settings from a Dalit's point of view. Zengin justly comments on Allen's reading of intertextuality: "meaning becomes something that exists in the network of textual links and can be found between a text and all the other texts, to which the text refers and relates" (299). Mambrol is also right to comment on the term intertextuality, in his blog text of web page, he says:

> A term popularised by Julia Kristeva in her analysis of Bakhtin's concepts Dialogism and Carnival, intertextuality is a concept that informs structuralist post-structuralist deliberations in its contention that individual texts are inescapably related to other texts in a matrix of irreducible plural and provisional meanings. The term is used to signify the multiple ways in which any one literary text is made up

> of other texts, by means of its implicit or explicit allusions, citations, its repetitions and transformations of the formal and substantive features of earner texts...(n. pag.)

The text of self-writing named as "Outcaste" or "Untouchables" which is not singularly of the author's or Damu's Dalit identity but of collectively dealing with all Scheduled Class community in general and Mahar in particular; thus a text leads another text and vice-versa. Here, the other, the term memoir in the title primarily refers to Damu's diary like documentary along with his orality texts and as it runs through the memory lane of the protagonist to become historical text of post independent Dalit community. They are functionally linked with each other and to Kristeva these texts are linguistic units that serve "as springboards in establishing different kinds of *novelistic utterances as functions*" (37).

Jadhav's *Untouchables* traces the demographic features of Mahar community and details thus:

> Among the erstwhile untouchable Dalit castes, the Mahar caste is the single largest in Maharashtra, a progressive province of the west coast of India, with Mumbai (Bombay) as its capital. Mahars are found in almost every village of Maharashtra, constituting around 10 percent of its population. Their quarters, called Maharvada, are invariably set outside the village boundaries. (6)

The subaltern condition is further documented in his life story referring to communal history even in pre-independent India: "Traditionally, the Mahar's duty in the village, as classified by British administrative manual, was that of 'an inferior village servant'" (6). On the one hand, the author explains how the community is socially suppressed and on the other he finds a solution, following the path of Ambedkar, in spiritual enlightenment that can be rationalised in the Buddhist revolt. He is of the view that social and religious sanctity (3) takes on this cruel caste system determining the continuity of deprived conditions of untouchables. Jadhav re-examines how 'the theory of *Karma*' stands maintaining the age-old caste system unchanged. But his reading of Buddhism makes him resist against the worst practice imposed by religious texts that advocate the 'four fold *Chaturvarna*' and traces the historical spread of the Buddhism:

> Certainly, revolts against the caste system did take place—the most notable being the one by Gautama Buddha in the fifth century B.C., which questioned and discarded the Chaturvarna and the caste system arising from it. Buddhism gained prominence over a large part of India and spread to other countries such as China and Japan, and to Southeast Asia, from the fourth century B.C. to the sixth century A.D (6).

The rise of the new religion represents 'the Light of Asia' which provides epistemologically a vital space for Dalits to be emancipating that is evidently shown in the life of Jadhav's parents and himself to be intellectually proving that his becoming of politically powerful is a real time achievement of a Dalit self. Sidonie Smith and Julia Watson define what autography points out: "'Autobiography,' now the most commonly used term for such life writing, thus described writing being produced at a particular historical juncture, ... with its concept of the self-interested individual intent on assessing the status of the soul or the meaning of public achievement" (2). Hence, Jadhav realises positively that his triumph is not of himself or of his family but of the outcaste community. At times, he celebrates himself being a Mahar while bringing out the Mahar legend of 'a handsome Mahar Warrior, Amrutnak' who rescued the queen of Sultan of Bedar. On his success when a reward was offered to him for his gesture of loyalty and bravery he selflessly got fifty two rights for his Mahar community. Jadhav with pride says: "The legend of Amrutnak is one of loyalty and self-sacrifice, which became a part of the

Mahar psyche" (7). He reveals that his self is instinctively individualistic, relational and collective (Nadeem, 227).

Jadhav's text is ethnic centred constructing the unique identity of both himself and his community. The life here is a triumphant journey, though it has thorns and roses, fall and rise as well. The text attempts to construct social recognition and social identity and it is always functionally reflective of the mythical and contemporary mind that is complex in nature exposing the three fold identities of individual (personal), relational (familial) and collective (social). The self-narrative involves a process which McAdams views: "Autobiographical narrative is 'a selective reconstruction of the ruminative past' (Qtd. in Nadeem, 224), and it is further critically studied as:

> The double process of identity exploration via narration and identity evaluation via reflection not only tie the three aspects of identity together but help evaluate them as narrators make a stance on the social values, roles and transactions they narrate. The act of reflection itself has an identity evaluation function. It shows the narrator's perception of the events initially by selecting them and by integrating them within an interpretive frame that includes their own value judgments. At the end, reflection culminates in a sense of closure and a final stance-making. (236)

Jadhav records these 'transactions' as socio-ethnic values stimulated through Buddha and Amrutnak, in the remote past Jyotiba Phule, Ambedkar in the past and Damu, his father in the recent past. And, his self-realisation is mythically, historically and socio-culturally done.

Indeed, the narrative is conditioned by both time and space shifts; in the displacement from village to the city, the Mahar family witnessed ups and downs, as they escaped from the prosecution in the village, but in Mumbay where Damu gained appreciation in whatever job he undertook. Analogically the Mahar warrior's guarding roles got recognised by British rulers offering them military jobs; Jadhav in *Untouchables*, gives such a historical note about his community:

> Mahars did find an outlet from their traditional village duties by serving as guards in the hill forts or enlisting in the military. The consolidation of British rule in India led to the Mahars' entry into the British Indian Army and paved the way female. Until then, women in general, and all untouchables, had been denied the right to learning. Education for the untouchables in the army gave them a new vision and a new sense of self-worth. They realised that the low esteem in which they were held was not an inescapable destiny but a stigma imposed on them by the priests. They felt the shame of it and were determined to get rid of it. (6)

The narrated self is multifarious and is able to recreate the memories related to the surrounding world and knowledge assimilated through texts in historical and cultural context and so education has been duly valued as a tool that would turn every Dalit empowered. This positive note is the core element of this auto/biographical narrative, *Outcaste* or *Untouchables*, which attracts the reader to witness the changing self as stated by István Dobos: "The fact is that the changing self-understanding of an autobiographer postulates a continuous process of losing and recreating the identity in the course of recollection" (10).

Moreover, the self in autobiography does not simply represent the individual life of the author as it is critically evaluated that 'instead of representing the personal life of the narrator, autobiographies can also be about something else, namely, about roles and parts played in belletristic and critical works and writings' (12). Hence, Jadhav's autobiography is historiographical to present Dalit life, especially of Mahar. Also it is a "social discourse" referring to "the historical, social and cultural processes that these texts initiate, first as actual cognitive performances, and, simultaneously, as social agency within the liberation movement of the Maharashtrian and Indian *dalits* in general" (Poitevin, 8). 'Another essential feature of the Dalit autobiographical narratives is that they do not isolate the individual from his whole historical environment, family, community and society at large' (10).

Jadhav, a well-educated and renowned Economist, follows the model propounded by Ambedkar to be engaged in a socio-political movement to liberate Dalit people and ensures the value of education by his writings and speeches contributing to Marathi Dalit history. The introductory text of *Untouchables* opens with a motivational note:

> Every sixth human being in the world today is an Indian, and every sixth Indian is an erstwhile untouchable, a Dalit. Today, there are 165 million Dalits, (equal to more than half the population of the United States) and they continue to suffer India's 3,500-years-old caste system, which remains a stigma on humanity. However, Dalits are awakening. We are struggling against caste discrimination, illiteracy, and poverty; our weapons are education, self-empowerment, and Democracy. (www.SimonSays.com 1)

What Ambedkar visualises about the caste free modern India is also Narendra Jadhav's mission that is reflected in the text, *Untouchables: My Family's Triumphant Journey out of the Caste System in Modern India*, and the journey he has endorsed in his life narrative is proactive in strengthening the Indian Constitution that ensures every citizen of the country right to equality as Article 14 codifies: "The State shall not deny to any person equality before the law or the equal protection of the laws within the territory of India" (Indian Constitution, Part III, Article 14).

To conclude, it has been evidently studied that Jadhav's auto/biographical text is an intertext that is a manifold adapted tale of the Dalits who still face the challenges of societal stigma in India. The author shares the adoring complimentary note about his father in the text and also diligently assesses the gradation imposed on caste system in India retold through three generations.

And, author's self which is so subjective but it objectively comprises Indigenous communities. Consequently, the socio-political aspects of this indigenous society intertextually make the author transact his self in three phases that are personal, familial, and social.

## Works Cited

Allen, Graham. *Intertextuality*. London: Routledge, 2007.

Barthes, R. *Image Music Text*. Trans. Stephen Heath. London: Fontana Press, 1977.

Dobos, István. .*Autobiographical Reading*: *Spectrum Hungarologicum*. Vol. 3.University of Jyväskylä, Faculty of Humanities, Hungarian Studies.www.jyu.fi/hungarologia 2010, 21 April 2021.

Eagleton, T. *Literary Theory: An Introduction*. Minneapolis: U of Minnesota P, 2008.

*Indian Constitution – Article 14* <https://samistilegal.in/article-14-right-toequality/#: ~ :text = ARTICLE%2014%20RIGHT%20TO%20 EQUALITY%3A&text = Article%2014% > 23 April 2021.

Jadhav,Narendra/dp/0670049727/ref = sr_1_21?dchild = 1&qid = 1619892490&refinements = p_27%3ANarendra + Jadhav&s = books&sr = 1-21, Accessed on 15 April 2021.

Jadhav, Narendra.*Untouchables: My Family's Triumphant Journey Out of the Caste System in Modern India.* New York and London: Scribner, 2005.

Kristeva, Julia, Alice Jardine, and Leon S. Roudiez. Trans. Julia Kristeva *Desire in Language: A Semiotic Approach to Literature and Art*. Edited by Thomas Gora. New York: Columbia U P, 1980.

Mahananda, Sarojb Kumar. *Towards Dalit Historiography: Imaging the Gandas through Various Narratives.* New Delhi: Archive Press, 2017.

Mambrol, Nasrullah. "Julia Kristeva's Intertxtuality." March 22 2016.Blog writing. <https://literariness.org/2016/03/22/julia-kristeva-intertextuality> 22 April 2021.

Nadeem, Nahla. "Autobiographical Narrative: An Exploration of Identity Construction Processes in Relation to Gender and Race". *Narrative Inquiry* 25.2, 2015, pp. 224-241.

Poitevin, Guy. *Dalit Autobiographical Narratives Figures of Subaltern Consciousness, Assertion and Identity.* Centre for Cooperative Research in Social Sciences. (Pune, India)2002 <http://www.ccrss.org> 22 April 2021.

Smith, Sidonie and Julia Watson. *Reading Autobiography: A Guide for Interpreting Life Narratives.* The U of Minnesota P, 2010.

Zengin, Mevlüde. "An Introduction to Intertextuality as a Literary Theory: Definitions, Axioms and the Originators". Pamukkale Üniversitesi Sosyal Bilimler Enstitüsü Dergisi Saýý 25/1, 2016, Sayfa 299-326.

# 27

# Trauma of Being a Dalit in Govardhan Wankhede's *My Life: The Journey of a Sociologist*: From Bleeding Dignity to Healing Humanity

*Dr Suchitra Gupta*

> My heart was heavy. It had lost faith in God. One can somehow get past poverty and deprivation, but it is impossible to get past caste. (Valmiki, *Joothan*: 18)

*My Life: The Journey of a Sociologist* is an autobiography of Dr Govardhan Wankhede and this autobiography unveils the layers of oppression, discrimination and deprivation faced by him in the span of his life. Dr Govardhan Wankhede, a former Professor and Dean, School of Education, Tata Institute of Social Sciences, Mumbai, is a prolific writer who has written extensively on the tyranny of hierarchical practices rampant in the society. He has to his credit 07 books, 14 Articles published in International Journals and many major interdisciplinary researches. Through his writings, he has voiced his concern on the issues of casteism and discrimination faced by the untouchables forcing them to live their life of indignity and inhumanity.

The book is not only a memorialisation of his life experiences but also a means of preserving community memories. It is also a documentation of the lives of the people of his populace. "Although there are a few autobiographies written by Dalit Litterati and activists, this is the first by a Dalit Academic Sociologist" (Shah n. pag.). A post-independence narrative, the book accounts his journey from a remote village in Maharashtra and ends with him making extensive contribution in the national and international academia in a self reflectory pattern. Distance in time and space often has a healing and amnesiac effect but this was not the fate of the author who gets "... overwhelmed and in tears while recalling my experiences of poverty, caste, discrimination, untouchability and the life conditions of other members of the community" (Wankhede, 17).

Set in 1950's, the autobiography concerns itself with the three generations of the family of the author, he being the first generation learner. He reflects on the metamorphosis of his life and his children who are fortunate enough to lead a comfortable life and study in one of the best educational institutes of India, having fluency in English, a language that symbolises class and culture. While tracing his life from childhood to his retirement as the Dean of the School of Education and as Chairman of the Centre for Higher Education, the narrative speaks volumes of the trauma faced by him as a Dalit.

Adhering to his call of bringing reformation in society, he narrates the major incidents of his life with the sole purpose of bringing and spreading awareness in society and of instilling hope among the deprived.

The author in his autobiography pens the trajectory of his life through three lenses: from the lens of a member of society, from the lens of sociologist and from the lens of an Indian citizen.

## As a Member of Society

Experiencing intergenerational trauma and agonised by the inhuman living conditions to which his community was exposed to, he dwells on the possible rationale behind the inhuman practices in the Indian society. Equating casteism with Hindu philosophy and religion he observes that birth and rebirth in Hindu thought and religion connotes 'Karma' or actions in past life that are judged by Gods. God's judgement is executed by a small section of the self declared superior population and going by their interpretation all sufferings are the outcome of the penalty of misdeeds that are decided by gods. "As a result, with the course of time, this thought had led to clear hierarchical and graded social division based on caste and gender" (Wankhede, 17). During the course of time, various movements and societies have endeavoured to heal the wound by bringing the marginalised section of society earlier known as "Untouchables" now called Dalits or SC into the mainstream. Yet a sizeable remainder of this populace continue to get exploited and are forced to lead a deplorable life.

(a) **His Childhood:** Reminiscing his childhood he talks of the social exclusion that leads to acute deprivation of dignity and total loss of identity and consciousness to question the existing social Hindu order. The houses in his village were congregated according to castes with certain areas reserved for the upper castes and some for the lower castes. The village was majorly occupied by the "middle-caste" (Wankhede, 23) like Malis, Kumbies and Marathas. The Marathas were located on a raised area. The Mahar community into which he was born lived in Maharwada that was situated on the eastern end of the village to ensure a considerable distance between the upper caste and the untouchables. This positioning of the houses was done very judiciously so that "the winds carrying the scent of the Mahars" (Wankhede, 25) do not pollute the upper castes as the winds in the village blew from west to east. Absence of toilets led men and women to adopt open defacation near the Maharwada to avoid the stench. The Mahars had no recourse. The Maharwada was further divided into two groups, the native residents and the immigrants. The immigrants were accorded lower status by the native Mahars.

Incongruously a Mahar who is required to keep the village clean, is himself surrounded by the stench and the filth, and is denied the right to food and clean clothes. "Children and women used to collect food from discarded leftover in a nearby waste food garbage" (Wankhede, 31).

The strong urge among Dalits to escape the oppressive, dehumanising socio-economic conditions led them into the grip of Christian missionaries. It is reported that 42% of Indian Christians are Dalit Christians. The strict social norms and familial pressure stopped the author from converting into Christianity. "Otherwise I would have been a Christian and have an altogether different life, education, job and thereby a different identity and existence" (Wankhede, 43). On a personal note, the author says that he faced discrimination at home front also. "Being the middle child I was neglected by my mother, father and elder brother. My parents lavished more attention, love and care to the elder and the younger one" (Wankhede, 39).

(b) **His Education:** His parents, though illiterate, played a pivotal role in the education of their children by providing a stimulating environment for the education. In the village there was little provision for the education of Dalits. The efforts of Samta Sainik Dal brought a pronounced impact on the lives of the Mahar community. The Mahars gave up their occupation overnight and almost all the children were enrolled in the village school. Reminiscing of his early schooling, the author says that he had to walk barefoot two miles one way every day with little or no food. For his high schooling he took admission at Akot. He opted for Arts stream as it was less expensive. Here living in a Maharwada was a nightmare with all the stench of excreta from public toilets flowing all around. All through his school, he "was disturbed, frustrated and despondent because of financial problems, family issues and the social inferiority complex" (Wankhede, 64). There was no joy and happiness of living but the fear "of being labelled as a gone case" (Wankhede, 65) kept him moving ahead. He continued with his education, doing odd jobs to earn money, fighting and struggling for books, clothes, food and money. He completed his graduation from Milind College at Aurangabad and post graduation in Sociology from the University of Marathawad.

An inner urge to study further propelled him to apply for MPhil course at JNU despite all opposition in the family.

JNU came as a game changer in his life both academically and socially. At JNU, for the first time in his life, he experienced freedom from religion, language and to some extent freedom from caste discrimination. The author categories his experiences and problems on the basis of culture, language and academics. The free and liberal atmosphere at JNU led him to compare JNU and Delhi to London, the city which ironically he had never visited. The open western life style, the use of English as a means of communication at JNU initially disconcerted him but gradually healthy and open discussions, debate, arguments at JNU blossomed his personality. JNU taught him "to question, to enquire, to listen, to talk, to argue, to research and to expand my span of knowledge" (Wankhede, 136). The research fellowship from ICSSR and UGC were great financial support to him in this period. JNU gave him an extensive national and international exposure by providing him an opportunity of attending and participating in World

Congresses and International seminars. His initial tenure at TISS, Mumbai furthered his research acumen. The author is reminded of Dr B. R. Ambedkar's thoughts where he considers "education as a great means of change, liberty and dignity" (Wankhede, 130). After a brief stint at Indian Institute of Education at Pune, the author returned to JNU and enrolled himself for a PhD degree which he completed in 1993.

(c) **Facing Social Discrimination:** "... the seeds of wild grass are seen nowhere but they exist everywhere, similarly caste is not seen everywhere but exists everywhere" (Wankhede, 164). The author all through his life experienced felt the shadow of caste. This rigidity of caste system compelled Girish Karnad to write "One's caste is like the skin of one's body. You can peel it off top to toe, but when the new skin forms, there you are again: a barber—a shepherd—a scavenger!" (21 qtd. in Sonker, 53). There are occasions when to save himself from indignity he hides his identity. The colour of the skin and the language spoken are the two parameters by which caste is judged and the author says that on occasions people could judge his caste. He lost his first love—a Brahmin girl colleague at IIE Pune at the altar of caste. On another occasion till his caste is unexposed, everything is good between him and his two friends—a Brahmin boy and a Sindhi boy at JNU. With the revelation of his caste, the indifference, sarcasm sets in the friendship.

A course on "Indian Education System: Issues and Strategies" was taught by him at TISS. Being an optional subject it was mostly opted by the students from SC-ST communities. Astonishingly he was informed that the departmental faculty discouraged the students from opting for this course. The author says "caste is always operative, openly or subtly. Though many will not accept being a castist or practicing untouchability but inadvertently all do" (Wankhede, 164). The author narrates another very shameful incident where in a programme at TISS Mr Daya Pawar, an eminent Dalit writer was invited as the chief guest. The other faculty members feigned excuse on varied grounds and finally the author being a Dalit, was assigned the job of entertaining the guest. At TISS not only he is denied timely promotion, he is forced to work in undignified conditions. "I did not get a room to sit in the office for ten years. Yet another person who joined as lecturer five years after I joined occupied the vacant room in my absence" (Wankhede, 131).

"In the Indian academic world, the network of established academicians belongs mostly to upper castes and particularly Brahmins" (Wankhede, 170). The author being a Dalit, considers it his good fortune to be able to not only retain his post but also to get promoted and to get retired from a prestigious institution like TISS.

He marvels at himself, his achievements and reminiscences upon his childhood struggles, his school days, college days, university days and the hurdles and difficulties faced by him. "This was certainly upward mobility in terms of education and occupation as well as the entry into a new world of academics, intellect and an elite class with Western sophistication. This was denouncing the traditional imposed life of helplessness, poverty, disrespect and dependence. This was freedom from the burden of caste, untouchability, humiliation, indignity and hunger" (Wankhede, 129).

Baba Sahib's message "Educate, Unite and Agitate" (Wankhede, 130) had brought a social revolution in India. At TISS, SC-ST Employees Welfare Association was formed and it appealed to the High Court Bombay to order TISS to execute the reservation policy and to initiate and form SC-ST Cell. The TISS had to comply.

(d) **His Service to Society**: As a Dean of Social Protection Office (DSPO), he lends a healing hand of humanity to all the deprived sections in society. He begins by filling the vacant SC-ST positions in the faculty and the administrative staff. The Ambedkarian thought of cutting slavery and injustice through education motivates the author to initiate for the promotion of education especially among the backward classes. He initiated the making of videos of entrance exam preparation, group discussion, mock interviews, orientation programmes with food and lodging facility for pre and post admission students. He also ensured that selection panel had SC, ST, OBC representation. These efforts had positive results. A good number (10-15 students) from deprived backgrounds got admission in the college. English Language Lab was developed and made available to all in the campus. This resulted in 3 to 4 students from deprived classes going abroad under student exchange programme. "It is so satisfying and exhilarating that all can do it, we can do it; they can do it, if given the opportunity with sincere efforts and facilities" (Wankhede, 174).

## As a Sociologist

In his autobiography, the author gives a classified account of hierarchy among untouchables. The untouchables of Maharashtra are divided into four major castes—Mahars, Mangs, Chambars and Dhors. While Chambars and Dhors practiced untouchability with Mahars and Mangs on one hand, Mahars practiced untouchability with Mangs on the other. There was no inter-dining and no commingle between these two communities. Dhors are inferior to the Chambars. Excepting Chambars the other three indulged in eating the flesh of the dead animals. This flesh was also dried and saved for rainy days when there was virtually nothing to eat. The author gives a very gory picture of his childhood when his grandfather puts a bundle of calf flesh on his head to take home. "The blood dripped around my head and body" (Wankhede, 35). The trajectory of these traumatic experiences is underlined by human ethical studies. A man undoubtedly belongs to a race but is not a human.

Furthermore as a sociologist the author feels that "Sociology in India is missing out in recording and analyzing such basic and harsh social realities" (Wankhede, 175). A dalit who after much struggle acquires a respectable position in society is tormented and labeled as an "SC elite" (Wankhede, 176) and of misappropriating hard earned money of the common man.

The reservation policy in India is based on its caste system. Countries like New Zealand, Australia, South America and Africa also have a kind of reservation as preferential treatment which is based "on race, ethnicity, religion and language" (184). The author asserts that the reservation policy in India sort of compensates for all the injustices and atrocities inflicted on the backward classes. The misconception of the common man regarding the time period of its effectiveness is again a testimony of casteist hierarchy. "It is clearly mentioned that only the political reservations would be for ten years and there is no mention of educational and employment reservations and would depend on how it is implemented and what the achievements are" (Wankhede, 185). The entire issue has unfortunately become political and thus, it lost its real intent of purpose. The inadequate nature of the policies for the upliftment of the downtrodden is his another major concern as a sociologist.

The lacuna in the policies did not allow the benefits to reach many of the Dalit classes. Ironically, political gleanings have led to a rise in the demand for reservation on various grounds. The author infers the trauma of casteism in the post-modern times has no closure, rather it keeps haunting like a ghost.

## As an Indian

At TISS, the author gets an opportunity to visit Germany for three months under the faculty exchange programme—DAAD.

In the aircraft, he reflects on going away from "my motherland, my culture and society that had always treated me like a second class citizen and hurt my dignity and respect in various inhuman ways" (Wankhede, 139). In Germany his Indian sensitivity gets a rude cultural shock on seeing the functioning of free and open societal norms.

He delivers a lecture on education of SC-ST in India organised by the Department of Education at J.W. Goethe University. The lecture was attended by students, faculty members and a few local Indians. The author says that in Germany "academics is taken seriously with due respect with special respect to the profession" (Wankhede 143). He says that he experienced excessive respect as a Professor all through Germany.

Being a Dalit and belonging to an oppressed Indian community, inspired him to do a comparative study of the social realities, of identity crisis and discrimination faced by the guest workers in Germany and Dalits in India, "This makes me more certain of the fact that discrimination is everywhere but in different forms with different basis" (Wankhede, 149).

One of the highlights of his academic journey is visiting various countries like South Africa, U.K., China, Italy, Australia, France and Switzerland as a participant or as a subject expert in numerous international seminars and conferences. Sadly, he says, he got more recognition abroad than in India. An ambitious Dalit became the sore throat of many in India which sequentially invited trouble.

The remonstrative voices of the Dalits that came across through literature and many socio-political movements urged the Government of India to come up with many reformation policies that have proved beneficial for the Dalits in regaining their self respect and equality of status in society to quite an extent. The beckoning leadership of Dr B. R. Ambedkar and his slogan "Educate, Agitate and Organize" has motivated the backward classes to arise and to struggle for their emancipation from all untouchability, inhumanity and indignity. They are emerging as intellectuals and creating new possibilities for social revamping in Indian society. The narrative indulges in the graphic portrayal of severest form of deprivation and discrimination. Nevertheless there is not a moment of despondency and despair in the entire narrative. In the struggle for survival the stress is on the fight and not on the fence, the stress is on the Holy Grail and not on the hedges. The work neither seeks pity nor sympathy but is imbued with the spirit of resilience and hard work.

## Works Cited

Ambedkar, B. R. "Annihilation of Caste." *The Essential Writings of B. R. Ambedkar*. Ed. Valerine Rodrigues. New Delhi: Oxford UP, 2002.

Shah, Ghanshyam. https://migrate.leftword.com Accessed 01 May, 2021.

Valmiki, Omprakash. *Joothan: A Dalit's Life*. Trans. Arun Prabha Mukherjee. Kolkata: Samya, 2003.

Wankhede, Govardhan. *My Life: The Journey of a Dalit Sociologist*. New Delhi: Aakar Books, 2020.

# 28

# Dalit Autobiography and Santram B.A.'s *Mere Jeevan Ke Anubhav*: A Critique

*Dr Ashok Verma*

Dalit Literature has certainly come of age now. It is no more an emerging area of creative expression and critical investigation, particularly in the 21st century; rather, it is already an established canon in itself. Though it is thought to have gained momentum from the Marathi literature of the 1960s, the seeds of Dalit writings had already been sown in the relentless efforts of great social thinkers such as Jotirao Phule, Periyar and Dr Bhim Rao Ambedkar who envisioned, in their oeuvre, a society where there is no scope for caste-based discrimination. In fact, the period between the late 19th century and the early half of the 20th century was particularly conducive to such thought when a wave of social change was underway, alongside the national freedom movement, among other things. One particular signature in this tradition is Santram B.A.—the founding father of the 'famous' *Jaat Paat Todak Mandal* (Association for the Annihilation of Caste)—who in his own way, pioneered the cause of the oppressed, in the early half of the 20th century and rigorously worked towards bringing about a revolution of sorts in the Indian society and sought to establish caste discrimination as anti-human practice. The present paper presents a critique of

Santram B.A.'s autobiography *Mere Jeevan Ke Anubhav* (*The Experiences of My Life*) from the perspective of the oppressed. Further, an attempt has been made to assess his contribution to the Dalit cause and movement. The paper also seeks to investigate whether it is worth to compartmentalise the Dalit stance along narrow, strict caste identities. Moreover, the paper underscores the difference between Dalit autobiography and swarna autobiography along their different cultural lineage.

Dalit autobiography has a distinct identity because of its uniqueness of experience. It serves a definite purpose of providing voice to that section of society which has always been relegated to the margins of the social order. Dalit writers have always emphasised upon this distinct function of Dalit autobiography which follows the socio-cultural trajectory rather the purely 'aesthetic' one of the mainstream Brahmanical tradition. Autobiography cannot be a mere life story; it has to a socio-cultural document. That is why they object when Dalit autobiographies are presented as autobiographical novels, there is a deliberate attempt at projecting the self-felt experiences as a work of fiction. Sharankumar Limbale takes a strong objection to this projection and says that his autobiographical experiences in *Akkarmashi* have been misrepresented as fiction, thereby putting a question mark upon their authenticity (*Mere*, 174). While challenging the nomenclature, Satnam Singh, a scholar who has worked on Santram B.A.'s works, quotes Manager Pandey who says that there is no such literary genre as autobiographical novel.

Another key difference between Dalit autobiographies and those from the mainstream literature is that of cultural tradition. Whereas mainstream literature (*Swarna Sahitya*) denotes Brahmanical tradition, Dalit Literature carries forward the *shraman* tradition—a tradition based on the values of liberty, equality and fraternity as against the Brahmanical tradition that is founded on discrimination, enmity and bondage. While the *shraman* tradition promotes unity in the name of buddhist sangh, brahmanical tradition propagates disintegration in the name of various castes and varnas. (*Mere*, 175)

Santram B.A. can safely be called the first Hindi Dalit autobiographer. If his autobiography is placed along the diachronic graph, it is the first Dalit autobiography, for sure, as there is no Dalit autobiography written before him. Ironically, however, Santram B.A. has been relegated to the anonymity owing to the politics that seeped into the entire Dalit discourse at later stages. The mainstream Hindi tradition comfortably slept over Santram's contribution as he was not from a 'high' caste. Similarly, the Dalits could not bring themselves to accept Santram B.A. wholeheartedly and conveniently ignored his contribution to the Dalit cause as he was not from a scheduled caste. Between the two NOTs, Santram's copious creative as well as critical opus remained and still continues to remain in obscurity to a large extent.

Satnam Singh rues over this relegation of Santram B.A. He rightly terms his autobiography to be the "first autobiography of Dalit Literature" and establishes him as the first Dalit journalist as well:

> It is sad that Dalit Literature too does not include him [Santram]. . . . Taking into account the year of its publication, *Mere Jeevan ke Anubhav* is the first [Hindi] Dalit autobiography. Santram was also a fearless journalist of his times. He wrote in all prominent newspapers-magazines. In 1914 he took out the magazine *Usha*. His *Kranti* was a famous magazine of its times. . . . In this context, he may be hailed as the first Hindi Dalit journalist as well. ("Introduction", i)

However, it is also true that there are many scholars who prefer to expand the meaning of the term in a more generic sense, thereby detaching it from narrow caste identities. Gangadhar Pantawane, a professor of Marathi, rightly defines the term when he says:

> To me, Dalit is not a caste. He is the man exploited by the social and economic tradition of this country. He does not believe in God, rebirth, soul, teachings of holy books, separatism, fate and heaven because they have made him a slave. He does believe in humanism. Dalit is a symbol of change and revolution. (3)

Kancha Ilaiah, a famous Dalit thinker and writer, too, in his *Why I am Not a Hindu*, coins the word *Dalitbahujan*, so as to interpret Dalit in a larger, wider context and avers that in spite of contradictions "there are cultural and economic commonalities as well as commonalities of productive knowledge which mesh them [Other Backward Castes and Dalits] together like threads in a cloth" (ix).

The above lines clearly establish vital linkages between various oppressed sections of the Indian society, thereby, not only contributing to the Dalit cause but also underlining the profound heterogeneity of Dalit identity. This approach of rejecting narrow caste-based identities is pivotal in constructing a broader Dalit identity and forwarding the Dalit agenda. Writers like Santram B.A. are to be incorporated within the Dalit fold. That would certainly enrich the Dalit discourse. While underscoring the essential humanistic approach of the Dalits, it will further give a fillip to the efforts for negotiating the systematic oppression of a large chunk of population in the garb of graded inequality. Therefore, it is high time that the Dalit world took cognizance of Santram's status as one of the earliest writers who worked diligently towards shattering of caste norms to establish an egalitarian, casteless society on a strong footing of equality. It is heartening to note that some progressive Dalit scholars have started showing research interest in his works, thereby bringing to literary limelight the works of one of the great proponents of a casteless society.

Having located Santram in the Dalit tradition and his autobiography as the first Dalit autobiography, the paper now seeks to underline the salient highlights of his autobiography which is a rich text offering a glimpse into the multilayered and multifarious oppressive system of caste Hinduism. While it details the accounts of caste humiliation that Santram had to undergo, it also depicts his incessant struggle against it and other levels of oppression. The autobiography, thus, becomes a *potpourri* tracing various memories about the disparate experiences—personal, familial, social, literary, political—associated with the author.

One interesting aspect of Santram's rejection of birth-based caste identity is that he chose to write his name as Santram B.A. where B.A. is a marker of his bachelor's degree. In other words, he turned his educational qualification into his surname. By this move, he launched a two-pronged onslaught at the prevailing caste system. One, he simply did away with his caste surname since he did not believe in caste identity, thus setting an example of practicing what he preached. Secondly, he underlined the importance and power of education in paving the way for liberation from caste identities. Thus, Santram gave his name distinct meanings by proudly and explicitly linking it to his education. According to a scholar, "His name appeared without his caste nomenclature and he proudly displayed his educational qualification and degree as his surname, signature, and distinct identity—Santram B.A.—which became an integral part of his name (Gopal, 8).

Apart from underlining the significance of education, this unique identity further allowed Santram to interrogate and negotiate the traumatic experiences of caste discrimination. Dalit autobiographies constantly recount experiences of caste-based humiliation, oppression and the author's struggle to overcome it. Santram's autobiography is no exception to this. In fact, it is replete with such instances of caste prejudices. At an early stage in life, he had to undergo caste humiliation at the hands of his fellow students at school:

> When I was admitted in class four in Ambala, my caste was also mentioned in the register. . . . My co-students constantly harassed me, calling me by my caste name *kumhar*. And why would they have not done so when even a saint and poet like Tulsidas ridiculed *kumhara*. . . . I took the students' taunts quietly and painfully. (*Mere*, 16)

This subjugation at the level caste continued throughout his growing-up years. Another instance that describes a similar kind of experience at college is pertinent to quote here:

> In my boarding house, the kitchen in which I had food was orthodox. . . . One day a few fellow students . . . quarreled with me and placed a note on my seat stating that since I belonged to a low-caste, I should have my food outside the kitchen or else they would take the matter to the principal. . . . I angrily declared that even if they take the matter to the governor, I will have my food inside the kitchen only. (*Mere*, 17)

It is noteworthy that there is great difference between the author's reactions in the above-mentioned two instances. While in the first, he finds himself absolutely helpless and therefore, takes the insulting remarks meekly, he stands his ground in the second and silences the objector. Evidently, Santram's growth from a shy school boy to a confident college lad has passed through many such bitter experiences.

Such experiences, while on one hand make Santram understand his lowly status as a low caste boy, they also make him more resolute to closely observe and analyse the state of affairs and fight such oppressive system. Here it is pertinent to note that his unique positionality allows him to take an impartial view of the problem and seek the means to redress it. He himself writes at one place:

> I was born in a caste which is neither as high as *dwija* nor as low as untouchable. This position enabled me to objectively

> survey the plight of the so-called *dwija* and untouchables. Right or wrong, but I have arrived at the conclusion that the untouchables and the shudras do not suffer as much from their poverty as from the humiliation at the hands of *dwijas*. (*Mere*, 129)

Charu Gupta, a scholar on Santram B.A., too rightly observes in this context: "Through such memories, Santram imaginatively weaves an 'I' out of the contours of caste stigma. Santram's retelling encompasses everyday caste humiliation, myths of food and skin colour, and a critique of caste intellectuals and scriptural Hindu texts, through which he shapes a multipronged critique of caste in private and public life" (9).

As Santram found the caste system oppressive and against the fundamental principles of human dignity, it was natural for him to get inclined towards Arya Samaj—a movement that was in its full swing across the Punjab during those times. Along with some progressive thinking friends, he founded the famous *Jaat Paat Todak Mandal* (hereafter *Mandal*)—an organisation that became the harbinger of social change. Under the banner of the *Mandal*, Santram vigorously and diligently worked towards the upliftment of the have-nots and setting the Indian society free from the dangerous caste system. Here it may be noted that after some years, Santram got disillusioned with the ideology of the Arya Samaj as he found some inherent contradictions in it in favour of the orthodox retrogressive Hinduism—the very thing it sought to attack originally. He, however, carried on with his mission relentlessly.

The primary focus of the *Mandal* was to do away with the birth-based caste system and one potential way of doing so was to promote inter-caste marriages. As such, it became the guiding and defining principle of all activities undertaken by the *Mandal*. Santram mentions in his autobiography many such references of inter-caste marriages facilitated and solemnised by the *Mandal*. One such example is as under:

> I had two friends Parmanand and Bhumanand. Parmanand was Arora by caste and Bhumanand a Brahmin. . . . Parmanand requested me to persuade Bhumanand to marry his younger sister. . . . Bhumanand agreed. . . . His father, family and friends opposed it and no one came for the wedding. . . . It was a brave act to break caste taboos at that time. (*Mere,* 28)

Not only did Santram preach in favour of inter-caste marriages, he himself came forward to set an example of inter-caste and inter-state marriage when he married a widow from Maharashtra even when he was committed not to remarry. His belief in the reforming power of such steps was unflinching. He narrates the incident thus:

> Bhai Bhumanand Ji was talking to the parents of one child widow from Maharashtra. I said to him: 'please spare me. I do not want to remarry.' He said: 'This match helps overcome caste discrimination, promotes widow remarriage and downplays regional differences. It's a good opportunity for you to actively contribute towards social reform.' (*Mere,* 64)

Charu Gupta finds the following specificities in Santram's second marriage that again reaffirm Santram's unswerving faith in the intercaste marriage to bring about a change for the better in the Indian social fabric:

> This was an interprovincial widow remarriage. It was also an intercaste *pratiloma* marriage—most attacked by the orthodoxy—between a Shudra man and a Brahmin widow, similar to Ambedkar's second marriage. In a sense, the central focus of intercaste marriages allowed Santram to underline how caste permeated our most intimate spaces, and to show that it was in such arenas that caste needed to be challenged the most. (19)

Under the banner of *Jaat Paat Todak Mandal* only, Santram invited Dr B. R. Ambedkar to deliver the presidential address at a conference in Lahore. Though the conference had to be cancelled due to the overwhelming protest Santram faced from his own Arya Samaji friends, this invitation became instrumental in Ambedkar's writing a seminal essay on the caste system i.e. "Annihilation of Caste" which was later published by him on his own. Significantly, Santram went on to translate "Annihilation of Caste" into Hindi and published it under the banner of *Jaat Paat Todak Mandal*. He also published it in Urdu in his journal *Kranti*.

Santram was in dialogue with major Dalit leaders of his times including Periyar, Babu Mangu Ram and Ambedkar. In an exchange of letters between Santram and Ambedkar, the latter wrote:

> I admire your efforts for breaking up the caste system. But allow me to say that I do not agree with the way you are attacking the problem. I do not see how you can break up caste without annihilating the religious notions on which the caste system is founded. I cannot develop the argument now. . . . In the meantime I must leave it to you to deal with the question in the way you like. ("Religious Notions", 5)

Significantly, Ambedkar argued that inter-caste marriage was the hallmark of *Dalit* progress and the most important solution to annihilating caste, since it challenged the relationship between maintenance of caste purity and control of women's sexuality (*Annihilation*, 59-64). Santram too, throughout his life, continued to work towards liberating the Indian society from the caste system and as such, he becomes an authentic Dalit voice in their struggle against the centuries old oppression of the Dalits in the name of caste.

Founding his anti-caste arguments on Ambedkar's premise that without eradicating the religious concepts that perpetrate caste system it is impossible to achieve annihilation of caste, Santram incessantly questions the notions of the *Manusmriti*. He also pinpoints the inherent discriminatory ideology of the caste Hindus, which is primarily due to the religious sanction of the caste system in such scriptures. Santram terms such ideology as "polluted and narrow" and creates a dent in the ideologically promoted hegemonic image of the caste Hindus and the Shudras in a dyadic relationship. This unwitting internalisation of their respective images by both the groups is primarily responsible for the plight of the low-castes.

On the question of conversion of Shudras and untouchables to other religions (such as Islam or Buddhism), Santram rips apart the dual standards of the caste Hindus and writes: "Hindus want to uphold untouchability and at the same time, they also want that the untouchables should not convert" (*Mere,* 123). Having seen through the inner working of the caste Hindu ideology, Santram boldly feels completely disillusioned with the national freedom movement. He feels that without wiping out the unjust caste system, the attainment of *swaraj* for a larger section of the Indian population would be mere eyewash. He cannot help write at such a point: "I was not so keen on Swaraj as for eradicating caste system and its natural successor, untouchability" (*Mere,* 127). He goes on to say that the British regime is indeed an unprecedented divine blessing for the *Shudras* and the untouchables. It is a fact that the fair chances of progress that the *Shudras* enjoy under the British raj have neither ever been nor can be under the Hindu regime.

A well-read man as he is, Santram draws his arguments from various sources and disciplines to bring to the fore the underlying dichotomy of the Hindu mythology and scriptures. Selectively quoting from ancient texts, he refers to the instances of *anuloma* and *pratiloma* intercaste marriages to substantiate his point-of-view. For example, Pramatta, a Brahmin woman, married a barber and gave birth to Matang, the great *rishi*. Arundhati, a Kshatriya, was married to Vashishth Rishi, son of a prostitute. Their son Shakti married Adrishyanti, a Chandal girl. Shakti's son, Parashar, the great *rishi*, married Satyavati, a fisherman's daughter, and was father of Vyas, the writer of Mahabharat.

Bhim married the demoness Hidamba, and Ghatotkatch was their child (*Humara Samaj,* 11-14). At one point he also questions the intentions of the 'great' mythological kings and wonders, "Why such Hindu kings like Ramchandra, Harishchandra, Krishna, Shivaji and Pratap did not think of . . . providing education and full citizenship rights to untouchables and Shudras?" (172)

Thus, disillusioned with the scriptures, he finds them essentially discriminatory and outrightly rejects any possibility of the role of such *shastras* in abolishing caste by saying that "attempting to take help of *shastras* in finding solutions to eradicate caste and untouchability is like washing dirt with more dirt" (172).

A staunch opponent of the caste system, Santram even approached Mahatma Gandhi to discuss the problem. He narrates an interesting incident in his autobiography wherein he got involved in an argument with Gandhiji over the issue. In fact, Gandhiji was in favour of maintaining a status quo in the existing *varna vyavastha* which Santram could not bring himself to agree upon. The entire episode is narrated thus:

> I led a deputation of the JPTM to Gandhi at Lahore and requested him to help our movement. But the Mahatma said that caste was a good thing as it eliminated hard competition in the choice of profession. . . . At this I replied—'Mahatmaji, it is a good thing for a Brahman, or Kshatriya, or Vaishya boy to follow the profession of his father, but how can it be in the interest of a sweeper boy to continue to remove night soil and clean latrines for generations? Mahatmaji, you are a Bania by caste; your hereditary profession was to sell salt, oil and flour. Why don't you go and earn your living by selling those commodities? Why have you come here to preach politics and ethics?' (139)

This episode clearly shows that Santram had guts to call a spade a spade fearlessly irrespective of the 'stature' of Mahatma

Gandhi. His autobiography is replete with such instances wherein he posed some piercing yet logical questions to the followers of the Brahmanical tradition. Obviously, he was working with the zeal of a missionary and was syncretic in his approach, drawing his arguments from various sources and traditions. This approach gave him a unique perspective. That is why he could not completely conform to a particular ideology whether of Arya Samaj or that of the contemporary Dalit movement. He maintained his distinctive position in his mission—the eradication of caste system.

Thus, Santram B.A. was a true humanitarian who waged a relentless battle against birth-based caste discrimination. Throughout his life, he kept on fighting against this "devilish arch-enemy" responsible for the division of the Indian society into numerous groups and sections. In the words of Santram himself, "I neither believe in Hinduism, Christianity or Islam as individual religions nor Indian and Western cultures as different cultures. I believe only in one religion i.e. Humanism and one culture i.e. human culture. To me, religion is a collective nomenclature for the basics that promote peace and spread happiness in the society" (107). This is a position maintained also by Dalit authors and thinkers in the *shraman* tradition. Santram B.A.'s autobiography, thus, often invokes narratives associated with Dalit movements. The whole argument can be summed up in the words of Satnam Singh who writes: "In this way, we can say that Santram B.A.'s autobiography *Mere Jeevan ke Anubhav* is the first autobiography of Hindi Dalit writing because it records the experiences of caste humiliation as well as those experiences that put up a strong fight against caste-based discrimination" (176).

## Works Cited

Ambedkar, B. R. *Annihilation of Caste: Speech Prepared for the Annual Conference of JPTM of Lahore but Not Delivered*. B. R. Kadrekar, 1936.

—. *Jatibhed ka Uchhed.* Translated by Santram BA, Jat-Pat Torak Mandal, 1937.

—. "'Religious Notions on Which Caste System is Based Should be Destroyed': Dr Ambedkar's Letter to Jat-Pat Torak Mandal." *Tribune*, 11 Dec. 1935, p. 5.

Gopal, Madan. "A Hundred Years of Writing." *The Times of India*, 16 Feb. 1987, p. 8.

Gupta, Charu. "Speaking Self, Writing Caste: Recovering the Life of Santram BA." *Project Muse*, vol. 40, no. 1, U of Hawai'i P, winter 2017, pp. 16-43. https://muse.jhu.edu/article/666049.

Ilaiah, Kancha. *Why I Am Not a Hindu: A Sudra Critique of Hindutva Philosophy, Culture, and Political Economy*. Samya, 2002.

Pantwane, Gangadhar. quoted by Brijesh Kumar in "Dalit Aesthetics—An Alternative Way of Looking into Literature." *International Journal of English Language, Literature and Humanities*, vol. 3, no. 4, June 2015. pp. 1-8. http://182.18.165.51/Fac_file/PUBLI391@673440.pdf.

Santram B.A. *Hamara Samaj*. Nalanda Prakashan, 1949. (English Translations of the textual references are mine)

—. *Mere Jeevan Ke Anubhav*. Samyak Prakashan, 2014. (English Translations of the textual references are mine)

Singh, Satnam. "Dalit Sahitya ki Pahli Swa-Jeevni: Mere Jeevan ke Anubhav." *Mere Jeevan Ke Anubhav*. Samyak Prakashan, 2014. pp. 170-176. (English Translations of the textual references are mine)

# 29

# Balbir Madhopuri's *Changiya Rukh: Against the Night*: Dynamics of Caste Prejudice and Dalit Resistance

*Dr S. Chelliah*

Dalit autobiographies have been originally written in different languages in India and out of these autobiographies, many autobiographies have been translated into few Indian languages, English and other languages of the world. Among these, there is only one famous Punjabi Dalit autobiography that must be read by every person just because the pain of being a low-born has been depicted in this autography and it inspires other people also. This autobiography *Changiya Rukh* was originally published in Punjabi in 2002 and it was later translated into Hindi and English and was published in English in 2010 (reprinted in 2019) by Oxford University Press. Khsushi Saroha writes about this autobiography:

> From my findings, all I can conclude is that while Maharashtra stands the lowest with regards to caste-based discrimination; and Uttar Pradesh if at all, does only slightly better; it is Punjab that has always given a comparatively habitable environment to the Dalits and continues to do so. (Saroha, 237)

The writer of this autobiography Balbir Madhopuri, born in a small village in Madhopur in 1955, is a firebrand figure who has published numerous books and has enriched Punjabi Literature especially the Dalit Literature with his unique works. His childhood experiences remained much bitter, his school life remained full of discrimination and even after getting a job; his caste kept following him at every step. He had to work as a child labourer and an agriculture worker. While doing agricultural work as a labourer, he becomes so distressed that he just writhes to get rid of this life. He writes, "It occurred to me that if I was unable to complete my education, I would have to face and bear all this all my life" (Madhopuri, 107). He earned his postgraduate degree in Punjabi and chose to become a writer. Balbir Madhopuri retired as a Deputy Director (News), All India Radio where he was an editor of a monthly magazine Yojana (Punjabi), Publications Division, GOI. Presently, he works as Director, Punjabi Bhawan. He is an Editor of *Samkali Sahit* there, a prominent quarterly magazine of Punjabi Sahit Sabha, New Delhi.

*Changiya Rukh* can be called the most circulated book in India and abroad and this book has been published in many editions and several languages of India and abroad. He has written novels, poetry collections and biography of Ghadri Baba Mangu Ram. He has written 14 books and 40 books have been translated from Hindi and English into his mother tongue Punjabi apart from numerous edited anthologies. He has edited 46 books also. His books have been included in the syllabi of several national and international universities. He has received many awards and honours.

Balbir Madhopuri has written his works dealing with the problems and discriminations of the Dalit people. The pain of Dalits can be seen in his autobiography in which he has described how the Chamar community of his village were considered untouchables and all those kinds of works were assigned to them which the upper caste people would never accept to do. Even after that, the upper caste people would think as if Dalits were their slaves and it is their birthright to command over them.

He has written in his autobiography how the children of the lower castes would go to the village *gurudwara,* not inside of the building, and the upper caste people would give them *prasad* in such a manner that Dalit children's hands may not touch the upper caste people. This is not a new thing in Dalit autobiographies as the same kind of incident has been described by Bama in her autobiography *Karukku* how an old Dalit man brought the eatables for the upper caste Jamindar with the help of a string so that his hands may not touch it. She notices this incidence one day while coming back from her school. She wanted to laugh to see "the sight of such a big man carrying a small packet in that fashion" (Bama, 15). But what her brother tells her, was very shocking to her. She writes about it in her autobiography, "Annan told me the man wasn't being funny when he carried the package like that. He said everybody believed that Naickars were upper caste, and therefore must not touch Parayas. If they did, they would be polluted. That's why he had to carry the package by its string" (Bama, 15). Mulk Raj Anand's *Untouchable* (1935) is another example in which the central character Bakha is brutally beaten by the upper caste boys just because he did not tell them his caste. He had to maintain distance from the upper caste people just because he belonged to an untouchable class.

Balbir Madhopuri writes in his autobiography how he had to face every kind of discrimination in the school. The Dalit students were allowed to touch the drinking water resources in his school with the pure manner. Madhopuri writes how a teacher Sodhi Master would send him and his cousin Roshi to their neighbouring village around two and a half kilometers to cut the fodder for his cattle and other personal works. Madhopuri and other Dalit students were sent for his personal works. Another teacher would send Balbir and other boys to distribute the postal letters in the nearby villages of which distance was one to five kilometers. He never dared to send the Jat students for that purpose.

The basic reasons behind all this remain that some upper caste teachers, nurturing the social system, think that the education will not help these Dalit students as they will have to do any kind of labour or they will do any personal job. It might have been the mentality of some teachers four -five decades ago that they did not want that Dalit children may get good education and become officers. Whatever the reasons may be behind all this but one thing is clear that the brilliant Dalits students like Balbir Madhopuri have had to suffer a lot.

Balbir Madhopuri's autobiography *Changiya Rukh* means a kind of tree whose branches have been lopped, trimmed or slashed mercilessly by someone. Likewise, some people who have narrow-minded mentality because of their caste prejudice, do not want the development of the Dalits. Ravi Bhushan observes about this autobiography, "Changiya Rukh is a powerful testimony to the suffering, angst and attempts at rebellion of the Dalit community of Chamars in Punjab but it is something more" (Bhushan, 3).

In the very first chapter of the book, Balbir Madhopuri writes how the people of his caste were not allowed to pull water from the common wells as there were different wells for the lower and upper caste people in his village. The quest of these people, both for water and identity, is reflected in the opening lines of the autobiography, "Sim simpaniya, Qugitihai aa...(Ooze O water, ooze/ the dove is thirsty...) (Madhopuri, 01).

Balbir Madhopuri writes in his autobiography how the Jats of his village did not like any kind of interference in their personal life. They wanted to see Dalits only as inferior and poor. If any Dalit child would wear new or neat and clean clothes, he was bound to beating. Madhopuri writes about it:

> If a low-caste boy were to come out in the lanes of the village, all bathed and dressed in new clothes, his hair combed, one or the other of the Jats sitting under the trees would get up and throw mud on him. If he protested, he was sure to be

> beaten up. If an untouchable appeared in the village dressed in the new clothes, he was certain to be given a beating on the pretext that the low castes were trying to become the equals of the higher castes; no one knew or could predict when such an incident would occur and where. (Madhopuri, 02)

Balbir Madhopuri narrates further how the Dalit children were badly humiliated when they would go to the *Gurudwara* for offerings. The Jats would feel irritated too see these Dalits children and would shout at them. Their frustration is clear in these words:

> 'Give these Chamar brats a shout and drive them off,' the Jatbhai of the *gurudwara* would say to whosoever stand near him and on the occasion of Sangrad—the first day of the Indian solar month—or Gurupurub—the birthdays of the Gurus,....We would all run away, in the flicker of an eye, trampling the *jootis* that lay strewn outside the *gurudwara*. But as soon as he turned the otherway, we would be back at the window, exactly like we had been earlier. (Madhopuri, 11)

The upper caste people called them names and used such a language that cannot be expected from a civilised society, "You can't control this litter. I myself will drive them away, the mother's—,' and he would jump up mouthing an obscenity, which we all completed in our minds" (12). This instance is not alone, there are other examples in this autobiography where the upper caste people abuse Dalits without any fear, "Which bitch gave birth to you? Stop, I'll cut you into pieces!" (Madhopuri, 41). The people of his caste would bear everything silently just because they were depended on those for the work as Jats had agricultural lands. "No one says anything to those who harass us day and night! Do we not belong here that they have made life so difficult for us? They scold and terrorize us all the time. Merely because they have land, they have become our god!" (32). Thus, they had to be depended upon their fate. Madhopuri writes about the hunger during the feminine when these Dalits suffered to the most possible extent, "The crux of the matter is that no one can fight fate. Feminine has reduced many to penury" (Madhopuri, 102). He writes on various themes pertaining to Dalits in this autobiography and the main reason behind it remains their poverty which is the root cause of several other problems. Himanshu Sharma observes in this context:

> The theme of deprivation, exploitation, poverty and social exclusion are dominant in *Changiya Rukh*. It is set in the village of Madhopur, Jalandhar in Punjab and it tells how the life of the Dalits is miserable and pitiable and they have to lead a life of humiliation, suppression and socio-religious discrimination. (Sharma, 220)

Balbir Madhopuri narrates that the corruption in India also does not let the conditions of Dalits improve. His uncle Rama's words aptly describe the pains of a Dalit. Madhopuri narrates in his autobiography, "Our condition will improve only when corruption is either eradicated or at least brought under control" (106).

> It was later that I realised that if we tried to overcome the barrenness of our lives, we had to make a more strenuous effort and with greater unity, and carry on our fight continuously and vigorously against the exploitative system. The tale of our woes is hundreds of years old. (115)

In his autobiography, Balbir Madhopuri mentions that there were some people in their caste named Khusia, Bhima and Piari who would carry the carcasses when any animals died in the village. It was very difficult for them to carry this carcass. Their work was very difficult. Madhopuri writes, "They tied the hooves of the dead animal together and passed a hold through them, which they then carried across their shoulders, so that they could walk easily and comfortably" (Madhopuri,

25). When the dead animal was big in size, four or five people would do this work.

Balbir Madhopuri has narrated how the elders in his family were much poor and conservative. He writes that his grandmother was a very interesting woman who would quarrel over trifles on the issues of money. She had spent her life in utter poverty. They would use animals' fat as a fuel for lanterns and would eat the same fat on the *chapattis*. He narrates about this chapter in "Dadi's Saga". Madhopuri delineates how his grandmother would scold his mother, "Daadi would scold and taunt my mother whenever she bathed us with hot water during winter. She would say, 'Don't use all the wood to heat the water! Couldn't you put it in the sun for some time?" (Madhopuri, 127).

Balbir Madhopuri's sufferings related to his caste did not come to an end even after getting a job in the capital of India, Delhi. He had to face many problems in getting a rental accommodation. In fact, people were felling reluctant to keep him on rent due to his low caste. He writes about his problems how a man from Himachal Pradesh questions him, "You have been living in Delhi for so many years and are still looking for rented accommodation! Do you have any bad habits ... drinking or ...?" (Madhopuri, 207-08)

This autobiography makes the reader feel about the pains of the Dalits. It is very easy to criticize or hate but it is very difficult to support and love somebody. All persons on this Earth are born equal and have equal rights to live on it. It is not good if we put the barriers of caste, class or religion among us and show discriminatory attitude towards others. Balbir Madhopuri's autobiography brings so many such issues together and gives a message to treat each and everyone equally and lovingly. Dr Sadhana Agrawal analyses about this autobiography:

> The autobiography *Changiya Rukh: Against the Night* has many very touching themes and even the opening of it makes

the point clear when Dalit leather-workers of their communities are not allowed to drink water from the common wells which were used by the upper caste people and that's why they had to be dependent on the well which were reserved only for Dalit people. (96-97)

## Works Cited

Bama. *Karukku* (2000). Trans. Lakshmi Holmstrom. New Delhi: Oxford U P, 2011.

Bhushan, Ravi. "Balbir Madhopuri's *Changiya Rukh*—A Critique of Dalit Identity and Politics." Edited by M. S. Thirumalai. 11.3. (2011): 1-8.

Sharma, Himanshu. "Prejudicial Caste Hegemony in Balbir Madhopuri's *Changiya Rukh: Against the Night.*" *Indian Dalit Autobiographies: Marginalised Voices*. Ed. Singh, Bijender. New Delhi: Authorspress, (2015): 219-225.

Saroha, Khushee. "A Regional Study of Dalit Autobiographies from Maharashtra, Uttar Pradesh and Punjab". *The Criterion: An International Journal in English*. 5.2 (2014): 228-238.

Agrawal, Sadhana. "Exploitation of Leather-Workers in Balbir Madhopuri's *Changiya Rukh: Against the Night.*"*Dalit Men's Autobiographies: A Critical Appraisal*. Ed. Bijender Singh. New Delhi: Kalpaz Publications, 2017. 95-102.

# Index

## B



## C

## J



## K

## T



## U